Bathsheba's Lament

By
Lorita Boyle

Bathsheba's Lament
Published by:
Intermedia Publishing Group, Inc.
P.O. Box 2825
Peoria, Arizona 85380
www.intermediapub.com

ISBN 978-1-935529-00-2

Copyright © 2010 by Lorita Boyle
Printed in the United States of America

No part of this publication may be reproduced, stored in a retrieval system, or transmitted in any form by any means – electronic, mechanical, digital photocopy, recording, or any other without the prior permission of the author.

All rights reserved solely by the author. The author guarantees all contents are original and do not infringe upon the legal rights of any other person or work. No part of this book may be reproduced in any form without the permission of the author.

The New Revised Standard Version, copyright 1989, 1995 by the Division of Christian Education of the National Council of the Churches of Christ in the United States of America. Used by permission. All rights reserved.

What Others Are Saying About *Bathsheba's Lament:*

"Lorita Boyle's gifted storytelling will touch your heart and change your life. She captures the deep places of every soul in this timeless novel! I hope it is the first of many still to come! Bathsheba's Lament is A MUST READ!"–Bodie Thoene, award-winning author of 60 novels

"The Bible sketches powerful tales of humans who either met God or refused to meet him. And the reader is left to question: What, exactly, is the rest of the story? How would I have acted? What would I have done? The genius of historical fiction is that it invites us, like Lorita Boyle has done in *Bathsheba's Lament*, to consider these questions by walking through the door of the imagination. Surely, Bathsheba is one of the most fascinating women in the Bible. Boyle skillfully invites you to step in between the biblical lines to meet someone who might be very much like yourself." – Karen Mains, author and Director Hungry Souls

"Although the Bible gives insights into David's grief and repentance after his adulterous behavior toward the wife of Uriah, we hear very little about Bathsheba herself. In this book, Lorita Boyle delves realistically into what this faithful Hebrew wife must have experienced in a culture where women were stoned for adultery, and often treated as chattel. However, the implications go far beyond the biblical context. Bathsheba, betrayed and abused by a man she both respected and admired, faced the same emotional turmoil that many abused women experience today. Her road toward forgiveness and healing provides hope and direction for anyone who has been crushed by abuse or betrayal." – Judith Allen Shelly, author of 20 books, including *Spiritual Care: A Guide for Caregivers*

Dedication

Tom – my honey. You're the best gift God ever gave me. Without your love, support, encouragement and patience, I wouldn't be writing this dedication and seeing this dream come true! It's fun to know that the adventure we call "marriage" keeps getting better as we trust and follow Jesus.

Acknowledgments

I've lived with Bathsheba for over ten years. The story came to me like the tiny mustard seed Jesus spoke of in Matthew 13, and it just kept growing within my heart and mind. But I expected someone else to write it. Although others did write about her, they didn't write the story I'd been given, the story God gave me to write. And I thank my Abba for the privilege and wonder of working and praying with him to create *Bathsheba's Lament*.

As her story grew within me, I shared it with growing passion and commitment. Those crucial twenty months of Bathsheba's life became known to many friends and family members. And as I told it, the details were refined and defined more clearly, so when I sat down to write, I had great clarity and understanding of my heroine. Thank you my dear family and friends who listened so well and encouraged me along the way, often with questions and/or your own thoughts and insights. You know who you are and you're too many to mention by name, but I'm grateful to each of you.

But writing is a craft, and I'm still a learner who is working at honing that skill. And as a student of writing, I'm especially indebted to some who so generously critiqued and gave me their expertise of the story. First, I need to thank Sandi and Scott Tompkins – your loving friendship and years of encouragement as a writer have been an invaluable gift. I especially thank you for your faith in and commitment to *Bathsheba's Lament* and directing me to a publisher. My friend, Julia Pferdehirt, gave me practical writing suggestions as well as encouragement to go deeper into Bathsheba's pain. She also affirmed the steps Bathsheba needed to take on her journey to forgiveness.

I also thank the generosity of author and acquaintance, LeAnne Hardy, who read my manuscript and gave me a detailed and helpful critique. My prayer-warrior friend, Edna J. Cash, read and prayed through my manuscript with loving care, affirming God's call to tell Bathsheba's story.

My husband and children also lived with Bathsheba's story, and I think there were times they were ready to have her pack up her donkey and leave. Tom – you're the best husband any woman could have, and this book wouldn't have been birthed without you. That is appropriate, as our three wonderful children wouldn't have been born without you, either. I love you Sarah, Jonathan and Brandon, and thank you for your support and encouragement. But I especially thank you, Sarah, for even though you've yet to read this book, you've been a patient listener, and an incredible cheerleader of my writing. I'm also thankful to Marshall, Stephanie and Piper, our children by marriage.

Thank you to my nephew, Tim Murphy, for my cover photo.

And thanks to W. Terry Whalin and Larry Davis at IPG.

Chapter 1

"It's spring, the flowers bud
  and fields ripen.
Israel's men march to war
  led by their mighty king
And fathers, husbands and sons
  die on enemy land
While women spin thread
  and lament their dead."

I stopped singing, the bitter taste of my words lingering on my tongue. As I spun, oil from the wool thread dripped from my fingertips like heavy tears. I jumped up and paced the room. Light spilled through our tiny window illuminating Papa's lyre perched on the stone and wood shelf. I reached up and drew it into my arms, cradling it like he once held me.

Sitting down on the rug, I smoothed my linen tunic and settled the lyre across my lap. Its weight was heavier than my own lighter instrument. I tuned it. Hearing its unique timbre, I was once again with Papa, playing and singing together with rampant delight. I took a ragged breath, and played a chord.

"It's good to hear your father's lyre again," Uriah said. His tall, broad form blocked the sun in the doorway, casting me in shadow. "It was in Prince Jonathan's camp I first heard Eliam's talent with lyre and voice." He gazed down at me, his deep set black eyes alight with remembrance. "That was before I discovered his war skills surpassed his musical ability. But years later, when I visited your family in Hebron, I always enjoyed hearing the three of you sing and play together. Except, of course, for the time you insisted I sing with you."

His deep, rolling laughter moved over me, and chased away my sadness. I stared up at him, touched by his determination to draw me out of my grief and into happier memories.

"Papa never told me you couldn't sing and when you tried you sounded so much like a howling jackal, I couldn't stop laughing." I grinned as I plucked each of the eight strings, so that it sounded like laughter.

"But I can weave a good story," he said, "a gift that helped me win Eliam's beautiful daughter."

I smiled up at him. "Yes, it did."

"I am a blessed man to have such a beautiful and talented wife who creates her own songs, as well as sings and plays the songs of David. You know, after Eliam and I joined David's rebel army, I learned the songs of David and the history of my adopted people listening to your father and David sing." He glanced down at me. "Can you believe I'm nostalgic for a time when we had no assurance of our survival from one day to the next?"

I nodded as my fingers picked up the chords of a dance.

He reached down and cupped my cheek. "Beloved, I came to tell you I'll be able to share your evening meal with you tonight, but I need to go back to the palace to finish our war council."

I gripped his hand and kissed his calloused palm. Uriah leaned down and caught my mouth in a gentle kiss before he strode away.

After I heard the gate close, I stood and put Papa's lyre back on the shelf. With a deep sigh, I walked out of our workroom and into our enclosed stone courtyard. I lifted my face to the warmth of the spring sun. Yet, even as I felt the sun's hot breath, I longed for winter's bleak weather. In those cold dawns I would nestle close to my beloved. With the spring, Uriah was off each morning to the King's palace to talk of war.

I slid down at the foot of our blossoming pomegranate tree. Before Papa's death, I'd held to my childish faith that both my father and Uriah were invincible. That our Lord's strong and protecting hand would always shield them from harm.

But Papa was dead, and my wounded heart was forced to recite the age old affirmation and lament: "The Lord gives and the Lord takes away, blessed be the name of the Lord." And fear and anxiety chattered like a flock of crows that have nested inside my head.

"Bathsheba, come, we'll go to the marketplace," Mama said. "There we'll hear the news of when our men must leave for war. We've all seen the king's messengers returning with the conscripted soldiers from each of our twelve tribes, so it must be soon."

I looked up to see Mama standing before me, her slightly bowed and petite form hidden behind the basket she held, her dark brown eyes full of anxious anticipation.

I shook my head. "I have no desire to learn of Uriah's departure any sooner than I must, Mama. Take Rachel with you. I promised to take Sarai some of this new wool we bought from the wool merchant a week ago."

"No. At another time I'd take your maidservant, but not today."

"You know as well as I that Grandfather will tell me the news as soon as he hears it, if Uriah doesn't tell us first," I said, pushing my fingers through my thick hair.

She reached down, gripped my wrist and with a strength that shocked me, pulled me up. "The women at the marketplace will have all the news, and I'd rather hear it from them than anyone else. Besides, you know how foolish men can be; they think to protect us by telling us nothing."

Her words made me laugh, but she frowned back at me.

"Oh, Mama," I said after I caught my breath. "You're the one who told me how men always keep their secrets, while women love to share theirs."

"Which is why we're going to the marketplace."

I realized I'd not win this argument and glanced over to see Rachel kneeling nearby, her lithe figure bent over the stone quern, grinding the barley.

"We'll be back soon," Mama called to her.

Rachel looked up from her task to smile. She'd pulled her reddish brown hair back from her round face, and her brown eyes sparkled. At eleven years old, her features were still more childlike than womanly, but her body was beginning to bud like blossoms on a tree.

Under the welcome warmth of the sun, Mama opened the gate and led the way down the dusty road that took us past our neighbors' stone and brick homes, to the city gate and marketplace. Soon we were weaving our way through colorful stalls filled with cloth, pottery and the pungent smells of spices, grain, and both dried and ripe fruit. As the voices of the sellers and buyers rose with dissonant force, we made our way to a fruit stall.

Before we reached it, our neighborhood's paramount gossip, Mara, overtook us. Her dark eyes were alight with excitement and her face was red from the burgeoning heat of the day.

"Have you heard the news, Anna?" Her thick hand grabbed my mother's arm. "Our men leave in three days to attack Rabbah. Now your dead husband, Eliam shall be avenged." Turning toward me, her eyes lit with malice as she smirked. "And you, will your man have any hope that when he returns from war he might finally find you big with his child? What terrible sin did you commit, woman, to be cursed with barrenness?"

My heart tumbled even as a round rock under my sandal unbalanced me. Mama clasped my arm and steadied me before I sprawled in the dirt at Mara's feet. Taking a deep breath, I stood up straight.

"What horrendous sin have I committed, Mara?" I challenged. "Friends tell me how you pester them with questions about me, trying to discover all my transgressions. Mercy, woman, don't you have enough to do taking care of your own five children? Why can't you be grateful for God's blessings to you, and stop harassing me?"

Her eyes bulged as she stared at me and her mouth opened and closed on air. She clearly didn't know how to react to my finally confronting her. For years I'd feared her sharp tongue, but today, well, today I was too worried about the coming war to be concerned about Mara.

"Look, Mara." I nodded toward a fat, grubby boy hiding behind a large basket. His drawn slingshot was pointing to some object I couldn't see. "Your son's up to mischief. Perhaps you should stop haranguing me and watch him?"

Her look was venomous. "Oh no, I won't fall for that old trick. Who do you think you are giving me advice on children? Why you—"

"Stop that boy!" the potter bellowed. "He broke my jar!"

The potter's shout seized Mara's attention, and she turned around to see her son sprint up the hill, ignoring the shouts behind him.

"Joseph!" She screeched as she lumbered up the path after him. She tried to get around the potter, but he was a raging lion.

"Oh no, woman," he roared, springing in front of her, he forced her to stop. "You'll pay for this water jar your son broke before you go anywhere." He pointed down at the remnants of his jar.

Under the potter's diatribe, her face bloomed into a moon of mortification. Turning back to Mama, I grinned. "Let's get our fruit and go home. Watching Mara reproached by the potter has been a delight. Thank you for insisting I come. I'm feeling better than I have for weeks." I took dancing steps toward the vendor's stall.

Brushing away the flies on the fruit, Mama picked out the plumpest dried dates and figs from the vendor, paid him, and put them in her basket. I looked back to see Mara grudgingly pay the potter and smiled at Mama. She winked at me as she balanced the basket on her head with stately elegance.

As we strode by the other women, I smiled and was encouraged to see answering grins from many of them. I also noted their voices gabbled about Mara, and not my barrenness. I silently thanked the Lord that today I wasn't the focus of their gossip.

As we walked home, I softly sang:

"But let all who take refuge in you rejoice;
    let them ever sing for joy.
Spread your protection over them,
    so that those who love your name may exult in you.
For you bless the righteous, O Lord;
    you cover them with favor as with a shield."

I prayed the Lord would surround Uriah and me with his favor, and would be both shield and protector to Uriah when he marched to war. I also prayed my womb would blossom with new life, so I'd no longer be a target of the verbal arrows of the women, especially Mara.

"Daughter, look, there's Uriah standing by the jewel merchant." She turned to me. "He's probably buying you a bauble to alleviate his war news. Go, join him, I can walk home alone."

I looked across and saw Uriah stooped so he might see something that sparkled in the vendor's hand. Through our years of marriage, he'd brought me many beautiful and costly jewels and ornaments from his share of the spoils of war. For him to choose to buy me something was a precious gift indeed. "No, I don't want to ruin his surprise."

Mother touched the necklace at her throat, lifted her arms,

and looked wistfully at the gold and silver bracelets and armlets that encircled and decorated them. Each one was different, and each beautifully wrought, some with precious stones, others without. "It was my beloved Eliam who told him how much you and I enjoy jewelry."

"I know," I murmured, touching her hand. "I miss him, too."

We hadn't gone far, when I heard Uriah's deep voice call my name. I turned and waited for him as he walked toward us, his usually serious features giving way to a pleased grin.

"We just came from the marketplace, where we found the fruit we needed to make you date cakes," Mama said. "Now I need to talk to Sarai, so you two go on home together."

Before I could stop her, she scrambled up the path and turned out of sight.

"You went to the marketplace?"

I heard the relief in his voice, and realized how concerned he'd been these last days when I'd refused Mama's entreaties to join her in shopping. "Yes, Mama wanted to hear when you'd be leaving for war." I looked up at him with apprehension. "Mara said you leave in three days?"

His smile slipped into a frown as his bushy eyebrows knit together over his deep-set eyes. "I suppose I shouldn't be surprised you know the news almost before I do? Yes, I heard it this morning, but I wanted to wait to tell you. King David told us our army marches in three days time. The first grain is harvested and our celebrations of Passover and the First Fruit Feasts have ended. Commander Joab agrees it's time to march on Rabbah and bring the Ammonite jackals to heel. We defeated all their allies last year, now it's time to lay siege to their defenses and defeat them in Ammon."

With a deep sigh, I nodded in agreement. "Does the king have any idea how long it will take to conquer the Ammonites?"

He grinned down at me, his eyes crinkling with humor. "Wife, I know God often instructs King David on whether or not we shall triumph in a conflict. But no, the Lord has not told us how long it will take to win our victory. Come, I'll walk you home before I return to the palace."

"I hope you won't be long. If we only have three more days, I want all the time with you I can have."

His eyes softened as he stared down at me. "My lamb, you're a delight to this grizzled old warrior's confidence. How many other young wives plead with their husbands to spend more time with them?"

"Only those with husbands as thoughtful as mine," I said. "But you know how I hate to see you leave me for war, never knowing if I'll ever see you alive and well again."

"Eliam's daughter used to accept the lot of a warrior's life and all its risks without question or complaint."

I heard his rebuke and stopped in the middle of the path, forcing him to stop as well. "That was before Eliam's daughter lost him to an Ammonite arrow."

Chapter 2

Mama and Rachel were inside weaving, and I was in the courtyard by our clay oven kneading bread dough when I heard someone at our gate. I looked up and saw Grandfather as he opened the door and strode through.

"Bathsheba, it grieves me to tell you I come as a bearer of bad news."

I stood up from my kneeling position and watched his blue-striped robe flowing around his gaunt frame as he paced our stone courtyard. His sandals stirred up small dust clouds that rose up about him like whirlwinds aroused in the desert. I clasped my hands in front of me and forced myself to silence as I waited for him to calm himself and tell me why he was so upset.

Finally, he stopped and stretched out his arms toward me. I walked into his embrace and kissed his wrinkled, white-bearded cheeks. "Grandfather, what has disturbed you so?"

"It's King David," he exclaimed, his brown eyes intent and piercing.

"The king? Are you allowed to be angry with our king?" I teased.

His deep brown eyes lit with humor before rage clouded them once more. "I just came from the palace. King David refuses to lead his troops to war!" He threw up his gnarled hands and looked to heaven. "How can our God-anointed king refuse to fight God's battles against his enemy armies?" He cast me a troubled glance. "He asked if I don't trust Joab. I told him it was under that schemer's command last year that I lost my only son." He put a fist against his heart. "I could see David's sorrow, for he loved Eliam, too. But he told me his mind was made up: Joab will lead the attack against Rabbah in three days while he as king oversees court business."

His shoulders slumped and his arms fell to his sides. "He won't listen to me, Bathsheba." His sorrow-filled eyes rested on my face. "How could he deny me, Ahithophel, his most trusted advisor and not take my godly and wise counsel? Doesn't he understand how it's more important for him to lead his army to war than to remain close to his home like some old woman? Yes, he's promised to send the ark of the covenant with his army, but it isn't enough!"

I gasped, shocked by both his vehemence and his treasonous words.

"You and I both know how our Lord of Hosts favors the king when he leads our troops," Grandfather said, "and we suffer fewer casualties under his God-anointed leadership."

"Does Uriah know about David's decision?"

"Of course," he growled, flinging up his arms. "Everyone knows, but only David and Joab are happy about it. Joab, the fox, sees it as another opportunity to establish himself even more strongly as Israel's greatest commander, beside David, of course." He shook his grizzled head. "I came to tell you because I know Uriah will say nothing to keep you from worrying."

"My husband is ever considerate," I agreed. "We both know how he always tries to shield me from anything that might disturb my peace."

He flicked my cheek with his finger. "But we know that as the daughter of one of David's mighty warriors, you were raised to show no fear."

"Yes, Grandfather." I leaned up and kissed his cheek. "But

we also know I still worry, don't we?"

His eyes glowed with pride. "Yes, daughter of my heart, but I'll never share your secret."

"Thank you."

Caught up again in his anger, he frowned. "Tell Uriah I'll see him tomorrow at the palace. I still believe that no king who's still full of vigor and strength, and no white beard like me, should sit at home with his women when his army goes to war!"

He kissed my forehead and swept out the gate. As I closed the door after him, fear clawed at my heart. "Lord," I whispered, "please convince David to change his mind. And help Grandfather to be wise in how and what he speaks to the king so he doesn't incite David to angry retribution."

* * *

"I heard what your grandfather said. I don't like this." Mama walked out of the room where she and Rachel had been weaving and patted her chest. "My heart is heavy with misgivings. David should lead his men to avenge my Eliam's death and all the others who died fighting! They must cut down every Ammonite warrior until they are like the dust we trample."

Her once radiant brown eyes were again full of grief and anger. "Eliam shouldn't have fallen by that cursed Ammonite arrow," she cried. "Isn't it sung how one of David's mighty men can stand against a hundred when. . ." she stopped, gazing at me expectantly.

"God strengthens his arms for battle." The childhood verse came easily to my lips. But although the Lord had strengthened Papa's arms for battle, he hadn't shielded him from deadly arrows. "Come, Mama, let's go to the tabernacle. We'll worship, and pray for Uriah's safety and victory for our army."

"Yes, we'll petition God to protect Uriah. Perhaps he'll answer our prayers for your husband's safety even though he was deaf to our prayers for Eliam."

Seeing her anguish intensified my own grief. Papa's death at the beginning of the campaign last year seemed to have sapped

Mama's enthusiasm for life, taking the spring from her steps and the joy from her soul.

To care for her, Uriah and I brought her from her home in Hebron to live with us. My grandfather had always treated her like a despised slave instead of a beloved daughter-in-law, and with Papa's death, this hadn't changed. In fact, he'd demonstrated his hatred of her by giving my father's and her home to his nephew and his family and moving them into her home the very day she'd left to join us in Jerusalem. I'd wanted to rebuke him for his disrespect, but Mama had stopped me.

Through this year, I'd watched streaks of gray invade her thick, black hair even as grief mapped her face with lines of sorrow. Over the months since Papa's death, her erect, youthful figure was often stooped under the weight of suffering, and her beauty dimmed, except for her rare smiles.

"I always feel better once we've been to the tabernacle to worship," I said.

Mama stared, but I could tell she wasn't seeing me. "When David leads, all of heaven's host goes before them. But Joab?" She lifted an arm and shook her head. "That one has too much innocent blood on his hands. Some men may trust him, but I don't, and I don't believe God does, either."

Her words echoed my own misgivings, leaving me no comfort or peace. I turned toward the gate and Mama and I left our courtyard to go to the tabernacle to worship and pray.

* * *

When I heard the rhythmic slap of Uriah's sandals upon the stone of our courtyard, I didn't run out to greet him, as was my custom, but waited for him in our bedchamber. I was perfumed, oiled, dressed in my best tunic, and adorned with the jewelry Uriah had given me. The thick slit between the rocks in the wall of our bedchamber let only a sliver of light into the room, so I'd lit a clay lamp which glowed with welcome on a small table by our bed.

Mama and Rachel had eaten earlier, and I could hear their

voices coming from our roof. I'd considered meeting Uriah there, as it was cooler, but it wasn't as private. I wanted privacy.

He stopped at the open door to our room. His dark eyes lingered on my face before moving down my body. "What's the occasion, beloved?" He sniffed the air and looked down at the feast laid out in bowls on a mat and then back at me. "I don't know if I'm hungrier for you or for this banquet."

Smiling with pleasure, I lifted my hand to him. "My husband, I'm here to offer you both."

Uriah closed the door, before he took my hand, knelt and gave me a long kiss. As he sat down, I got up to fetch the water bowl so I might wash and dry his hands and feet. When I was done, I sat next to him.

"I have something for you," he said, his eyes lit with anticipation. He drew some jewelry out of the pouch at his side. "I bought this for you as a parting gift, but also to thank God for your nineteen years of life. This morning, your mother told me in passing that she'd given birth to you on this day."

I stared at him and took the beautiful necklace from his hand. It was a silver chain with a round, polished amethyst in the middle. "It's beautiful." My hands shook as I slipped it over my head.

Uriah gently lifted my hair from around the chain. "Yes, I knew this stone would be lovely on you." He kissed my neck. "And it will look even better when it's the only thing you're wearing."

* * *

After Uriah had enjoyed both his meal and his wife, I knew I couldn't sleep before talking to him about David. Unsure how to approach him, I sat up and said, "Uri, Grandfather told me King David plans to stay in Jerusalem instead of leading his troops to war. He was very concerned when he heard this, as am I."

"And why is that? Is David not our king?" he asked with quiet force. "And as king, he'll choose whatever he deems best for himself, his God and his people."

His answer was expected. "Yes, beloved, but Grandfather says the Lord made David king so he'd fight his holy wars in the spring, while ruling in the city during the seasons of peace, and I agree with him."

Uriah pushed himself up and leaned against the stones at our backs. When he looked down at me, his eyes held a subtle accusation that made me squirm.

"Wife, as I've told you, when I was a young man and converted to the Hebrew faith, and swore my oath of fealty to our God and to David, it was before he became king. What I didn't think I needed to say was it doesn't matter if I agree with his decisions or not. As a loyal subject to my God-anointed king, I'll faithfully give him my obedience and allegiance."

"As I do, as well," I said. I couldn't fight his warrior's commitment, or his heart of loyalty to our king, nor did I want to. I knew even with my fears, trust was my only option. I'd voiced my doubts, and he'd listened. It had to be enough.

With a sigh, he reached for me and drew me into his arms. "Please, beloved, you and I both know that God called me to be a warrior, and gifted me to be one of the best. I serve King David with deep gratitude and respect. He's king, friend and a warrior worthy to be praised and followed. With or without him, we go to defeat the Ammonites. We can't allow them to rise up again to try and destroy us. I also go to avenge the death of your father." He rubbed my back, as if to comfort. "Before David and his council today, all his captains affirmed our vow of holy war and that we wouldn't return to our homes until the Ammonites are defeated and all our men come back in victory."

"Then I pray the war will go well and quickly." I put my hands on his chest and leaned back to gaze at him. His eyes glowed with determination and confidence. I reached a hand out to stroke his black hair, touching the gray strands at his temples that reflected the wisdom of his years. Uriah's strength was that of a trained soldier. A man who practiced his trade during the long months of winter so he'd be prepared to fight when summoned. Yet, I also knew if he were granted the grace to do so, he'd leave fighting and become a man of the land.

"Beloved, I vowed to be with child before you left for war this spring. But again, God has not allowed me to honor this vow, and I grieve."

"My lamb, do not despair," he said, wrapping his arms around me and hugging me tight. "You know that Sarah, the wife of the father of your nation, Abraham, was ninety when she bore Isaac." He looked deeply into my eyes. "Sometimes, God asks us to wait for his best gifts, as I waited for you. Can't you be satisfied with my love while you wait for our child?"

I couldn't help laughing. "Uri, you're not Abraham and please God I'm not Sarah. I'm sure to be dead before I reach ninety whether I have children before then or not. I do appreciate your encouragement, but you don't hear the accusations I hear from the women almost every day." I leaned back to see his face. "Don't their husbands tell you of their reproach?"

"No, they've never said a word." A wolfish smile curved his lips. "They probably know if they spoke one word of censure against you, they'd be dead, or gravely wounded."

"Well, some of the women have encouraged me to have you take another wife—"

"No!" He grasped my shoulders. "I refuse to even think about taking another wife." His voice gentled and he massaged the places where he'd gripped me. "Forgive me, beloved, but I can't believe my jealous wife would truly desire me to take another."

"You're right. I hate the very thought of it."

"I'm glad to hear it. For I know I have quite enough women in my life with you, your mother and little Rachel."

Did he tease me? I frowned at him. "Husband, can you jest about this?"

"No, not about your barrenness." He stroked my back. "But I believe I've learned wisdom from my own life and watching David. Truly, David's court often seethes with the intrigues of his many wives and concubines and their sons and daughters. No, I want nothing to do with another wife," he said vehemently.

"I've no desire to come home from the battlefield only to enter another in my own house. I'd think our good king would welcome a return to war instead of staying at the palace where he's sure to be drawn into the bitter skirmishes between his many wives and their offspring."

"Grandfather takes great delight in being in the midst of all the palace intrigues," I said. I touched his cheek, tracing the thin scar from his left ear to his mouth. "Oh, beloved, I admit I fear for you as I never did before Papa's death."

He put his fingers against my lips. "Our Lord's given me not only a warrior's body, but a mind for strategy, even as he's given this to Joab. We never take unnecessary risks."

I nipped his fingers lightly so he drew them from my lips. "Uri, war is always a risk for those who fight."

"Yes, but when I go to war, I hold your beautiful face before me like a talisman, and I trust in our God." He kissed my lips and smiled at me. "My lamb, I'm sure I'll return to you after this campaign. And in God's good time, he'll open your womb and give us the children we desire."

"How is it you have such faith?" I cupped his cherished face in my hands and kissed him back. "Who knows, perhaps tonight the Lord will remove his reproach and quicken your seed within me? It would give me such joy to know I was nurturing new life while you fought for our king and our God."

"May God grant you the desire of your heart, beloved."

"I pray he will, but my heart has little hope of it."

Chapter 3

I spent the next two days preparing for Uriah's departure, taking comfort in serving him in this way. Mama and I had gone into the storage room on the other side of the courtyard from our work room and my bed chamber to find the extra wineskins and cooking utensils Uriah would take with him to war.

In a small alcove next to the storage room was the pen where our goat, Delilah, was kept. Rachel milked her each morning and evening, and we made cheese for Uriah to take with him out of all the milk she gave us.

While I went about my chores, I sang, hoping to alleviate the pain I felt knowing he'd soon be gone. He was with Joab, David and other commanders at the palace, to hold their final war council with the king, before the army left for Rabbah. I'd finally accepted David would not change his mind, and lead his army to war.

"Daughter, have you checked his extra wineskin for leaks?"

I smiled at her. "Yes, Mama, and the bread should come out of the oven shortly, and Rachel is milking Delilah so we can make even more cheese."

"Good," she said, and smiled at me. "Do you know you have flour all over your face? Would you greet your husband on his last night home looking like that? Go and clean yourself up."

"He's never minded a little flour. But I promise to clean up as soon as the bread is done," I said as I batted at a persistent fly.

"I'll take the bread out. You know how much I love the taste of warm bread."

"So do I, but I can see you don't want to share, so I'll go get ready for Uriah."

I left her to prepare for my husband's last night with me. I knew I'd get little sleep, not only because of our love-making, but because Uriah rarely slept well the night before leaving for war.

* * *

The next morning, after I kissed him good-bye, I clung to Uriah for only a moment before he left to join his men. Mama, Rachel and I soon followed to stand with all the people of the city to watch our army leave for war. However, this year it wasn't King David in his shining chariot who led the procession, but the brightly robed priests. The air shimmered as their shofar blasted a trumpeted challenge and they carried the ark of the covenant on poles before all of Israel. The gold ark glittered in the brilliant sunshine, and we all bowed as it passed by.

I was comforted with the promise of God's Presence and mighty power held within the ark, yet I still wished it were David who led his men. After the priests passed, Joab, Uriah and other of the king's mighty men followed on horseback, their heads erect, they looked neither to the right nor the left. Pride filled my heart as I watched Uriah ride by.

The warriors from the tribal clans marched in lines behind them. It was a thrilling sight, but dust rose around us like a heavy cloud, and we quickly lifted our veils. I closed my eyes against the grit that burned my eyes and the threatening tears.

"It feels like it was years ago and not just last spring that we watched a similar procession move through the city," Mama said beside me.

I glanced at her and saw how tears pooled like unwelcome rain in her eyes. I nodded, reached out and grasped her hand.

* * *

I stood in our bedchamber, and hugged my husband's old tunic to my breast. I breathed in his musky scent, and prayed.

"You did well in preparing Uriah's war provisions, daughter, and you didn't cry for all to see you, as I did," Mama said as she walked into the room.

"No one saw you cry. And you should be proud, because you were the one who trained me to do this as the daughter and wife of warriors."

"Sometimes I wonder if there was something I forgot that may have distracted Eliam, causing him to fall in battle." She stared at me, her eyes stark with distress.

I dropped Uriah's tunic and gaped at her. "Mama, Uriah told us exactly how Papa died." I grasped her hands and squeezed them for comfort.

"One of David's mighty men should not have fallen so easily by a cursed arrow of an Ammonite dog." Her voice was low and fervent, her brown eyes full of grief and anger. With a small cry, she wrenched herself out of my grasp. "You've no idea what it's like to lose the husband of your heart."

I watched her run out of the room. I wanted to follow and comfort her, but my own fears kept me planted atop the dry earth of our floor. I thought of Papa. He'd been more than Mama's husband; as she'd been orphaned as a child, he'd also become her father, lover and friend. His death was an open wound that resisted healing. All my prayers for God to touch and succor her had seemed to go unanswered.

"God," I whispered. "Please be Mama's comforter, and please, please bring Uriah safely back to me. For even as your ark goes with the army, you march with them as well. Strengthen the arms of your servant, Uriah, that he might do battle for you. Let him lead his men with courage and wisdom. Protect him from the Ammonites, and when you've given your army the victory, bring Uriah home to me."

Chapter 4

Our army had been gone a week when loud wailing invaded our city, signaling that the war had claimed its first casualties. Weaving, I jerked up to my feet as fear clutched my heart with talons of despair. Would a messenger stop by our home? Or would the harbinger of death pass us by? Silently I prayed for Uriah.

"So it begins again," Mama lamented, her eyes stricken. "Last year I was in Hebron when a messenger of King David came to bring me to Jerusalem and the king. There, David honored me by personally telling me of Eliam's death. May you never be called to the king to hear such news about Uriah."

"Amen."

"I know we should send Rachel to find out who's grieving their losses, but my own grief is still too fresh," she whispered. "Especially as I hear the keening cries of our friends."

I took her cold hands in my own. "Then we'll stay here and grieve together."

Her mouth opened, and her loud cry joined the grieving wails of our sisters in the city. I swallowed my tears to clear my throat, and cried aloud with her.

* * *

After Uriah left, Grandfather came to see me at least once every week to make sure I was doing well, and to give me the consistently good news of the war. He said even though we had some casualties during the first battles, there had been few since, and all of Joab's reports were of our victories against the Ammonites.

It had been over three weeks since the war began when Mama and I had taken a moment of rest from our daily tasks, and the heat inside our weaving room and sat under our tree. We heard a knock on our gate and looked up and saw Rachel as she ushered Grandfather into our courtyard. Mama immediately jumped up and scurried back into the room.

"Shalom, Bathsheba, I bring more good news from the war," Grandfather announced. He strode up to me, his face alight with joy. He reached his hand to me, pulled me up and into his arms.

"Joab's messengers say our troops have chased the Ammonites behind the walls of Rabbah again. Our enemies rarely send out forays against our forces encamped around them, but when they do, your husband always distinguishes himself in battle."

"This is welcome news, Grandfather," I said, kissing his cheeks.

"I just saw King David. Again I urged him to join his troops at Rabbah. But he sees no need to join his men with such good reports from Joab." He stroked his white beard. "You'd think he's lost his stomach for war, the shepherd boy who went from killing lions to killing a giant, to defeating thousands and becoming our anointed king.

"Uriah, even more than the king, is doing the job our God gave him to do." He began to pace. "I don't understand why David must suddenly covet peace and a warm bed instead of the rigorous life of a warrior."

"Perhaps David's tired of war, Grandfather," I said. "He's been fighting since he was a young man. I'm sure I'd be tired of war if I were him, and would rather write songs of praise to our

God than draw sword against our enemies."

He threw his head back and cackled. Finally he stopped and stared at me. "You are a woman," he scoffed. "Of course you'd rather write music than fight. Now, I must go see Absalom to give him the news from the war. He's asked me to bring him the news if he isn't in court to receive it himself, and this morning he wasn't in court. But first I wanted to reassure you that Uriah is well, and the war moves forward." He took my hand in his own and patted it. "So, do you miss that great ox of a husband?"

I smiled, relieved at the change in topic. "I'm sure I miss him far more than you."

"Perhaps, but ever since Eliam's death, Uriah has become more like a son than a grandson." His slight body shook with a bark of laughter. "Uriah promised to kill me a hundred Ammonites himself in revenge for Eliam. From the reports, he's already fulfilled his promise."

"And knowing how he's always at the front of any fighting, I'm at the tabernacle at least twice a day praying for his safety."

"Oh, he'll stay alive, girl. I, too, petition God for his life at the tabernacle. Well, now that I've given you the news, I must go see Absalom. Of all David's sons, he's the one who has the most promise. It's too bad he was born a few months after Amnon. However, he grows in stature each day, demonstrating his father's intelligence and charm and his mother's shrewdness."

"I admit he's handsome, but his arrogance also seems to grow with his years."

"He's second in line to the king," he retorted. "Surely his arrogance can be forgiven. It's Amnon who struts around the city like a young lion amongst his pride."

I laughed at the vivid truth of his image. "Yes, but then he is David's cub, and undisputed heir to his kingdom." I was always uncomfortable with Grandfather's awareness not only of David's secrets, but many of his sons' as well.

Once I married Uriah and moved to Jerusalem, Grandfather told me many stories of the king's family. Hearing them, I decided to keep my distance from the king's court, and the politics and intrigues that infused it. Uriah often said he preferred the battlefield, where the lines were clearly drawn between enemies, to the court, where enemies could hide behind the smiling face of a friend or relative.

"Girl, are you listening to me?" Grandfather barked.

His raised voice startled me. "I'm sorry; I was remembering something Uriah said."

"And not what I'm telling you? Absalom always listens closely to all I say." He turned his back on me and was off in a cloud of dust, not waiting for Rachel to open the gate for him.

I was staring after him, shocked I'd offended him, when Mama spoke from beside me.

"Don't worry daughter. Your grandfather must always be the center of attention, unless David or one of his sons is around," she commented dryly. "But it was good to hear we're winning the war."

"Yes, it is good news, but I was hoping for a short campaign, and Uriah home by now."

"Wars are never short, daughter, even if they are only weeks in the fighting."

I glanced at her and sighed. "You're right. No war is short to those who wait for the return of their loved ones, or for those, like Uriah, who are fighting for us."

* * *

When I went two days past the time my menses should have come, a wild hope sprang up in my heart that God had answered our prayers and given me a child. I didn't say anything to Mama, afraid to do so would somehow break this joyous expectancy. But I worshiped at the tabernacle all morning and sang at our home all through the afternoon as I went about my work, and laughed when Rachel left her spinning beside me to dance to my songs.

But on the third morning past my due day, I awoke to the wet, sticky evidence that Uriah's seed had not taken root within me, but been rejected by my cursed womb. I lay in grief on my bed, the weight of my barrenness like a mantle of death that covered me.

"Come, my lazy daughter, it's time to get up. Do you not have a new song to sing this beautiful morning? I've loved listening to you sing these past days."

"There will be no more songs, Mama. My menses has come to prove me barren again." I sat up, the hard stones digging into my back. "Mama, even though I've searched for years now, I know of no sin I've not repented from, can think of nothing I should have done that I didn't do. And you, Papa and Uriah have all testified to this, and have I not always worshiped God with all my heart, soul and strength and made the requisite sacrifices?"

"Yes, you've done all that, dear one, which is why I believe it's not your sin but mine."

"Mama?" I asked in shock. What could she mean by her words?

She shook her head, her eyes darkened with pain. "I won't tell you today of my past, but soon. Now, clean yourself and finish grinding the wheat while Rachel and I go to pray for Uriah at the tabernacle."

I stared at her. From her closed expression I knew I'd have to wait to hear her story.

Chapter 5

Rachel went to the market, and I swept the stones of our courtyard when Mama walked out of our work room where she'd been weaving.

"It's time we talked, dear one. Time you knew the truth."

I stared at her, noting the pain in her eyes, the way her chin trembled. I set the broom against the stone wall. "The truth?" I asked her, puzzled.

"Yes, come and sit with me on your bed."

I followed her into my bedchamber and sat beside her, both curious and anxious at her words.

"Years ago, I promised your father I'd never tell you of my past. But he's dead and you're alive and in agony over something for which I'm to blame. I can't watch you suffer any longer, always questioning God and grieving for your loss. Although I know Uriah will love you whether you ever give him a child or not."

"Mama, what are you saying?" I murmured.

Her eyes looked past me, and widened, as if in horror. "I was a child of about four years when the Philistines raided our village and took me captive." Her voice shook with emotion. "My memories are of blood, fire and the smell and taste of ashes and fear, and black smoke billowing around me like death itself."

Her gaze caught mine and I gasped at the agony radiating from her eyes.

She leaped up and began to pace. "I know my father and mother were killed, but God has mercifully robbed me of that memory."

"Mama, you don't need to tell me."

"Yes, I do." She wiped her tears with the back of her hand. "My captors beat me when I wept, so I didn't. They took me to the Philistine city of Gath, where I was sold as a slave to a wealthy Philistine with two wives. I worked in the fields, helped grind the grain, and learned to weave. After my menses began, and I developed. . . ." She stopped, took a ragged breath. "My master repeatedly raped me. My cursed beauty condemned me to concubinage."

My eyes burned with unshed tears. How had she survived a life of such suffering?

Slumping down to the rug on the floor, she wrapped her thin arms around her knees and rocked her body, staring past me. "He wasn't a gentle man. To survive, I learned how to escape within my mind to a place far from his hateful touch. But God was merciful: I bore him no children.

"The other wives hated me for my beauty, but especially for my race. They beat me when the master was away, and made my life a misery. They accused me before him of laziness and lying, but my expert weaving made him money, and my body served his . . . appetites. Thus, he ignored their accusations and refused to get rid of me. So, the wives plotted my death."

Caught in her story, I exclaimed. "How did you find this out?"

She glanced up. Her haunted eyes pierced me. "Before my master took me as his concubine, I'd saved the life of his firstborn son from being bitten by a poisonous snake. He was on the ground playing with rocks when a snake slid toward him unnoticed. I was beating a rug with a big stick, saw the snake, and hit it with my stick until it stopped moving. I learned he never forgot I saved him."

She stopped rocking. "His mother told him their plan to poison me, and one morning he caught me outside our courtyard coming back from drawing water. He told me of the wives' plan and offered to sell me again to save my life." She glanced over and gave me a wry smile. "I didn't know why, but I decided I wanted to live. So, when my master left the next day to visit a nearby village, his son took me to a caravan outside of town and there he sold me to the Philistine slavers."

My throat was too full of unshed tears for me to speak.

"A few days later, as we marched through the arid wilderness, a loud war cry ripped our peace. David's men were ravenous lions pouncing on their prey. Roped with other frightened slaves, we fell onto the rocky ground. There was no escape. I knew I'd flown death by poisoning only to be cut down by bandits.

"Suddenly their shouts became understandable words. I screamed for mercy in the same tongue, shocking them and myself." She looked at me, and I saw the remnants of an old joy in her bright eyes. "The Philistines were killed. I was the only slave taken to David's camp. I knew what they'd do with me, and searched for a weapon to defend or kill myself. I'd sworn I'd never be raped again. I knew even if I was of their race, they'd despise me as a Philistine slave.

"It was your father who squatted down in front of me and assured me I wouldn't be harmed. It was a wonder I could understand him. I nodded my comprehension, although I didn't believe him."

A sudden smile wreathed her face, highlighting her still vibrant beauty. "He stood up and left me, but soon returned with an old woman with gray, wooly hair and a dark face radiating kindness. She said her name was Martha, and I'd live in her tent while I was with them. She promised she'd treat me like the daughter, Anna, she'd lost to a fever months before.

"Anna had followed her husband into the wilderness, even as the widowed Martha followed her daughter." She stared at her hands resting on her knees and her eyes softened with the memory. "God knew old Martha had a kind and generous heart, and he used her to touch my bruised, broken heart with love.

"You see," she said, glancing over at me again, "even though I still had nightmares of being taken, I had no memory of my Hebrew name, my tribe or the place from which I'd come. I only knew it had been about fourteen years since I was captured. Martha decided she'd name me 'Anna,' for her daughter. She told me it meant 'grace' and it was God's grace that brought me to her. Months later, I knew it was also his mercy.

"That first night she took me to her tent, fed me, and helped me bathe. While she combed out my clean hair, she questioned me about my past, gently pulling out strand upon strand of my story. She thought I was asleep when Eliam called her from her tent to tell him about me." Mama gifted me with a smile of pure wonder.

"Oh, my daughter, old Martha took my answers and wove the truth of my past into something delicate and beautiful, not the ugly, knotted cloth I saw. And she talked about God's goodness in bringing me to her tent to comfort her after the loss of her daughter. Her voice, Bathsheba, her voice awakened the whisper-soft tongue of my mother, and I fell asleep that night feeling safe and loved for the first time since being captured as a child.

"I stayed with Martha and helped her with her work, and she taught me about God and gave me the stories of my people I'd forgotten, or never heard. I also listened to David, who with a voice strong as a waterfall and just as melodious, sang praises to God under bright morning skies as well as evening canopies of radiant star and moonlight. And Eliam often joined him in song and with his lyre."

She reached forward, took my hand and held it in to her cheek. "Eliam came by, played his lyre and sang to us. Then Martha allowed him to walk around the camp with me, but never out of her sight." She squeezed my hand. "I knew I could never marry, as I was unclean and barren. Besides, I'd never known gentleness from a man and feared to be touched." She kissed my hand and let it go. "Ah, but your father was so handsome, and his strength was like a standing bear, but he never touched me in any way. So I believed God wouldn't mind if we talked and walked together. But in time, I learned your father wanted more."

Her voice vibrated with wonder. "He decided he wanted the beautiful captive for his bride, even knowing my shame and my barrenness, and suspecting my fear of men." She wrapped her arms around herself.

"Ah, but when your grandfather heard of Eliam's plan to wed me, he was furious. He sent a message through a spy of David's to request a visit to David's camp. Eliam made the arrangements, and when Ahithophel arrived he threatened to proclaim Eliam dead to him if he married the prostitute, Anna."

I gasped in horror. "Oh, Mama, no."

She looked at me, her eyes aglow with pride, and her arms reaching toward me. "Oh, Bathsheba, Eliam stood up to his father with such confidence. He told him if he, Eliam, could defy Saul, the King of Israel, to follow David, he could certainly disobey his father to marry the woman of his choice. You must understand," she implored me, grabbing my hand, "Eliam knew his betrothed had been married off to another. Once Eliam had left King Saul's army to join David's rebel men, Ahithophel's friend had called Eliam a traitorous outlaw and promptly married his daughter to a man faithful to King Saul.

"Ahithophel didn't deny this, but reasoned he could find another, more appropriate bride for him. Eliam assured him no good Israelite of reputable family would ever consider marrying his daughter to Eliam as long as David remained an outlaw. Your grandfather wouldn't listen.

"He blustered and raved, but couldn't deny Eliam was right. However, when your father made it clear he'd take me as wife, your grandfather tore his robe, put ashes on his head and in a loud voice he cursed Eliam and me. Ahithophel declared him 'dead' to him and his family and stormed out of the camp." Slow tears etched the lines of grief on her face as she clutched my hand. "Dear one, how could I *not* love a man who forgave my past, and wanted to protect and care for me?"

"Of course you'd love him, Mama." I loosened her grip and drew her into my arms and hugged her close. She felt small and fragile in my arms. Yet, I knew her to be a woman of incredible strength and love.

She drew back and faced me. "Because of Eliam's loyalty to him, David gave us his blessing, even knowing how Ahithophel had bitterly cursed us."

"David's blessing must have been more powerful than grandfather's curses," I said. "Look how you two loved each other, and how God blessed you with me."

"Yes, you're my miracle child, and the reason why your grandfather reconciled with your father," she agreed. "After three years together, I didn't give Eliam a son, but God blessed us with a beautiful, loving daughter. I prayed everyday God would use you to help reconcile your father to his father, for I saw how the estrangement grieved Eliam. I named you Bathsheba, meaning 'daughter of the oath,' and I swore to God if Eliam's parents accepted you and him, it would be enough, they never had to accept me. . . and they didn't."

"But Mama, you should have been loved and accepted, too. You had no other family." My mind raced with the implications of her words.

"You know you were born in Hebron, after we'd settled there with David. When you were four months old, Eliam granted my wish for him to take you to be introduced to your grandparents. Your grandmother walked into their courtyard and discovered her estranged son standing there with the tiny bundle of her only grandchild in his arms. It was her cry of joy which brought your grandfather to the courtyard as well. He saw you being held by your grandmother, with Eliam smiling down on you both."

Mama smiled radiantly. "Eliam told me how Ahithophel roared 'leave,' and grabbed you out of his wife's arms. He held you up and looked astonished when you gurgled and laughed at him. Your tiny hand caught hold of his beard and pulled. Staring at you, Ahithophel's countenance changed from belligerence to bemusement."

Her low laugh filled the room. "Ah, daughter, you captured his heart with just one glance, and he's never stopped loving you since. And your grandmother loved you, too. And when I heard how God answered my prayer, I rejoiced to see how you had lived up to your name. Although I never told Eliam what that oath was. I could accept Ahithophel's silent censure because my beloved was reconciled to his parents, and you became their treasured grandchild."

"But Grandfather ignores you and refuses to talk with you even to this day."

"Yes, but you're the joy of his life, and as precious to him as you are to me," she said. "And you know how your father adored you."

I smiled with remembrance. "Oh, yes, Mama, and I miss him so much, I can only imagine how great your grief has been."

"And it was because of his great love for both of us that Eliam chose Uriah as your husband. You see, your father knew if anything happened to him, he could trust Uriah to care for both of us. He knew your grandfather would never take me in, and I have no other family."

"You'll always have a home with us, Mama," I assured her, "but it hurts me to know how much pain Grandfather has caused you. Could I not talk to him?"

"No," she said, violently shaking her head. "Don't ever speak to your grandfather about me. I refuse to cause any dissension between you two. As it is, I'm afraid it's his curse upon your father and me that has caused your sorrow." She bowed her head and wept softly.

I threw my arms around her again and hugged her tightly.

"But God had mercy on you, and you had a child. Why wouldn't he have mercy on me, too?"

She pushed away and looked at me, her face lined again with sorrow. "Because God knows it's more painful for a mother to see her child suffer loss than it is for us to bear it ourselves. Bathsheba, if I could, I'd take all the reproach and pain of your barrenness onto myself."

I gazed at her, feeling a great welling of sadness. She'd endured such cruelty in her life, and I felt her pain like a hot coal on my skin. "I can't believe our God would withhold children from me just to punish you. Even as he was merciful to you and Papa, I believe he'll be merciful to us. You know Uriah's confidence that some day we'll have children."

"Yes, and have I not beseeched God each day for a grandchild?"

"Oh Mama, you've suffered so much, losing your family, becoming a slave and concubine. Please forgive me for all my complaints when my life has been filled with the love of my family." I wept over her many losses, the grief of my barrenness overwhelmed by my awareness of her suffering.

"Rest now," I said, gently smoothing the tears from her face as she lay down on my bed. "I know you must be exhausted." I kissed her and left the room.

I walked into the next room, and returned to my weaving. As the rhythm of the task took over, I pondered all she'd told me. Even though I'd assured her I couldn't believe our Lord would punish me, my mind examined her words. Was Grandfather's curse falling upon Uriah and me? My heart quickened its beat within my chest.

"I've been barren for four long years now, even longer than my mother." I whispered.

"What is it in my life that is holding back your blessing, God? Please show me."

Words from one of King David's psalms came to mind and I quietly sang:

"Search me, O God, and know my heart;
    test me and know my anxious thoughts.
See if there is any wicked way in me,
    and lead me in the way everlasting."

David's words became my prayer, before another song moved from my heart to my lips:

"How precious is your steadfast love, O God!
    All people may take refuge in the shadow of your wings.
They feast on the abundance of your house,
    and you give them drink from the river of your delights.
For with you is the fountain of life;
    in your light we see light."

As the thread spun under my fingertips, I prayed. "Oh, God, please gift me with new life from your fountain of life."

Chapter 6

I called for my ritual bath seven days later when the late afternoon sun moved in its slow dance toward earth. According to our laws, to once again be considered "clean" and able to rejoin the community, I needed to take my *mikvah*. This bath had become my monthly acknowledgement of the defeat of life within me.

The irony was even as Uriah became more renowned for his victories at war, I experienced defeat at home. And as I prepared for this bath, I considered how I might approach Grandfather to ask for his blessing on both Mama and me.

"My lady," Rachel's greeting drew me back from my thoughts. "The courtyard is cooler than your bedroom, and the tall, enclosing walls keep you well-hidden. Would you like me to help you with your mikvah there?" She grinned at me impishly. "Your grandfather has already visited you today, so we know he won't interrupt you."

I smiled at her teasing remark. "You're right, with such a hot day, it would be nice to bathe where I can catch a breeze to help cool me; even the water is warm from the sun."

Rachel drew pitchers of water from the large jars we used specifically for our purification rites. I disrobed and stepped into the round shallow bowl we used for our mikvahs. As Rachel slowly poured water over my head, I closed my eyes. Tears mixed with the purified water as it streamed down my face and body.

As I washed myself, I thought about my weaving. My hands were swift and sure with the distaff and my eyes saw the symmetry of colors and patterns before they took shape on the loom. Although my gift for this was not as great as Mama's, she'd taught me well.

My eyes still closed, I lifted up my face and praised God for giving me a husband who loved and cherished me, even though I was barren. A man who refused to find another wife to bear him the babes I hadn't.

Self-pity gripped me. I missed Uriah. With all my heart, I wished I was preparing myself for Uriah's homecoming, not mourning my loss of hope. When would he return? I yearned for the touch of his hands and the gift of his seed. But what good was seed when there was no fertile soil to nurture it?

My woman's body was a mirage in the desert. From a distance, it promised life-giving water and shaded trees, but up close, there was nothing but gritty, arid sand. Where was my beloved? I needed his loving reassurance that someday the Lord would bless us with a child. Where did Uriah find the faith to believe what I couldn't?

"Are you ready for the rinsing water?" Rachel asked.

I nodded. She slowly poured more water over my head and down my body. As I rinsed, I silently blessed Uriah and his unshakeable faith and steadfast love. Yet, grief lingered with me like an unfinished song. I quickly completed my mikvah and went inside.

*   *   *

Mama had helped me comb my hair, and we'd just sat down to our late evening meal when we heard someone knock at the courtyard gate. I sent Rachel to answer the summons and looked toward Mama.

"It's late for someone to call upon us," I said. Anxiety for

Uriah welled like a hidden spring within me.

"Do you think it's Ahithophel with news of Uriah?" Mama asked, her eyes dark with fear.

Like a startled doe, my heart leaped within me. I knew if he'd received news he'd immediately come to me with it, no matter what the time.

I heard a man's voice, but not Grandfather's. I waited for Rachel to tell us who it was. She walked into the room.

"It's King David's captain of the palace guards, Benaiah, with one of his men. He's asking for you, mistress," Rachel said, her voice high and questioning.

Puzzled and frightened by Benaiah's presence, I looked toward Mama, who shrugged her shoulders and shook her head. Neither of us could discern a reason for his late visit, unless. . . .

Mama and I walked out to the courtyard and bowed our heads in greeting.

"Shalom," I said.

Benaiah, a friend of both my father's and Uriah, stood straightly erect, his countenance foreboding. The brilliant blue of his tunic, with the gold fringe and tassels of his captain's rank, showed brightly against the flat yellow of the sun's dying light.

He bowed his head. "Shalom," he greeted, his dark, rugged face etched in stern lines. "I'm sorry to interrupt your meal, but I've come with a personal request by the king for you to attend him, Lady Bathsheba. King David asked me to give you this cloak and tell you it's light, but warm, and will keep you from being chilled when evening comes."

The king sends a gift as well as a summons? Why?

"Why does King David ask for my daughter, my lord?" Mama asked, bowing.

Her boldness surprised me, yet I also heard her fear. I knew if it hadn't been Benaiah, she'd never have the courage to ask. But he'd shared countless meals at our home in Hebron, and even here with Uriah, Mama and me.

"That is the king's business, and none of yours, woman," he

said, although not unkindly. But his eyes stared at her with clear rebuke in their dark depths.

"Forgive me, my lord," she murmured, bowing to him, her face ashen from his censure.

"I should change before I go into the king's presence," I said. I wanted to draw his attention away from Mama. I knew I must obey the king, but I was dressed in my old, worn tunic that I slept in. "Surely I should dress more formally for our king?"

"No. Take the cloak and we'll be on our way."

He handed me the blue cloak. I had no choice but to accept it. Yet, why would the king be concerned I might get chilled? How long would I be with David? I touched the cloak, surprised at its soft and supple weave and noted the hood. It also had an ornamental pin attached, that was a rich gift in and of itself.

"Rachel," Mama ordered, "go get your mistress' sandals." She turned to me, "Come here, and let me help you with the cloak."

I stood in front of her as my legs trembled under me. She slipped the cloak over my shoulders and drew the hood up. Drawing the material together beneath my chin, she used the lovely pin to keep the ends together. As she closed the fastener, I could feel her hands shake. "I'll wait for you, daughter. I fear. . ."

"I know," I whispered. "We fear news of Uriah's death."

"Here, lady, your sandals," Rachel said.

Mama took my arm so I wouldn't fall while Rachel slipped them on.

Benaiah turned to leave, and I followed him from our courtyard and out into the road. My heart beat to a rhythm of dread. I gripped the soft fabric of the cloak and followed the king's captain. The other guard marched behind us.

As I walked, my mind raced. Did David think it would be a mercy to my grandfather if he told me of Uriah's death instead of Ahithophel? David had called Mama to him to tell her of Papa's death. Was Grandfather with him even now?

I trailed Benaiah as we climbed up the road toward the cedar and stone palace. It rose above us in regal splendor. As we drew closer, I offered thanks we'd seen no one. Fear would have silenced any greeting I might have given.

However, once we passed through the gate house, Benaiah led us not to the main entrance, but toward a smaller side entrance. A guard stood at attention by the door and saluted Benaiah. Why didn't we go to the main gates?

"Uzi," he commanded our rear guard, "stay here with Samuel."

Upon entering the palace, I followed Benaiah down a short hall and up a flight of steep stone steps lit by torches in the wall. I lagged behind as fear slowed my steps. At the top of the stairs, Benaiah waited for me in a shadowed hallway. He nodded to me and I continued to follow him down the hall.

The crisp fragrance of cedar blended with the fragrant burning oil in lamps on stands. I looked down at the polished wood and almost ran into Benaiah when he abruptly stopped at an ornately-carved door. Two tall and grim-faced soldiers dressed in the brilliant blue color of David's personal guard stood on either side of it.

"I'll leave you now, lady," Benaiah said. He inclined his head and left even as one of the soldiers knocked once on the door and opened it.

I watched Benaiah leave and shivered. My feet felt heavy and numb. I didn't want to enter this room to hear my beloved husband was dead. I wanted to run back home.

A firm hand moved against my back and pushed me into the room. Shocked and offended, I wanted to rebuke him, but the door snapped shut behind me.

Trapped, I stood just inside the room. I looked around, expecting to see Grandfather. What I saw shocked me. The room wasn't furnished for a kingly audience... it was a bedchamber. Throwing back my hood, I saw no kingly chair on which David would sit while holding court, but a large, raised bed. Clay lamps filled with aromatic oil glowed in the corners, as well as on stands beside the bed. Pillows of red, purple and blue decorated it.

I took a hesitant step inside. Across the room I saw an open door. Where did it lead? Dare I go and look?

Had I not been called to King David at all? Did this bedchamber belong to one of his wives? But why would a wife of David summon me? It made no sense.

"Lord God," I whispered, breathless with panic, "help me. Why have I been brought here?"

Chapter 7

I shook with fear, unable to walk farther into this foreign bedchamber. A thick veil of confusion wrapped around me, and I was paralyzed with dread. The silence devoured my courage like a voracious rat. I turned away from the bed and noticed a rectangular table. Upon it was a lamp, a bowl of fruit and a golden pitcher with two gold goblets. Two blue and purple woven backed chairs stood near the raised table. The strong scent of the perfumed lamp oil nauseated me.

"Bathsheba, you're here."

I recognized King David's deep, resonant voice even before I looked up and saw him stride toward me from the open doorway. I immediately prostrated myself.

"Please, my lady, let me help you rise."

How could I rise and receive his grievous news? I wanted to cry out to him to let me remain on my face and wail out my sorrow for Uriah. But he hovered over me. I couldn't keep my king waiting. I pulled myself to my knees. The king took my arm and lifted me from the thickly carpeted cedar floor.

I stood before him with my head bowed. I was surprised when he put his fingers beneath my chin and lifted my face up to his scrutiny. I closed my eyes, as heat flowed from my head to my toes. I was flooded with shame. Only a husband took such liberties with a woman.

I sensed his avid gaze upon me, even as he removed his fingers from my chin. Why was he staring so? My heart thundered within my breast as fear pierced by lungs like a cold knife, and left me breathless.

"Do you like the cloak? I wanted to be sure you stayed warm, and didn't catch a chill after taking your bath," he assured me. With a quick movement, he undid the ornament holding the cape. He drew it from me, and it fell at my feet.

His words startled me. I looked up to see lust blazed within his eyes, twin fires of destruction that roved over my body. I stumbled back from him. Horror lanced through me with the strength of a spear thrust. The king had watched me bathe?

"When I inquired about you today," he said, "and was told your name, I recollected you. I saw you again as a little girl who hid behind your mother when I came to talk with your father in Hebron. Although there were times when I coaxed you onto my lap when I sang. Do you remember?"

He laughed with delight, and the sound confused me even more. Would he laugh and share remembrances with me as a child if he truly wanted to seduce me? Yet, he stared at me with the ardent gaze of a lover.

"And now look at you," he said. "You've grown into a beautiful woman, with your glorious black, curly hair, your lips as red and shiny as pomegranate seeds, your brown eyes sparkling with hints of emerald and gold, and your lush body flushed with desire."

Sweat bloomed on my forehead, as nausea moved up my throat. Truly, the king didn't call me to him to tell me of Uriah's death, but was trying to beguile me with words. Can he honestly believe I'm flushed with desire and not humiliation? *Oh God, his summons had nothing to do with Uriah and everything to do with the man, David.*

A different kind of fear filled my soul, leaving me bereft of words or reason. His large, calloused hand reached out and stroked my cheek. I shivered with revulsion, but he seemed not to notice, or perhaps mistook it for an answering passion? Lord God, no!

"My heart leaps like a gazelle within me just touching your soft skin. Here, feel it." He took my hand and placed it over his heart. It raced beneath the light material of his tunic, even as my own heart flew within my breast. But mine sped from alarm, not desire. And like the gazelle he described, I wanted to turn, leap and run from the room.

"As soon as I saw you bathing I knew I had to possess you, if only for this night."

I couldn't breathe! It was true. Because David saw me in our courtyard, he now wanted to lay with me, a married woman, married to Uriah, my beloved.

"No!" I gasped. I tried to pull away, but he wouldn't release me. His grip tightened painfully on my hand. Would he strike me for my instinctive denial? Anguish made my heart stop. "My king, I cannot do this," I pleaded.

He released me, only to take a lock of my hair in his hand. "Ah, it's still damp, and look how the light highlights the blackness with shades of blue. I remember your hair was curly as a child. But as a woman, it's more lovely, and curls around my finger with a desire all its own."

His soft words of praise shook me more. "Surely my king," I implored, "you would not take the wife of your friend, Uriah, who even now fights for you at Rabbah."

I took a step back, hoping he'd release my hair, but he only tightened his grip, and grabbed my hand to draw me closer. My throat constricted. I must scream. I opened my mouth, but fear and hopelessness stopped me.

Why scream? His guards wouldn't risk death to answer my cry for help. They'd even pushed me into the room, knowing their king waited for me inside his *bedchamber*. I shivered with the sudden certainty that death would surely engulf my family and me if I refused my king. No one refused God's anointed one anything. Was there no honorable escape from him?

Searching for a way to divert his lust, I said, "Your wives are beautiful with a radiance that rivals the very sun. I beg you, my king, send me home and call one of them to you. Do not—"

He placed a hand against my lips. "Quiet, my beauty, I am your king. Before every allegiance in your life, your allegiance to me comes first."

Stepping back, I escaped his muzzling hand. Desperate, I tried to reason with him. "Does my allegiance to you come before my allegiance to God?" I dropped to my knees and bowed my head before him. He released my hand. "My king, do not do this. I'm a faithful wife."

With strong, ruthless hands, he gripped my arms and lifted me so I stood before him. But my legs folded beneath me. Before I slipped to the floor, he clasped me to his breast. His arms were bronze bands of unyielding strength. I closed my eyes and swallowed the bile that rose in my throat. He held me so tightly against his chest I could barely breathe.

"I'm your king. You'll do as I say, and you'll not deny me."

Hearing the harshness of his words, I knew his lust ruled him. He refused to listen to my entreaties or my arguments.

Forcing my face up with his hand, his lips grazed my closed eyes and fastened on my mouth. His passion not answered in my lips, he kissed my neck and loosened the girdle from my tunic. He leaned down and pulled up the hem of my garment.

"Lift up your arms, Bathsheba," he commanded. I kept my face down and my eyes tightly closed, but I lifted my arms. The tunic slipped past my head. I stood naked before him as the searing heat of my shame blazed through me.

He stepped back, and wild hope spun through me. He was going to let me go! I glanced up and cringed as his ravenous gaze roved over me with possessive zeal. I tried to cover myself, but he gripped both my wrists.

"No, do not cover such perfection from my eyes."

In silent desperation, I implored God to stop David. He did

not stop, but kept his grip on one wrist and pulled me toward the bed. Everything in me cried out to fight him. But no one fought God's anointed king and lived, especially not a defenseless woman.

"Bathsheba, I will have you."

He caught me up in his arms and dropped me on the bed. The pillows surrounded me, suffocating me. I lifted myself up to get away from them and looked toward the door.

"Don't think of running, little gazelle," he said with a harsh laugh. "You know my guards would stop you. But, most importantly, you'd displease your king."

I leaned my head forward so that my hair shielded my face from his gaze. I knew if he could see my face now I'd betray my loathing. Help me, God! Like the sweet scent of incense, a picture of my mother rose into my mind: Anna, the Israelite slave who'd had the courage and spirit to survive the repeated rape by her Philistine master. Anna, the woman who'd captured the heart of my father with her brave, valiant soul. If she could endure such suffering, then I, her daughter, could survive the betrayal and defilement of my king.

The rustling beside me spoke of his disrobing. I kept my eyes closed. The strong scent of cinnamon in his royal perfume was as overwhelming as his presence as he joined me on the bed. With a silent cry I asked the Lord to take me to that secret place Mama had found when she'd been raped. The place where my mind could find peace, even as my body was taken captive and abused. But I couldn't find it.

* * *

"Leave now, woman," he ordered.

No tenderness or compassion touched his voice. I had been nothing but a receptacle for his adulterous passion which was now spent.

I trembled with crushing pain as tears filled my eyes. My soul foully wounded, I silently cursed him as I crawled to the edge of the bed.

Mother, was this how you survived? Did you curse the man after your body was forced to accept the most intimate of embraces?

"Get dressed. One of my guards will see you home."

Shame's fire engulfed me. I wanted to scream for him to keep his guards, who were no guards to me. Had they not been the ones that brought me to be defiled by my king?

I shook as I pulled myself up to a sitting position. Dizziness attacked like a swarm of bees, dimming my vision with black spots. My legs were long weights attached to my numb body. I fought for the strength to swing them over the side of the bed.

I stood, and swayed in my weakness. *Oh, God, don't let me fall.* I took deep breaths to calm the nausea that swept over me.

I staggered over and picked up my discarded tunic. With hands awkward in haste, I slipped my tunic over my head. Where was my belt? The cloak? Panic threatened as I searched the floor. I found my belt and tied it, but where was the cloak? I needed it to cover and hide myself. No one must know my disgrace; they mustn't see I'm an adulteress.

A well of sulphurous bitterness poured through me. I bent down and grasped at the splash of color that was the cloak. Pulling it on, the open pin scratched a path across my palm. With a silent cry, I quickly closed the pin and wiped my bleeding hand on my tunic. I ignored the throbbing pain, and gripped the hood and pulled it over my head.

Humiliation screamed I must cover myself. Grief wailed I must rent my garment. *Oh, God, help me.*

"I said leave, woman!"

His harsh, merciless command straightened my back and strengthened my legs. A river of hatred roared through me. I stumbled over something on the floor as I staggered toward the door, but I didn't look to see what it was. I swiftly righted myself, and reached for my escape.

I opened the door and lurched past the two guards. Were they the same men who'd earlier pushed me through the door? Had they knowingly thrust me into their king's adulterous arms or were they ignorant of their king's wickedness? Were there other women who'd been forced through that door?

My stomach rebelled at the thought, and I gagged. I rushed down the hall. Would one of the guards follow me home? Had David arranged for a guard to take me home even before I arrived? Feeling the hard wood beneath my feet, I stopped abruptly and looked down. My bare toes curled under me.

I'd left my sandals with the king.

I couldn't return for them. I'd never willingly return to my tormentor.

Scrambling down the hall, I abruptly stopped when I reached the end of it. Where were the stairs? I shook and with a small whimper, slid to my knees on the floor.

A strong hand gripped my arm. I cried out and pulled away. The hand released me as I cringed against the wall.

"Don't be afraid, my lady," he whispered. "It's Benaiah."

It wasn't David. A relieved sob escaped my lips.

"Come, you turned the wrong way. Follow me, and I'll lead you safely home."

There was no safety at home; why should I go there? But I had to get away. I pushed myself up from the floor and followed him. Staring down, his strong, sandaled feet moved along the cedar hall and stone stairs. Before we left the palace, he grabbed a torch and led me out into the night.

I hated the light he held up before us. I wanted only that the darkness would envelope and hide me. The sun had forsaken the sky and the moon was asleep beyond the hills. I was relieved. I wanted no light to reveal my dishonor to my family or my neighbors.

"You'll be blamed, of course," taunted the accuser in my head. "You're a woman and the temptress Eve's daughter. You bathed in the courtyard."

"But I didn't know the tall walls of our courtyard couldn't shield me from being seen from the palace," I inwardly wailed.

"David is your anointed king. God's chosen one cannot sin, can he?" the voice reasoned.

My mind tumbled into the depth of an abyss. *Oh God, I hate your king.* A deep chasm of loathing opened inside me. "How could your anointed one so wickedly betray me and my beloved? Oh, God, how could he do such a thing to me?" I whispered to the night.

I limped down the path, as tears formed tiny rivulets down my cheeks. Suddenly, I tripped on a stone and fell to the hard ground. Pain set fire to my foot, and my torn hand screamed in agony as I used it to try and catch myself. A strong hand gripped my upper arm and gently pulled me up.

"No," I cried out, violently shaking my head. "Don't touch me. I'm unclean." He released me. I trembled where I stood. *Oh, God, give me the strength to go on.*

"I'm sorry, my lady."

I heard the compassion in his low voice, even as he held up the torch so that my way would be better lit. Was he sorry for my fall, or sorry for his complicity in my disgrace? He'd been the one who'd taken me to David. Surely he'd betrayed his friendship with my family by doing so. Or had he? Hadn't he obeyed his king's command even as I was forced to do? What choice did Benaiah have but to obey David? Not to do so was death.

All through my life, I'd held King David to be second only to God in my reverence and devotion. As a child, I'd learned how to worship by singing David's songs. Often I'd watched him dance and sing with joy before the Lord and his people, in the tabernacle he'd built for the ark of the covenant, and in the streets during our holy celebrations and victories.

I exalted David as your beloved king, even as I exalted you, God, as my Lord.

My mind reviewed the years that were my life. I perceived how in my child's heart, I'd never separated God from my king. Even as a young woman, I'd not thought to separate God from the wise and luminous King David.

How could the king I knew and loved become a ravening destroyer? *I'm now an adulteress, worthy of death by stoning. Not because of my sin, but my king's.*

"Where are you, God of Abraham, Isaac and Jacob?" I whispered as I looked up to the vast, starlit sky. I clapped my hand over my mouth to stop my keening. I wanted to wail my pain and awaken the sleeping world around me to my devastation. But to do so would only hasten my death.

"Where am I without you, God? All I can feel are the oozing wounds of my shame."

Chapter 8

When we reached the gate of my courtyard, Benaiah bowed to me, turned and strode away. I was left in darkness, both within and without.

I turned away from the gate, even as it creaked open. Mama slipped a warm arm around me, pulled me into the courtyard and shut the door.

Hearing the door close behind startled me. I wrenched away from her. "Don't touch me. David has made me unclean," I croaked. The truth of my words chilled me to my core. "Before God, I'm an adulteress. I'll never be clean again. Never. If I don't kill myself, there'll be others who will. This is the law." I gasped and shivered. "Will Uriah be called home to help stone his wife?" *Oh Uriah, beloved, please forgive me.*

"Quiet! Come, I'll wash you."

I stared at her, starlight my only illumination. Awareness radiated from her eyes.

"Have you so quickly forgotten my story that you're surprised I discerned what happened to you?" She reached her hand to me. I didn't draw away. She tenderly took my wounded palm and cradled it in her own.

"After you left, Rachel mentioned she'd thought she'd caught a glimpse of someone on the roof of the palace, but when she'd looked, there was no one there. So, when you didn't return with news of Uriah's death, I started thinking. Soon it came to me why David had called you to him." Her deep sigh wafted over my face like a zephyr, but it did nothing to warm me. I felt frigid to the bone. "He'd seen you bathing from his roof and desired you.

"Dear one, I know what it's like to be called to a man against your will. To lie silent beneath him when every part of you is crying out to resist this abomination." She moaned and shook her head in silent remembrance. "I considered going for Ahithophel, but by the time he got to the palace, I knew it would be too late. I also feared what David would do to all of us if your grandfather confronted him. I sent Rachel to bed, and I've knelt by the gate praying as I waited for you."

There were no words. My grief and shame drew me into a void of silent agony. I doubled over and wept.

Her hands gripped my arms and she shook me. "This is not the time to give in to tears. Come inside. I'll clean you and then tend your wounds."

Blistering anger flowed through me like molten rock, burning my throat as words spewed out. "Wounds? You think to 'tend my wounds'? I'm an adulteress! I'm condemned to death by God's own law! As soon as it becomes known I was with David, I'll be stoned, even as I've no doubt the king will be forgiven. Let me die, Mother. A quick tumble from a cliff will be much less painful than seeing Uriah's anguish when he learns of this betrayal."

"No, it would not," she snapped. "If God is merciful, Uriah will never know of this. Now, follow me, we'll talk in your bedchamber. We mustn't awaken Rachel, or our neighbors with your ranting."

A short burst of hysterical laughter escaped me before I clamped my teeth shut on another. "Oh Mother, it doesn't matter whether they hear it from us or from one of David's personal guards. One way or another, I'm sure his sin will find us."

Without another word, she undid the pin, took my cloak and grabbed my arm, hauling me into my bedchamber. "I'll go get the water for your cleansing while you take off your tunic."

"Mama—"

"Silence! I'll be back in a few minutes."

I collapsed onto the edge of our bed and curled into a ball. With a fist in my mouth, I forced back the hysteria that roiled in my gut and up into my throat. I tried to shut my mind against the memory of David's touch, even as I silently cursed the man who was no more the shepherd-king to me.

No, but he was the man who had total power of life and death over me, and over my family. The man I couldn't accuse unless I wanted to embrace death and watch my family die, too.

So Rachel had even caught a glimpse of someone, but didn't tell me? I never should have listened to Rachel. But I'd never seen anyone on the roof before, never imagined someone could see into our courtyard from that distance. Fool!

My head against my knees, I surprised myself as I offered whispered thanks. "Thank you, God, there will be no child to die with me. I praise you I am barren." Tears flowing, for the first time I thanked God for the curse that was now a mercy. I heard a sound and looked over to see Mama carrying a large basin with a pitcher within it.

"Come, I'll help undress and wash you. I see your poor feet have been badly abused, too. What happened to your sandals?" She shook her head. "No matter, sit on the bed and I'll clean your hands first. How did you wound your palm?" She took my hand and stared at it with concern before gently patting it with a cloth. "Ah, I see, it must have been the clasp. This is a wicked scratch. I fear it may leave a scar. My poor child, what cruelty you've suffered this night. I'm so sorry."

Her soothing words moved over me, lapping at my pain. But I couldn't move. Perhaps, if I curled up on the bed, I could try again to escape to that place where memories had no power to wound and kill? Might the Lord be compassionate this time and help me find that place?

Mama's gentle hand rested on my shoulder. "I know your pain, my daughter, but you must do as I tell you. Sit up and I'll help you wash, and then I'll give you a potion that will help you sleep. There's a chance no one saw you go to David or return, besides his guards. If the Lord is merciful, no one needs to know what happened. Come, step into the basin."

I unfolded my aching body, drew myself up. With a gentleness born of her own violent past, Mama carefully helped me to stand in the basin and washed me. I grabbed the cloth from her and scrubbed at my body, determined to eradicate every trace of his seed and scent from me. I scoured my skin until Mama grabbed my hand.

"Daughter, you'll bruise yourself if you continue. Stop, dear one."

"Don't you understand?" I demanded. "I must get rid of every evidence of his touch." Hatred rose like a canker to mix with my humiliation. "My anointed king violated me, Mama. The poet, whose songs of worship could lift me to the very presence of God, is the same man who has condemned me to death by his lust."

In my despair, the words from a song filled my mind, and spilled from my lips:

"Be gracious to me, O Lord, for I am in distress;
    my eye wastes away from grief,
my soul and body also.
    For my life is spent with sorrow,
and my years with sighing;
    my strength fails because of my misery,
and my bones waste away. . ."
    But I trust in you, O Lord;
I say, "You are my God."
    My times are in your hand;
deliver me from the hand of my enemies and persecutors. . . ."

Even as the words started to comfort me, I recognized their source ... David. "He's even robbed me of the songs that would console me," I moaned. Hysteria rose with the bile in my throat. I dropped to my knees and retched in the water basin until my body was empty of everything but despair.

"Dear one, you're sick of heart and body and you've rubbed so hard your skin is red and raw from your scrubbing. I'll soothe you with anointed oil, and then get the salve for your other wounds."

She wrapped a cloth around me and helped me rise. Leading me to bed, I sat down and was seized with violent trembling.

"I think I must wait to put the oil on you, I can't risk you catching a chill. Here, I'll help you slip this soft tunic on and lay you down."

The tunic came over my head and she helped pull my shivering arms through the holes. She put a wool covering over me. I kept shaking.

"Rest if you can. I'll go prepare a potion for you to sleep, and then attend to your outer wounds with my healing lotion."

I shook and rocked myself. Would I ever know my husband's touch again or would he come back only to kill his adulterous wife? "Lord God," I whispered. "How can I endure this misery? Be merciful and let my mother prepare a mixture that will help me to sleep unto death."

She returned with a cup and the jar of healing balm. "Drink this while I tend you." she grabbed my arm and pulled me up. She helped hold the cup steady while I drank the bitter brew. She cared for my wounds and after she put the balm on my hand, she wrapped it with a strip of linen.

"The potion should help you sleep through the night, even with your pain."

"The pain I have can't be touched by this bitter cup," I lamented. "If only you had given me enough to let me sleep forever."

"Stop talking like a fool," she said. "Now, lie down and rest.

You'll be asleep soon."

"Stay with me?" I pleaded. She slipped next to me on the bed and her slim arms drew me up against her, cradling me like she used to do when I was a small girl. Her warmth, and the comfort of her next to me, acted with the drug to relax me, but fearing my dreams, I fought sleep.

Chapter 9

I awoke slowly. I was lethargic and my ears felt stuffed with wool. My eyelids were heavy and my sight clouded. I attempted to rise, but fell back as my head spun. My mind refused to focus. My palm throbbed with pain and my feet hurt. My mouth tasted bitter. *What was wrong with me?*

With vivid clarity, I saw David. I squeezed my eyes shut and wished again for the escape of sleep and the blessed forgetfulness it brought.

"Good, I see you're awake," Mama said, staring at me from the foot of the bed.

"I sent Rachel to the well," she told me, "so we could talk without her overhearing us. I told her King David called you to him at Ahithophel's request. How David praised Uriah's war feats with his own lips. She believes you arrived home soon after she went to sleep. I also told her to keep your summons to herself, as we didn't want others to be jealous that their husbands and sons hadn't been shown the same honor."

I laughed bitterly at the irony of her excuse. Dizzy, I slowly sat up and leaned against the stone wall behind me. "And what excuse did you give for my sleeping so late?"

She shrugged her slim shoulders. "I told her you were too excited to sleep last night because of your pride in Uriah. I said we'd do the chores and let you sleep in this morning."

"And how will you explain my bandaged hand, sore feet and missing sandals?"

"I will tell her you accidentally scratched your hand taking off the pin, you scraped your feet on some of our stones, and I insisted on giving you my new sandals."

I glared at her. "Ah, Mother, you lie well. I never knew you had such talent."

"These days I rarely lie, but there were times in my life when it was how I survived."

I heard the pain in her voice, and cursed my self-pity and thoughtlessness. "Forgive me." I reached my wrapped hand toward her. "I shouldn't have been so critical."

She gently touched my hand and knelt by the bed. "If we're to survive this, you'll have to learn to lie and lie well." Her dark eyes were alive with determination. "Last night you weren't ready to answer my questions. Now, I must ask them and have the answers before Rachel returns. Daughter, did any of our neighbors see you taken to the palace?"

I forced my mind to focus on the night before. "No, I think everyone was inside eating their evening meal or abed. We met no one on the road when we walked to the palace." A detail caught me. "Mama, Benaiah and the other guard didn't take me to the main door, but to a door on the side of the palace. I wondered about it, but only thought he must be taking me by a quicker way. But it was so others wouldn't see me, wasn't it?"

"Yes, I think you're right. For that I praise God," she said, relief evident in her voice. "But were there guards at this door who saw you?"

"One, but I'd never seen him before, nor the other two guards who stood before David's bedchamber door." Unthinking, I pulled my wounded hand through my hair, stopped, and grimaced.

"So, you saw no one, but could someone have seen you?"

I trembled. "I don't know. But if so, would anyone have

recognized me in the cloak? All the time we walked, I had the hood over my head. Even in the palace." I tried to remember more. "I also had the hood on returning home. Truly, Mama, I don't believe anyone but the guards could recognize me." I lifted my knees to my chest and wrapped my arms around them. "I ... I don't think anyone saw me, but how can I be sure?"

"All right. Now, tell me everything, dear one."

As I recounted all that happened to me, tension gripped me like a string on a bow.

When I finished, she stared down at me and her eyes darkened with anxiety. "I wonder if you should talk to Ahithophel? He's a wise man, and might be the only one we could trust to find out what rumors there may be of you in the court."

"No!" I exclaimed. "I can not confess to Grandfather what happened. We both know if he knew David had violated me, he'd want revenge. I can't risk his death and ours by telling him."

A long sigh escaped Mama and she bowed her head. A moment later she looked at me, her eyes full of grief. "You're right. One more question, daughter. Did David say anything about calling you back to him?"

"No," I spat. Rocking myself, I hugged the wool closer. "He obviously saw me bathing from his roof and desired that 'beautiful woman.'" I stared down at my body, hating it. "I detest myself for bathing in the courtyard. Yet, Mama, how could I know this time would be different? I've taken my mikvah there before."

"Yes, dear one, but before King David's been gone to war with his troops, not on his palace roof looking down on his city."

I stared at her in horrified wonder. "You're right. He called me to him only to satisfy his sinful lust. I was nothing to him but a moment's pleasure. And when he was done, he demanded I leave." I jumped up and paced.

"Oh, Mama, he shared memories of our home, and his visits with you and Papa," I cried. "And then he said my loyalty was first to him before anyone else. You know I would have fought him. But I feared if I did, I would have forfeited my life and the lives of my family."

"You're right. Your silence and compliance saved us all." With a gentle hand, Mama caught my tears as they trailed down my cheeks. "I'd save these tears, but I'm sure you'll cry more than can be held even in the largest bottle."

"I want to die," I choked out. "To Uriah I was beloved. But now, I'm no longer Uriah's faithful wife, but an adulteress. My sentence is death. How can I live with myself even if no one discovers this sin?"

"Oh, dear one, I feel and understand your anguish." She put her hand lightly upon my bowed head. "I know why you want only to escape through death. But if God is merciful, no one will speak of what happened and you'll live to welcome your husband home and back to your bed."

"How can you say that?" I cried, jerking my head up to glare at her. "Our marriage bed has been defiled. How can I welcome him into this body that's been desecrated and made forever unclean?"

"You have defiled nothing," she cried, shaking me by the shoulders. "You had no choice but to submit to David. In this time, before Uriah returns home, you'll work to forget what happened. You'll think only of your husband, and how happy you'll be when he comes back to you. And you'll welcome him to your bed and deny any thoughts that would sicken your soul."

Staring into her eyes, I could see her great strength of mind. She'd accept nothing from me but my acquiescence. "I can't do it. I can't welcome Uriah into my bed knowing—"

"You'd rather see him killed?"

I lurched back and gasped at the stark truth in her blunt words.

"If you tell him the truth do you think he won't confront David? And if he confronts his king, he'll die, and I don't doubt you'd die, too." With trembling hands, she drew me to her breast and wrapped her arms around me. "Please, daughter, you and

Uriah are all the family I have left. Do nothing to risk your lives."

Tremors tore through me, and I collapsed against her weeping. She held me tightly. Within a few minutes, she pushed me out of her arms and wiped her eyes.

"Rachel will return soon," she said, her voice vibrating with unshakeable resolve. "I'll help you dress, brush your hair and fix your eyes. She mustn't know you've been weeping. When she returns, you'll act as if you've received a great gift: the praise of your king for your warrior husband. Now, arise and act the daughter of the great warrior, Eliam. The beloved granddaughter of Ahithophel, David's wisest counselor."

I knew she was right. I couldn't waste more time for tears or doubts. If I valued the life of my family and myself, I must do as she said. Swiping at the tears with my hand, I smiled bravely. "I'm also the daughter of Anna, freed slave and beloved wife and mother. The most courageous woman I know."

Her eyes softened. With a quick movement, she hugged me, and I felt her strength of purpose as she crushed me to her. Leaning back, she reached up to touch my face.

"Yes, you're the daughter of Anna, the beautiful slave who captured the heart of a great man and loved him with all her soul. Dear one, if I could survive being a slave, you can survive this. Just remember, when your pain grows too great that you think you can't bear it, pray to God for help. He'll strengthen you. And I'll stand and support you with all that I am."

Her strength of mind, courage and great faith glowed from the depths of her dark eyes. I felt her will that same courage into my cowering heart. I'd never esteemed my mother more than at this moment. I was humbled by the witness of her life and suffering, and how she'd lived fully in spite of her past.

"I love you, Mama, and I bless you. But I fear I don't have your courage and I can only see darkness ahead."

Chapter 10

As each day passed, and we heard no gossip about me, our fragile hope grew that my sin wouldn't be discovered. However, I'd found it impossible to forget David's abuse.

While I spun the wool thread that morning, the memory streaked into my mind like lightning that blazed across a turbulent sky. I shook from head to foot, as a wave of weeping enveloped me.

It was Mama's warm embrace that brought me back to myself.

"Dear one, I'm here," she whispered. "Please, come out into the sun, it will warm you and the light will do you good."

"But if David is again on his roof?"

"I've told you, not once in the last week have I seen him there," she reassured me. "Surely you can come with me outside, at least for a few minutes?"

"I'll feel the sun later, when we walk to the tent of meeting. Mama," I said, "you know how hard it is for me to go where I might see King David. Can't you and Rachel go to the tabernacle without me this afternoon?"

"Bathsheba, each day I've told you the same thing: if we don't continue with our regular attendance at the tabernacle every morning and afternoon, the very suspicion you fear will be aroused. All know how much you love worshiping our God and will wonder why you aren't with us. And your grandfather, especially, will question you."

I bowed my head. "You're right. But it's so hard to be there now, when I experience only grief and despair. How can I find the peace I crave when the priests sing and play so many of David's songs of praise, which only remind me of the man who abused me?"

"I'm so sorry, dear one, but I do believe there will come a time when you'll again find joy in the worship of our God."

"Oh, Mama, I pray you're right."

* * *

In the second week after David called me to him, our neighbor, Lilith, stopped by. I was standing in the doorway of our weaving room. As I watched her walk into the courtyard, fear moved through me with the coldness of a winter wind. Would she say something about seeing me go to the palace? If she did, what would I say?

"Shalom, Anna," she called as she walked toward Mama. Younger than my mother, she was also rounder and taller, with long, grey-streaked brown hair. She smiled warmly at us. "I've come to ask you if Ahithophel has told you how the war goes? You know my husband, Barak, fights alongside Uriah, as Barak is under his command. He says Uriah is one of King David's finest warriors, and he's learned much from him in the winter months when they practice for war." Turning, she saw me standing nearby. "Bathsheba, what has your grandfather reported about the war?"

"His reports are all good," I said with a forced smile.

Mama drew her away from me back toward the gate. "Yes, Ahithophel comes every week to give us the news, and it's always good. If you like, next time he comes, I'll be sure to come over after he leaves and give you his report?"

"Yes, I'd like that very much. Well, I must go and tell Abner and Sharon the good news."

"Your son, Abner, has been growing so tall," Mama said. "Soon he'll be taller than his proud Mother." She puffed out her chest and smiled. "Yes, he grows in strength and wisdom each day. Thank you, Anna, I look forward to hearing more of Ahithophel's reports."

She almost sprinted out the gate, a huge smile on her face.

"I thanked the Lord that Lilith didn't come to gossip about me," I said. "And ask about my trip to the palace."

"Yes, God be praised," Mama agreed. "For when I saw Lilith enter the courtyard I feared the same thing. And to please her, I'll tell Lilith all your grandfather's reports. That way, if she does hear any rumors, perhaps she'll come and question us before spreading them all over Jerusalem."

"We must keep praying there'll be no rumors to tell."

"But if Lilith has heard nothing, and we've heard no word from your grandfather," Mama reasoned. "Surely, your secret has proved safe with Benaiah and his guards?"

"Every day we worship at the tent, I go to my knees praying for mercy, as I know you do as well. Could God be answering our prayers?" I didn't tell her that each time I was in the women's court, I avoided looking over to where David and his sons worshiped. I knew I'd be sick to my stomach if I saw him there, worshiping as if he'd never sinned against me.

* * *

In the late afternoon, Grandfather arrived. I'd just finished a row of weaving. I put it down and walked out to greet him.

"Granddaughter, you look pale," he said. He grasped my hands and kissed me on the cheek. "Are you ill?"

"No," I said. "So, have you brought me more good news?"

Not able to look him in the eye, I hugged him. As I held his wiry frame close, I fought the tears that threatened. I pulled out of his arms and turned away.

"Yes, yes, always there is good news about the war, thank our God."

"And now, are you on the way to worship? Do you know

if David will be there?" The question simmered up like boiled meat.

"Of course! He may shun leading God's army, but he's faithful to go to the tent of meeting many times each day." He scratched his beard. "But he's written no new songs. Everyone expected David to use some of his time in Jerusalem to write more songs. But he's been busy with his sons, working with them to learn more about his kingdom business. Well, I must go." He reached a hand to me. "Come, walk me to the gate. I know you must be missing Uriah."

"Yes." I walked up and took his hand. He gripped my hand, causing me to grimace at the pain with my still tender scratch.

He frowned at me and lifted my hand, staring down at the scar. "When did you get this? I don't remember it."

"A few weeks ago," I stammered. "It's nothing, just a scratch that didn't heal well."

"You must watch it closely. Scratches like that have caused deaths before."

"I know it well, Grandfather." I hoped he didn't hear the bitter irony in my voice.

At the gate, he hugged me and swept out into the road. As I watched him stride away, Mama came and stood beside me. "I'm glad he came, although I feared when he noticed your scar that you might tell him the truth."

I laughed without humor. "Ah, Mama, he's right. This scratch and what came before it might still cause my death."

* * *

I awoke to Mama shaking me.

"Bathsheba, wake up, dear one, you're having a nightmare."

When she let me go, I shuddered. "Oh Mama, David was chasing me through the rooms and halls of his palace, and I couldn't get away. It was so real. I wanted to scream, but when I did, no sound came out of my mouth."

I shivered as tears blurred my vision. "How do I fight dreams, Mama?" I asked, desperate for an answer. "How do I stop them from terrifying me with images too vivid to forget?"

She touched my cheek with a trembling hand. "I don't know, my child. I'm so sorry, but I have no charm or potion to rescue you from dreams. I can only ask God to send his angels to protect you from these nightmares."

"Yes, please pray."

Not able to sleep after Mama had awakened me, I waited for her to go back to sleep. I slipped out of the bed we shared and walked out our open door. I leaned against the wall, safe from any prying eyes.

I looked up at the sky, alive with glittering stars. The thought came to me that if Uriah were awake, he'd be looking at the same stars, the same sky. I missed him so much, but I also dreaded his return. Could I kiss him, embrace him, welcome his intimate love with the same joy and delight we'd always experienced? My heart feared our reunion even as I longed for it.

* * *

"Come, Bathsheba, I know you were up for hours during the night, but it's time to get up and worship at the tabernacle."

I rubbed my eyes. I hadn't gotten back to sleep until close to dawn.

"We must thank God you've escaped all rumors."

"Can we truly be sure of this?" I asked.

"I believe so. But whether I'm right or not, we will worship the Lord. For even if he chooses to take our families or our husbands in war, we will proclaim our Lord worthy of all praise. Hasn't he given us an abundant harvest this year? Does not his faithfulness comfort us in all our afflictions? And most importantly, we go to affirm his love for us endures forever.

"Think, daughter," she chided me. "Our Lord has never demanded we sacrifice our children to his flames, or give our daughters to feed the lusts of men at his temples. And I saw both abominations and more when I was a slave in Philistine."

"All right, I'll go with you. But I've been thinking I should go to the tabernacle at Gibeon and make a blood sacrifice."

"No."

"Mama, I know there's no sacrifice for my sin other than my own life. But, if I offered God a sin offering, perhaps he'd forgive me and enable Uriah to never know?"

"You've committed no sin that demands a sacrifice," Mama said adamantly. "Say no more about it. Besides, it would only lead others to wonder what your sin must be that you'd make a special trip to Gibeon to make a sacrifice."

Was she right? I saw the stubborn tilt of her chin, and knew to say more was pointless.

"Now dress and I'll tell Rachel to get you a date cake you can eat before we leave."

Soon afterward, we followed many others up the hill to the tent of meeting. David had created this "tabernacle" to be a place of constant worship to our God, with music and prayers that were given as an offering to our God day and night. I walked into the courtyard of women with Mama and Rachel and stood there among the other women. The music created by the voices and instruments of the Levites seemed to flow over me and reach to the heavens, bringing me a comfort I hadn't expected. I swayed to the music and breathed in the welcome scent of incense. Then I closed my eyes so I could better absorb this precious gift of consolation.

But when they began a song of David's, the despair in my heart reached up my throat as if to strangle me. I trembled as I understood that the king's poems could never bring me comfort and joy again. Yet, I knew the words so well they resonated in my mind, even when I wanted to reject them in my heart.

David's eloquent entreaties to God to rescue him from his enemies and be his savior and deliverer, spoke poignantly to my own condition. But it felt blasphemous that the man who'd written such powerful poetry, and known for all the years of his life the faithfulness and enduring love of his God, should be the wicked one I prayed to be delivered from. . . and wasn't.

The choir began to sing a well-loved song of David's, but

even as they sang aloud, my heart rose up with a song from the Sons of Korah, and I silently repeated the words, as if they'd been created to express my own anguish:

> "As the deer longs for flowing streams,
>   so my soul longs for you, O God.
> My soul thirsts for God, for the living God...
>   My tears have been my food day and night,
> while people say to me all day long,
>   'Where is your God?'
> These things I remember as I pour out my soul:
>   how I went with the throng,
> and led them in procession to the house of God,
>   with glad shouts and songs of thanksgiving,
>   a multitude keeping festival.
> Why are you cast down, O my soul,
>   and why are you disquieted within me?
> Hope in God, for I shall again praise him,
>   my help and my God....
> Vindicate me, O God, and defend my cause
>   against an ungodly people;
>   from those who are deceitful and unjust deliver me...."

Leaving the women's courtyard more than an hour later, the words of Korah kept whispering through my mind, and my lips moved in silent lament.

Chapter 11

With a cry, I scrambled out of bed and stumbled out to the courtyard. Mama sat on a rug near our round, clay oven, shaping a lump of dough. She looked up and smiled before a look of concern moved over her face.

"Was it another nightmare?"

I nodded as I stood, my whole body trembling. "This time I dreamed that Uriah died, Mama, but it wasn't by the sword of the Ammonites. I dreamed King David stabbed him with his great sword. Then he stood and sang a song of praise as Uriah bled to death at his feet."

She dropped the dough, ran to me and embraced me tightly. "Oh, dear one, such a bad dream you had."

"I know," I whispered. "I think I startled myself awake with my cry of horror."

"You've seemed to be doing better at night, to be sleeping better."

"Yes," I agreed. "Because in the last four weeks we've heard no rumors of my visit to the palace. No one has come forward to accuse me. But I still awaken feeling tired each morning, whether I've slept well or not." I hesitated, then added. "Do you think that David has forgotten the wife of Uriah?"

"We can pray he has," she said. "Now, go and wash your

face, and comb your hair before a bird comes by and claims it for a soft nest."

"All right, I'll go tame this bird's nest, and wash my face clear of all the dregs of my nightmare. And then you must tell me another of your incredible tales of your time in Ziklag, like when you and Abigail chased the lion out of town with only a broom and a torch. But I warn you, someday I'm going to write Abigail and ask her how many of your stories are true."

"Would I lie to you, daughter?"

"To distract me from my problems? Yes," I told her with a small smile.

* * *

Grandfather had just left after giving me his weekly report of the war, when Mama walked out from her weaving with Rachel in tow.

"Rachel, you go and tell Lilith the good news, and then I want you to go to Sarai's and bring me back some beads she promised me."

"Yes, mistress," she said.

"And if you want to play with her little Tirzah before you come home, that's fine," she offered.

"Oh, thank you, mistress," she said with a wide grin, spun around and ran out the gate.

I watched her go with a smile, glad that one of us in this household could live happily without care.

"Bathsheba, come with me, I must talk with you," Mama said. Her voice and demeanor changed abruptly. "Even though it's hot, we'll go in your bedroom. We'll need the privacy."

I stared at her in sudden apprehension, but followed her. She sat in Uriah's chair and pointed for me to sit on the bed.

"Bathsheba, you have been very tired lately."

"Yes, Mama, you know my nightmares."

"Are your breasts also tender?"

I looked at her closely. Why was she questioning me like this? "Well, yes, they've been more tender. But before my menses begins, I'm often sore, and I'm due any day."

"Daughter, you're already late for your period."

Her words shocked me, even as her piercing gaze unsettled me. "Mama, just last month I was a few days late. And you yourself told me how strong emotions in a woman's life can change her time, and I've been miserable."

I watched with fear as her brown eyes filled with deep sadness. She took a deep breath and exhaled slowly. "Bathsheba, I believe you're pregnant."

"No!" I cried. I jumped up from the bed to confront her. "I'm barren. I can't be with child." I glared at her and grabbed my stomach. "How can you even think this?"

"I know for these past years of barrenness you've been more regular than not, your menses coming about every twenty-eight days." She reached out a hand and leaned forward to touch my cheek. "According to my reckoning, you're almost a week past your time."

I looked into her dark eyes and saw her fear. I swallowed down the bile that rose into my throat. "No! The Lord wouldn't close my womb to Uriah, only to open it to my rapist. You must be wrong." I took a step back from her, shaking my head from side to side. "No! You're wrong!" I fought hysteria as it reached out to capture me.

"Dear one, I've prayed I'm mistaken," she cried, "pleading with the Lord to deliver us from this calamity that could cause your death." She bowed her head. Looking up she stared into my eyes. "I can't avoid the signs; you're tired, your breasts are sore, you often cry, you frequently relieve your bladder. . ."

"Of course I cry." I grasped the one thing I could explain. "What woman wouldn't cry if she'd been treated as I was?" I turned to leave. I couldn't listen to her ranting. She was wrong. She had to be wrong.

With a shake of my head, I ran out of the room, grabbed our basket from beside the door and was almost at the gate. Mama's hand gripped my arm with tensile strength. I stopped. Turning, I saw tears sliding down her gaunt cheeks.

"If you're pregnant, we must decide what to do," she said softly. "No one must know about this child."

I stared at her, my body tense, ready to escape. "You're wrong, Mama. Truly, I thought I was with child last month and was so happy until my menses came again. You just wait, it will come tomorrow, or the next day."

"Did you have these symptoms last month?"

I thought about it and knew I had not. "Tomorrow. We'll talk tomorrow if I still have not bled."

She hesitated a moment and shrugged. "If you need another day before you can admit to the truth, I'll give it to you," she said quietly. "But if by tomorrow afternoon you have not begun your menses, we must plan what to do."

I shivered from my head to my feet and ran out the gate. I'd go to the marketplace. I didn't care if Mara or someone else was there to taunt me. Their ridicule would be better than Mama's frightening words.

* * *

I was startled awake by a noise. As I lay trying to discern what had roused me, a wave of nausea moved over me. I took small breaths to combat it.

"What's wrong?" Mama whispered beside me.

"I heard something and woke up and now I feel nauseous."

"Ah," she said quietly, "I'll go get the bowl by the oven and return."

She crawled out of bed and was soon back with it. She placed it in my hand after I carefully sat up. I prayed I wouldn't be sick, and the queasiness slowly dissipated.

Mama lit the oil lamp by the bed before she crawled in bed and sat up beside me. "This was the only symptom of pregnancy you hadn't had. . . nausea. But now it's arrived and your bleeding has not. Bathsheba we must talk. We should do it now while everyone sleeps, including Rachel in the next room."

"Mama, I've thought of nothing else since you said this

to me, and could not sleep for hours thinking about it. If I'm pregnant and it's found out, I'll be stoned."

"When I was in Philistia," Mama whispered, "the women told me of herbs to bring on cramping, herbs I know I can get in our market. But I fear you taking them, for they sometimes cause the death of the mother as well as the child."

Without thought, my hand slid protectively over my womb. I looked into her grief-filled eyes. I was shocked how cold fear blended with warm hope within me. "If I'm truly with child, how could I kill the babe I've wanted all these years? A child innocent of the way it came into being?"

In the innermost part of me her words echoed with truth. The Lord had quickened my womb. What tragic irony, there was to be a child, but one conceived in pain, not love. A child with no future, because its mother had no future. The Law was clear: I must be killed. I wept in my despair.

"If I'm stoned and my child dies with me, let it be upon David's crowned head. But, I will not be the cause of my child's death."

Mama put her arm around me and cried softly. I wanted Uriah with me more than I'd ever desired him before; to love and comfort me. To somehow make everything right. But nothing would ever be right again, and in my heart, I feared his return.

Could I lie to save his and my life? To save the life of this forbidden child God, for reasons I couldn't understand, was knitting together within me? "Oh Mama, I hurt. For years, I pleaded to God for a child, and bled every month from his silence. Now, I discover I'm pregnant, and can only be afraid for its life and my own."

She held me more tightly. "I think it's time we called for your grandfather," she said.

My weeping ceased. "No!"

She gently released me and her eyes searched my own. "Then we must tell David. Perhaps he can send us away until after the babe comes."

"I want nothing to do with that man."

"Daughter, we need help. If not your grandfather, it must be David. He's the king, with the power and resources to help you. Perhaps, if you went away and had the child, and gave it to another to raise?"

Her words were a chisel to my heart, each word cutting out a piece of it. If I wanted to live, I knew she was right. But how could I give away my heart's desire – my babe?

"Perhaps we could tell your grandfather and Uriah a relative of mine discovered I still lived and wanted to see me? We'd say you decided to come with me. Yes," she said, slowly nodding her head, "this lie might work. But we'd need David's help. I'm sure he'd find someone willing to take us in until after the baby was born. Someone to adopt the child, or. . ." She gazed intently at me, her eyes suddenly lit with inspiration. "Or we could bring the babe back with us. We'd tell Uriah the mother and father had died and we were the closest family members?"

I was amazed at how intricate a lie she could weave so quickly. A lie certain to unravel if Uriah decided to join me after the campaign, which he'd surely do. But, if David were part of our conspiracy? Surely he'd keep Uriah away until the babe was born and we returned?

"Do you truly believe we could do this?" I asked in breathless hope.

"With David's help, yes. But first, you must inform David you're pregnant," she said. "I'm thankful Eliam taught you to write, so we don't need help sending a message to David. I'll take the missive to the palace, and personally tell Benaiah he must give it only into the hand of the king, and no other."

I gazed at her with equal measures of fear and awe. I didn't believe her plan could work, but I knew to go to anyone but David would prove disastrous. "He was the one who forced himself on me, causing all this trouble. He must help us through it."

"Let's pray first, Bathsheba."

"Yes, Mama." I felt an urgent need to pray. Should I pray for a miracle? But, what would the miracle look like? Wasn't my pregnancy a miracle? Confusion wrapped around me. I felt dizzy with all the doubts and questions that were like an enemy army invading my soul.

She hugged me. "We'll pray God will help you miscarry."

"Oh dear God, no," I gasped, pushing out of her arms. "I can't. Mama, I understand your desire to protect me, but life's finally taken root inside me, which is the bitterest joy I've ever known. I can't petition God to take the life I've just discovered, even if the existence of this child kills me. Mama, I can't pray for the child's death."

Her eyes radiated an inner fervor. "Rather this child's death than yours."

"Mama!"

"All right, daughter. I'll pray for God's will, and I know his will is to spare your life," she proclaimed. "You're all I have left. I'll fight for you like a lioness protecting her cub. So, this morning I'll tell Rachel I'm going alone to the marketplace. However, I'll go up to the palace first. I'll find Benaiah and give him your message."

"But what do I say?"

Her eyes sharpened with awareness. "Say only what you must; 'I'm pregnant.'"

"Yes, you're right. What else is there to say?" My hands trembled as I took hers in my own. "And may God be with us, dearest Mother, for without his intervention, I'm dead."

"You'll never speak of death to me again," she cried, her voice filled with anger. "I remember the stoning of one of David's soldiers and another man's wife. I ran away and vomited, not able to remain amidst the crowd of rabid executioners.

"Eliam came to me after it was over. He understood my horror at the scene, but he felt their sin deserved the punishment. No, daughter, you will speak no words of death. God knows I've had too much death in my life already."

I remained silent, my heart filled with misgivings. If my father were alive, would he number among my executioners, or would he show mercy to his only child? Surely, he'd show me mercy. But would my heavenly Father?

Chapter 12

We've had four days of excruciating silence. Mama and I have wondered if Benaiah has yet to find a time to give my missive to the King. And I've been nauseous each day.

This afternoon, she sent Rachel to the marketplace again so we could talk without her overhearing us.

"Surely we should have heard from the king by now," she said, pacing before me. I washed out my tunic in a bowl in the courtyard. She stopped, her face etched with fear. "When I gave the sealed note to Benaiah he gave me a look; a look that makes me wonder if he didn't guess its contents."

"God, have mercy." My hands shook as I squeezed out the water from my tunic. Did Benaiah guess the truth? The weight of Mama's stillness oppressed me. I stood up and shook out my tunic, hanging it on a hook in the beam that helped support our roof.

We heard running feet stop outside our gate, and looked at each other in apprehension.

Rachel opened the gate and ran to me. "Mistress," she cried. "I just saw our master, Uriah, going into the palace gate. I had just left home when I looked up the road and saw a man on horseback. He looked like our master, so I ran closer to better see him. As I watched, he turned toward the palace. It was Lord

Uriah!" The purity of her love for him glowed in her joyous smile. I wished I had her unsullied joy. Yet, my heart leaped with anticipation.

"He didn't see me. But he looked well, my lady, even if he was dusty and seemed somewhat travel weary. Truly, he had no obvious wound." She stopped to take a breath. "I thought to wait outside the palace gate for him to finish his business with the king. But I knew you'd want to know he's returned to Jerusalem, so, I came home. Did I do right, mistress?"

"Oh, yes, you did very well, Rachel," I assured her.

"Surely the king must have honored him by calling him to the palace to report about the war," Mama added.

"Yes, Mama, I'm sure you're right." Suddenly, nausea overwhelmed me. I ran to the corner of the courtyard under our tree, fell to my knees and was sick.

"Mistress?" Rachel cried in concern.

"It's all right, Rachel, your lady hasn't felt well all day, and although she's happy to hear of Uriah, it is very unexpected. Perhaps if you go inside, you can get her a small cup of sweet wine? It will help her feel better."

"Yes, I'll do this."

A moment later, Mama's cool hand settled on the back of my neck. I remained on my knees; my head bowed more with fear than with the nausea.

"Are you feeling better?"

"Mama, what if I'm sick like this around Uriah?" I whispered, trembling. "I can't seem to control it. It attacks like an enemy warrior with stealth and suddenness, leaving me trembling with weakness."

Rachel's sandals slapped against the stones and stopped. A cup appeared in front of me.

"Take a sip of this," Mama said.

My hands shook as I gripped the cup and tasted the wine. When she leaned over to help me rise, I clung to her. She led me into my bedchamber and helped me lie down.

"Rachel," Mama said, turning to face her. "Please go now to the market, if your master is coming home tonight, we'll need you to buy more fruit and also buy some lamb for a stew."

"Yes, mistress," Rachel said, a lilt back in her voice.

I curled up on the bed. "How soon do you think it'll be before Uriah arrives?" I turned to look at her. She sat beside me, her face stark with anxiety.

"I don't know, daughter." She rubbed my arm as she stared out the slit in our rock wall. "Surely he'll come to you as soon as he's reported all the news of the war to David? I should've known David's answer would be to send for Uriah." Her hand stilled on my arm. "If Uriah lies with you, then David is absolved of all guilt. And what man in love with his wife questions the timing or size of his child?"

I laughed bitterly. "I always knew David was a brilliant strategist, but I never recognized his ability extended outside of politics and the war room."

"Well, you must admit it's better than having us leave our home to go hide in the hill country while you await your child's birth." She patted my cheek. "Come, I'll help you prepare for your husband's return. We must take advantage of the opportunity David has given you to lie with your husband."

I stared at the hand she placed in front of me, but I couldn't grasp it. "I know you've told me again and again that when Uriah returned I must act as if nothing happened. Mama, I am delighted he has returned." I looked up at her and saw her dark eyes lit with both pity and resolve. "But, I've never lied to him before. I fear I won't be able to lie to him now."

"Would you prefer death?" she snapped. "Don't you see this is your only hope to save yourself, the babe and the life of your innocent husband?" She grabbed my hand and pulled me up. "We must believe David has given us the best solution for all. Besides, I won't allow you to die for lack of courage. Even our God will forgive a lie that embraces life over death."

"Do you truly believe this, Mama?"

"With all my heart and soul, daughter. Come, Uriah mustn't return home from the war only to find his beloved wife sick and depressed."

"Even if she is sick and depressed?"

* * *

Mama and I were making the lamb stew, and Rachel was milking Delilah when we heard a knock at our gate. Anxiety and joy warred in my heart. Was Uriah already here?

"Surely Uriah wouldn't knock?" Mama asked.

Rachel came to find us. "Mistress," she said, excitedly. "The king has sent you a gift."

I walked into the courtyard to see a young man. His stern look grew into a smile of admiration as I stopped and nodded to him. My eyes noted the blue girdle he wore around his white tunic, which signified he was one of the king's servants.

"My lady," he announced. "The King of Israel, may he live forever, asks you to prepare yourself for your husband's return. The king is speaking to Uriah the Hittite even now, expressing his pleasure in his warrior's most valiant deeds against our fierce enemy, the Ammonites." He cleared his throat and continued. "King David honors you and your husband by sending a gift of food to you from his own table. The king is sure this gift will meet with your approval, and he sends his deepest compliments to you, his faithful servant and wife to Uriah."

I swallowed the bile that rose at his message. Did David's words not mock me? I was his "faithful servant" not Uriah's faithful wife. David had stolen that from me.

I glanced at Mama, and forced myself to respond. "Thank you, and please advise your king that I'm most grateful for his gift, and pray he'll give Uriah the honor due him."

He bowed and went to the gate, beckoning to another servant, who carried a large covered bowl on her head. Even as she entered, another servant came with another bowl. The strong aroma of meat stew and fresh wheat bread filled the courtyard. I prayed I wouldn't be sick in front of David's servants.

"Here, you may set the food down on this table," Mama said, pointing to the table in the room that served as our dining area.

After the servants put down their burdens, they bowed and left.

Rachel shut the door behind them and turned. "Mistress, what a great honor our good king has bestowed on you and our master," she said in awe.

I could only nod my head at her and call up a weak smile.

"Rachel," Mama said. "Go milk Delilah before her bleats of discomfort assault our poor ears."

"Yes, mistress." She was clearly disappointed we weren't more excited by the king's gift.

"You're right, Mama," I quietly admitted as we walked into my bedchamber. "This is how David plans to make sure there'll be no scandal. Uriah will come to my bed, and in due time, all will rejoice at the news that I'm with child."

Mama took my hand. "And you, daughter, are you ready to welcome Uriah home?"

"I have no choice, do I?" I answered. "And truthfully, I long for Uriah and his comforting presence, even as I fear his touch, and how I will respond to it."

Chapter 13

Rachel came to my bedchamber to tell us that Lilith had arrived and was asking for us. We walked out of the room to find her standing by the gate; her face alight with curiosity.

"What's the occasion, Bathsheba, that you should receive a gift from the king?" she asked excitedly.

I had to smile at her enthusiasm. "Uriah's returned to Jerusalem and is even now giving the king his report of the war," I said. "King David's honored us and Uriah by providing food from his own table to welcome Uriah home."

"That is very good of the king," she gushed. "Bathsheba, do you think after Uriah returns home, he might take a moment of his time to come and tell us how Barak is doing with the siege?"

"Yes, Lilith," I said. "I'm sure Uriah will be happy to give you news of your good husband."

"But if Uriah wants to spend all his time with his wife," Mama added with a sly grin. "Then Bathsheba could ask him and tomorrow come and tell you?"

"Ah, yes, you're right, Anna," she agreed with a knowing smile. "If I were Uriah I'd want only to spend all my time with my lovely wife."

I felt my cheeks bloom with color.

"The food smells delicious." Lilith said as she sniffed the air.

"Lilith, the king was so generous with his offering, would you like some of the stew?" I asked her. "I was just wondering how we were to eat it all. You see, Mama and I had just begun making my own lamb stew after we heard Uriah had returned to Jerusalem."

"Really, you would share what was given to you from the king's own table?" she asked in wonder. "Oh, yes, Bathsheba, we'd be delighted to share in your feast."

"Rachel, go and spoon out some of the stew for Lilith and her children," I said. "Your Sharon is growing into a lovely young woman, and Abner seems to get taller every time I see him."

Soon, Rachel walked carefully toward us with a clay bowl full of steaming stew and handed it to Lilith.

"Mmm, this looks very tasty. Bless you for your kindness to us," she said with a smile that took up most of her round face. "And don't forget to ask about Barak?"

"I won't forget," I assured her.

She carefully walked out of our courtyard and through the gate, with Rachel following and going with her to open Lilith's gate across the road from us.

"Now," Mama said, turning to me. "I think you should lay down until Uriah comes. You'll need all the rest you can get before he arrives, because you're sure to get none when he joins you in your bed."

I smiled at her, suddenly anxious for Uriah's arrival. Surely I could welcome him home with joy if I concentrated only on my deep love and need for him?

I could hear Rachel's running steps. Soon she was standing at the door, her smile becoming a frown as she looked in on me. "Are you unwell again, lady?"

"No, Rachel," I said with a reassuring smile. "I'm only resting so I'll be able to stay up into the long hours of the night loving and talking with my husband."

A lovely red stain grew upon her cheeks. "But I will get to see him, too? You won't send me to bed before he comes to us?"

"Yes, little one, Uriah will come and greet you, too."

"Rachel," Mama said, putting her arm around her. "While your mistress rests, I think you and I should sample that stew and bread while it's still warm, don't you?"

"You wouldn't mind, lady?" she asked, looking over at me.

"No, you two eat. I'll wait to eat it with Uriah."

She smiled shyly. "I'm looking forward to tasting the stew. It does smell wonderful."

"Yes, it does," Mama said. Keeping her arm around the young girl, with a nod to me, she led her out of my room, but didn't close the door so I would have more air.

As soon as they left, I closed my eyes, but knew I couldn't sleep. So, I lay there and prayed that Uriah would soon come home, and God would remove all memories of David when I welcomed my husband to my bed.

* * *

I awoke feeling nauseous. I lifted my head and pulled myself up slowly. With a groan, I remembered Uriah was in Jerusalem. But he wasn't in our bed.

I looked to see if his imprint was on the bedding, sniffed the air for his beloved musky scent that often was perfumed with spices and leather. I smelled only my own sweat. Fear tore at me. Why had he not returned home to me? Perhaps he'd talked with the king into the early morning hours? Surely he'd be home soon?

The sense of gnawing hunger drew me out of bed. The last week it had amazed me how I could be nauseous, and soon after hungry. I became aware of the noise coming from outside our courtyard, and the clack of the loom being worked in the next room. Was Mama weaving?

With an effort, I stood up and took off the fine linen tunic I'd worn for Uriah. There seemed no reason to keep it on when I didn't know if he was coming home soon or not. I slipped on an undergarment and my light tunic, thankful to realize I was only slightly dizzy. Walking out of the room, I turned to the left and looked through the door to see Rachel working at the loom.

"Good morning, mistress," she greeted me. Looking up from her task, her eyes were dark with sadness and her ready smile was missing. "I tried to stay awake to greet our master, but I fell asleep. Your mother told me Lord Uriah didn't come home last night at all, and I was to let you rest. But my lady," she said, her voice filled with awe, "your mother has gone to beg him to return home. She said to obey King David and hold to his oath of marriage is greater than his oath to holy war, and you have need of him."

At her words, I was abruptly reminded of the vow Uriah had made before he'd left for Rabbah over two months ago. Mama must have remembered his vow last night, but believed he'd relent and come home as King David had told him to do.

"How long ago did she leave?" I asked. *Oh, Mama don't you know Uriah well enough by now to know he'd never forswear an oath?* Yet, I knew her boldness was born out of desperation for my life and the babe's.

Rachel put her finger to her lower lip. "Not long. Can I get you something to eat? Your mother told me to serve you when you awoke."

"No, thank you, Rachel, you continue your weaving. I'll get what I want." I needed to do something to help me stop worrying about Mama.

Rachel's desire to please had always touched me. And although I hadn't thought I needed a maidservant, two years before Uriah had insisted. Rachel's father had died in battle, and Uriah contracted with her mother to take her as my handmaiden. In this way, he helped support her widowed mother, and gave me more time for my music. Uriah's generosity to us both had made me love him all the more.

Unwrapping the bread, I tore a small piece off, filled a goblet with foamy milk and slowly walked out to the courtyard, nibbling the bread and sipping the milk. I stared at the door to the courtyard, willing Mama and Uriah to walk through it, yet fearing it wouldn't happen.

As I waited, a memory touched my mind. Uriah and I had been married just over a year and we were living in a tent near our barley fields. Uriah had been helping our workers cut our grain, as he always did in the early spring before going off to war.

I was delighted when he told me how much he'd enjoyed his year of grace from fighting after he married me. How being a part of planting and harvesting each of our crops had brought him more pleasure than he'd ever found in war. While spending that year with me, he'd experienced a contentment he'd never known.

However, he knew as long as he was one of King David's soldiers; he must always be faithful to fight for his God and his king. But he'd prefer to live peacefully with his wife, caring for his fields and home. Yet, his honor compelled him to remain King David's captain-warrior.

Bitter tears scored my cheeks as my heart cried out with the truth. No entreaty by Mama would bring Uriah home. He'd never dishonor his vow of holy war or his men by doing this. Bless her, but Mama had gone on a futile mission.

I took a slow, deep breath, refusing my desire to weep aloud. I was the daughter of warriors. Now, I needed to think of how we might allow Uriah to keep his honor and still come home. Was there a way, or had his vow closed every door other than an all out victory which would probably take months to accomplish?

Feeling suddenly drained, I went back into our bedchamber and sat in Uriah's chair. The chair I'd hoped to see Uriah in this morning.

* * *

I was still in Uriah's chair when I heard Mama call to Rachel as she entered the courtyard. Next, I heard Mama and Rachel speaking softly and the door of the courtyard open and close once again.

"Mama?"

She stood with shoulders bent in the doorway. "I sent Rachel to the well." Her face was pale, her eyes looked wounded. She slowly shook her head. "He refused to come home. He told me he'd been summoned by the king to give him the war news and this he's done. His eyes filled with anger when I entreated him to come home to you. I told him we knew the king had encouraged him to do this as well, and had even sent us food last night from his own table."

A sob caught in her throat. "Oh my daughter, he rebuked me for my words and said even with King David's encouragement and now mine, he couldn't disavow his oath of holy war. He said as much as he wanted to come home and enjoy his wife he could not do this. The ark and David's army are in their tents before our enemy's stronghold and the Ammonites have still to be vanquished. He'll return home with David's army when they're victorious. He told me he'd said this to the king himself, and knew you'd understand as well."

"Yes, Mama, the memory of his vow came back to me this morning," I said. "And no matter what happens to me, I'm glad my husband refuses to break his oath. At least one of us can hold his honor without guilt before God."

"Oh Bathsheba," Mama groaned. She shocked me when she knelt down in front of me and put her head in my lap. Instinctively I put my hand upon her head and stroked her thick hair, as she'd done to me so many times. Her shoulders shook. A few minutes later, she raised her tear-stained face to look at me.

"He slept with his friends of the palace guard last night in the courtyard," she said. "David has asked him to dine with him tonight and promised to send him back to the front tomorrow so he might return to his men."

"Did you think to ask him how much longer he thought the war would go on?" I asked, my mind grasping at the hope that if the war didn't last much longer . . . if he was home within another month?

"No." She sat back on her heels. "I went to plead with him

to come home, and begged him to do it for your sake. I told him how you were sick with worry for him." She hiccupped on a sob. "When I first came to the palace, I didn't see Uriah, but I saw Benaiah. I gave him my request to see Uriah, and he arranged for us to talk in a corner of the king's courtyard. I think your grandfather saw me talking with Uriah, because I heard his voice, but my back was to the palace, and when I turned to leave, he was gone."

"Perhaps King David called Grandfather to him so he might see Uriah and hear his reports as well," I said. "I know Grandfather would be pleased to see his grandson and hear from him personally about the war."

She stood up and paced. "But now we must think of another way to help you. Perhaps my first plan might work?"

"Mama, I've been thinking," I said, standing so I might face her. "And the only other plan that would work to allow Uriah to hold his honor would be the one you originally thought of – that we'd leave and go to another town where supposedly you have family. Truly, I can think of nothing else."

"But would the king agree to help us with this?" she asked.

"Who knows? But I've no idea what town we could go to."

"Oh, Bathsheba, I have such fear," she murmured, touching my hair.

"As do I. Mama, I want to see Uriah before he leaves Jerusalem, although I don't want to risk him seeing me." I took her hand, and held onto it tightly. "God alone knows when I'll see him again. If the war goes on much longer and I'm here when he returns, then it may be he'll return only to discover my sin. Mama, I must have at least a glimpse of him before he leaves Jerusalem."

"Stop talking so!" she snapped, shaking my hand free. "David's plan was sound, but he didn't know how honorable a warrior is our Uriah." She rubbed her forehead as she thought.

"David could also call Uriah back as a liaison between him and Joab," she said. "And if he served David as a liaison, surely the need to fulfill his oath would be gone? For it's not as if he would always be with the army."

"Yes, surely David could do this, as we know he can do anything he wants. Did I not learn this well?" I said, staring at the scar on my palm.

"Bathsheba," Mama said, catching my attention. "What do you think?"

"This is the best plan I've heard. But do we dare request this of David?"

She leaned over and hugged me. "For you, I'd dare anything. After Uriah leaves, I'll go to the palace and look for Benaiah again."

"First we must ask God for wisdom," I said. "Perhaps God will answer this prayer." Yet, he'd opened my womb to David, and Uriah wasn't coming home, at least not during this visit. But soon?

"Yes, dear one, but you're looking so pale. Rest awhile, and then we'll go to the tent and pray." She kissed me and walked out of the room.

I sat back down in Uriah's chair having little hope our prayers would be answered.

Chapter 14

Absorbed in my desperate prayers, the sound of loud voices gradually caught my attention. I recognized Mama's subdued voice followed by Grandfather's angry shout. Grandfather never talked to Mama, and yet it sounded like he was cursing her? I jumped up and immediately fell back into the chair. I fought lightheadedness, and slowly rose again.

"Who do you think you are, woman, to try and talk Uriah into disobeying his oath to his God and his king to come home to his wife?" Grandfather roared.

I said a prayer for strength as I walked into the courtyard. He paced in front of Mama, his face red and distorted, and his hand fisted and raised. "Do you want your son dead? Has God not struck down others who break their vows? I pray God might strike you down for asking such a thing!" He brought his hand down as if to give her a backhanded slap.

Mother didn't cower, but stood facing him, her countenance serene and without fear.

"Stop, Grandfather," I yelled. "It was me. I was the one who asked Mama to go to Uriah."

Mama stared at me, and opened her mouth to deny it, but I shook my head to keep her silent. She'd gone to protect me, and should not take the blame.

Grandfather's hand fell to his side as he stared at me, his eyes wide in accusation. "You?"

Cringing from his horrified look, I tried to explain. "Rachel saw Uriah ride into the city yesterday afternoon and followed him to the palace. Soon afterwards, King David's servant came here to tell us the king would send Uriah home, and he would be with us soon. The servant also brought a gift from the king, an offering of food from his own table. He and two other servants left us the feast." I swallowed bile, as my body shook. "But Uriah never came home. This morning I asked Mama to find Uriah and bring him home, if only for a few hours. He refused."

"The king encouraged Uriah to come home? He even sent food here?" Grandfather asked, aghast. "He never told me."

"Will you go now and accuse the king of incurring the Lord's wrath even as you have accused us?" I challenged.

"I don't understand." He looked down and shook his head.

"You saw and talked with Uriah. What else did he tell you?" I knew I was more hungry to hear all of Uriah's words, than to blunt Grandfather's accusations.

He glanced up at me, his dark eyes full of confusion and anger. "I saw your mother talking to him, but I was summoned to the palace. Soon, Uriah joined King David and me to talk about the war." He smiled proudly. "Uriah confirmed the war is going well, and the siege is working. He commended the men under him for their bravery and willingness to follow him wherever they were called to engage the enemy. He reported our casualties have been minimal because of Joab's sound strategy, and the obvious blessing of our Almighty God. He also said David should have another crown for his head and more slaves in a few months, if God continues to bless us."

"That's wonderful news," I said, even as my heart grew faint. If it took months to win Rabbah, then the life growing within me would surely be my death.

"Yes, it is, but what Uriah told me when King David excused us was not," he snarled. "When we came to the courtyard, I pulled him aside and asked him what your mother had said to him. He told me she'd asked him to break his vow and come home to you, Bathsheba. I was irate, but he tried to placate me. Benaiah's arrival stopped our conversation as he came to tell Uriah the king wanted to talk with him again. I left and came here to confront your mother."

I ached. After more than twenty-two years, Grandfather finally speaks to my mother only to accuse and curse her again. "Well, now you know she saw Uriah at my request," I asserted.

"And I understand it was you who went against everything you believe to encourage your husband to come home to you, even knowing this is against God's will."

My face heated with shame. I wanted to scream I wasn't the one who'd gone against God's will, that it was his "noble" king who'd done this. But to protect us all I agreed with him. "Yes, I made this request of my beloved, believing if the king could so encourage him, so could I."

Grandfather straightened up and pointed a condemning finger at me. "Woman, I'm thankful my grandson is a man of integrity, even if you have no honor in you," he accused. "All these years I was concerned Uriah would prove to be a man worthy of your esteem and love, when I see now it is you who isn't worthy of Uriah's respect."

His words were a heavy hammer, each word a blow shattering his love and respect for me. What could I say? He was right. I was an adulteress, unworthy of any esteem or love. I wrapped my arms around myself and bowed my head.

"You will not speak to my daughter like that," Mama rebuked him. She strode up and stood between Grandfather and me, facing him. "You know nothing about what she's suffered, and you were right all along. It was I who decided to go to Uriah this morning. Bathsheba was asleep when I left. She had no knowledge of what I planned to do."

"Mama, please," I pleaded, trying to pull her back. When she didn't move, I shifted so that I stood beside her.

"No, dear one." A cloak of dignity covered her as she stood facing him. "I refuse to let this man think you're not more than worthy of all the love and kindness Uriah has shown you. I'm used to his rejection, even his cruelty, but I refuse to watch him reject you when you did nothing wrong. If Eliam were alive, he'd make sure nothing came between the two of you. I must honor his memory by doing the same."

"You think, woman," he sneered, "you can bring any honor to my son in death when you brought him no honor in life?"

Mama staggered back.

"Grandfather, no! How can you say such a thing?" I cried. "Mama is a friend of the king and his wife, Abigail, and is honored by all who know her. Uriah has told me many times how thankful he is to be the son-in-law of my blessed and gracious mother."

I watched his face as hate gave way to rage. "Eliam shouldn't have gone against me to marry this. . . woman. She's brought nothing but dishonor to our name."

"No, it's you who dishonor the memory of my father by saying such a thing."

"You would speak to me about my honor?" Grandfather demanded.

"Only as it affects my mother," I said. My body shook and I knew if I didn't sit down soon, I'd fall. Mama stepped up and put her arm around me.

"We stand here talking about honor, and you're blind to how you're upsetting Bathsheba," she rebuked. "Go, old man, and don't return until you're ready to give your granddaughter the respect she's due."

I glanced at him as she led me into my bedchamber. He looked taken aback, angry and puzzled. Poor man, we'd never quarreled like this. Yet, I couldn't let him speak to Mama as he did, when he knew nothing of the truth that compelled her action.

"Do you need the bowl?"

"Please." I grabbed the bowl from her hands. I hated this; it felt as if all my innermost parts would be forced up with everything else.

I wiped my mouth with a cloth and looked up to see Grandfather. He watched us from just outside the door.

"Why wasn't I told you're sick?" he asked, his wrinkled face now creased even more with lines of worry. "How long have you been ill? Is this why you wanted to see Uriah?"

After sipping sweet wine from the cup Mama gave me, I said. "I've only been sick a few days, Grandfather, and I don't believe it's life threatening. I just ask for your prayers."

"Please, leave now and let your granddaughter rest." Mama's voice was a quiet command.

From where had all this courage come that she continued to challenge my grandfather? Of course, she was defending me. Mama had always been my protector, even more than Papa ever had. I sighed as she gently helped me to lie down. I looked to see Grandfather standing at the foot of our bed staring down at me.

"I'm sorry you're ill, Bathsheba. I imagine having Uriah with you would bring you comfort, but you know. . ."

"I shouldn't have asked for Uriah's presence," Mama snapped. "Now leave her be, and take your curses with you. Bathsheba needs your blessings right now, not your curses." She sighed deeply. "Have we not suffered under your curses long enough?"

He bristled, and his mouth became an angry line. He didn't respond, but turned on his heel and stomped away, a trail of dust followed him.

"You should never have tried to take my sin upon yourself, dear one," she said. "I've taken his curses and rebukes before, and I can take them again, but you don't deserve them."

"Perhaps not, but it stopped him from striking you. Oh Mama, I hate this sickness."

"I'm sorry to have upset you." She took my hand and stroked it.

"We both know it wasn't your fault."

"You're right, it's all David's fault. And even he knows he can't command Uriah to return home, he can only encourage. To command him would raise too many questions."

I didn't answer, but wondered if even now Uriah and David were talking together in the palace. Was David still trying to convince him to come to me? I was sure he must be. He'd be desperate to find a way to persuade Uriah into my bed.

"Merciful Father," Mama prayed, squeezing my hand, "bring Uriah home. I know you'd forgive him breaking his vow if it meant saving her life, and her babe's. Have mercy, Father, mercy on Uriah, on Bathsheba, her baby and me. Please, bring him home."

Chapter 15

I slept past our evening meal and into the night. When I awoke, I could see by the light of the lamp that burned that Mama was slumped in Uriah's chair, sound asleep. I tried not to disturb her when I arose.

"Can I get you some bread and wine, dear one?" Mama asked, sitting up.

"Uriah never came," I whispered.

"I prayed for us all. I even went to the tent and worshiped there while you slept." Mama pulled herself out of the chair and stood. I could see there were tears in her eyes. "I'll go and get you something to eat. Often the nausea is worse when the stomach is empty than when it has something in it. I don't know why this is, but I remember it from carrying you."

"Thank you."

I sat on the bed and leaned against the cool, stone wall. I still felt tired, but I wasn't sure if it was the nausea, or my heavy heart.

"Here, eat this."

I pushed back the hair that had fallen in my face and did as she asked. As I ate, a strong longing gripped me. "What if I went to Uriah? Would he turn me away?" I shook my head at my stupidity. "Of course he'd turn me away, and I'd only grieve us both even more. Mama, I don't know what to do. Help me, what should I do?"

"I've been thinking about our idea to ask David to bring him home and be a liaison to the army and the king," she said quietly. "I'm sorry, dear one, but I don't think the king would take advice from us. But, if you confided your condition to your grandfather?"

"No. We both know Grandfather would want only revenge for how David dishonored me." I combed my fingers through my hair and began to braid it.

"If only I had a family and hadn't been orphaned," Mama said. "Or, if Eliam were still alive, he'd know what to do." She stopped. "Ah daughter, if Eliam were alive and knew David had raped you, well, it has been wise not to have told your grandfather, who is much like your father."

I shuddered with awareness. "Every time I begin to sing one of David's songs, I see his face again, feel the pain." I slowly untangled the braid I'd just woven. "All my life I've sung the songs of our king, and been comforted by them. I've taken up my lyre or danced with tambourine in hand, rejoicing in our God. Even when I've fallen on my face before God in reverence and awe, I've quoted David's words. And now his words feel as barren as I once was, and I find myself silent before God, except to plead for mercy.

"How can words and music which once filled me with life and drew me to God, now instill such anger and sorrow? Mama, how could David, who's been so abundantly blessed by the Father, and been given so much through his gracious hand, the king who has multiple wives and concubines, be the same man who took from me the only gift I had. . . my honor?"

She moaned. "Haven't I wrestled with the same questions? I've known David many years, and Eliam knew him longer than I. Because of his many gifts, we often forget he's flesh and blood, like every man. He's God's anointed king, yes, but as we both know, he's also but a man. All men are capable of the most heinous sin, even as they are able to bless and be generous." She sat down by me and grasped my hand.

"Oh daughter, you *are* beautiful. David saw you, in all your loveliness, and decided he'd have you. He's a man who, for years as king now, has taken all he wanted, even women.

"Abigail once told me of one of his concubines. She'd been promised to another man, whom she'd come to care for. But David saw her in a crowd when he was riding home from war and desired her. So, he sent two of his guards to bring her to the palace where it was discovered she was unwed. He then took her and made her his concubine."

"She was unwed? Mama, he knew I'm Uriah's wife!"

"Bathsheba, men who have power often abuse it, and those with great power are tempted to abuse it all the more."

"Destroying the lives of those entrusted to their care," I spat, jerking my hand away.

"Yes, but I'll not allow David's sin to destroy you."

I laughed harshly. "And how will you save me, Mama?"

"I don't know yet, but with the help of the Lord God, I will find a way. I must."

I bowed my head on my knees. I couldn't listen to her words of imaginary hope. Exhaustion and despair covered me, grinding me down like wheat under a millstone. A part of me wanted to run to Uriah and pour out my heart to him, praying he'd forgive me, and come home with me, to remove the nightmare and shame of David's touch.

But I knew with a deep, inner surety I couldn't do this. It wasn't only fear for Uriah's death that stopped me, but concern for my own life, and the child's. My heart assured me Uriah would only blame David. But my mind argued that because I'd bathed in the courtyard, he could accuse me, too. If he did, would he reject, and maybe even kill me?

Tears dropped onto my legs, and I whispered. "Uriah, you take my heart with you to war, beloved, even as I war with my own heart. Lord of Hosts, protect Uriah, he's innocent and good and fights and lives for all that is honorable."

"Amen," Mama said beside me.

"I feel so cold. So very cold and hopeless."

"Come, I'll lie down with you." Mama crawled into the bed. "Perhaps the morning will bring good news. But for now, let me hold you so you might sleep again. In sleep is blessed forgetfulness."

I slipped down and Mama put her slender arms around me and held me tightly, my back to her front. She hummed softly, as if I were once again her little girl who'd awakened in the night with nightmares. But I was no longer that child, but a woman with a woman's fears. And anxiety knotted my stomach and tormented my thoughts, denying the quick forgetfulness of sleep.

* * *

Sometime during the night, sleep did claim me and when I awoke, Mama was gone. I tried to gauge how my body was feeling. The nausea was there, but I thought if I moved very carefully, perhaps I wouldn't be sick.

"So, you're finally awake," Mama said, standing at the door. "Here, I have some bread and goat's milk for you." She handed them to me.

"Rachel is on the roof, beating some rugs, so we must speak softly. Your grandfather came by earlier to tell us Uriah would go with David to worship at the tabernacle, before he leaves to return to Joab. He thought you might want to know this so you'd be sure to be at the tent when Uriah comes. He doesn't believe Uriah would look for you amongst the women, but you could easily pick him out among those closest to David. I was shocked that he spoke to me, and showed such compassion for you."

Her words pierced my heart with ragged pain. "Uriah and David worshiping together? By the Lord God, it's blasphemy!" I exclaimed. "King/adulterer and innocent husband prostrate before God? Can I stand to see Uriah beside the man who has ripped apart our lives?"

"Yes, you can, if you truly want one more glimpse of Uriah. Besides, the women will notice if you aren't there today and comment about it. I'm sure Lilith has told everyone about Uriah's return."

"Oh Mama, I feel such deep despair. My beloved is so near; does honor forbid a touch or even a word of farewell, if I should wait outside the tent for him?"

"Do you think he could look at you and not see your pain and wonder at the depth of it? Would you send him back to war wondering at the source of your agony?"

I bowed my head under the weight of her truth. "No, Mama, he must never know my grief."

Chapter 16

Arriving at the women's court at the tabernacle, Mama, Rachel and I quickly lost ourselves among the women. Because it was early morning, the heat was not stifling, but it still beat down with bright persistence.

I wove my way through the women to a spot where I had a clear view of the place where David always worshiped with his closest family and personal guards. Even though Joab had taken the ark from the tabernacle to the battlefield, this was still the place where all in Jerusalem worshiped.

Standing on tiptoe, I caught a glimpse of Uriah walking behind David, his dark, grey-streaked head erect, and his countenance somber. He looked up, as if he felt my gaze upon him. I quickly brought my feet flat to the ground, so I was well-hidden behind a number of taller women. I couldn't risk his seeing me. I couldn't trust myself not to run from the tabernacle weeping, and have him wonder why I left in such distress.

"Did you see him?" Mama whispered.

"Yes, just his face, but it's enough."

As I tried to focus on God, I felt hot tears burn behind my eyes. I shut them tightly, and willed them not to fall. My heart felt bruised and beaten, my emotions in turmoil. Music swirled around me – melodious voices gifted in drawing us into God's presence sang a Davidic song. I prayed I wouldn't become sick, and amazingly did not.

After close to two hours of worship, I had to leave. I quickened my steps and looked down so I'd catch no one's eyes. I didn't want to greet anyone.

Lilith had stopped by yesterday morning to ask about Uriah, and Mama had told her of Uriah's vow and his decision to remain at the palace. Lilith had been disappointed not to have news of Barak, but also pleased that Uriah had kept his vow and honored God and his men by not going home.

Arriving home, I ran and grabbed a piece of bread as Mama followed me into the room.

"Dear one, I'm so sorry. I know seeing Uriah was both gift and grief."

I nodded, unable to speak.

"I asked Rachel to follow Uriah and watch for him as he leaves, so we'll know when he has left us again for war."

"You did tell her to stay far behind, so he wouldn't see her?" I asked, afraid. "If he saw her, he'd know I'd sent her, which might distract him when he returns to war."

"Yes, I told her to stay out of his sight," Mama assured me. "Although she couldn't understand why. But she promised to obey, even though I know she wanted to greet and touch her master, even as we did."

"Ah, Mama, I feel exhausted, but my mind is spinning."

"I know, as is mine. I'm sure Rachel will be here soon. There can be little else for the king to say."

I stared at her. "Nothing more for him to say, but what will he do? His plan to have Uriah lie with me was thwarted by Uriah's steadfast honor. Now what will he do to cover his sin?"

"Perhaps he's already come up with the same solution we did? Or he might call back Uriah to join his palace guard again for the duration of the war," Mama said. "Surely, David could tell Joab he needs Uriah's strength and wisdom here in Jerusalem.

He could explain that because the siege is succeeding so well, Joab could easily release Uriah to serve David at the palace."

"But would Uriah do this when the victory isn't won? Oh, Mama, I fear there is no sure way to circumvent Uriah's vow."

I heard the door creak open and watched as Rachel ran through it. She stopped abruptly when she saw us, flushed from running; her long, dark hair was in a tangle around her anxious face.

"My lady, my master has left. I saw him as he put a kingly scroll in the pouch at his belt and got on his horse. I followed him up the road, away from the palace, that leads through the fountain gate. I came home as soon as I could with the news." Out of breath, she stopped.

"Thank you, Rachel," I said, "you did well."

"Come, have a date cake," Mama said, "I'll work with you on our pattern. You're doing well, but I have more to teach you."

I watched Mama and Rachel walk into the weaving room. Suddenly, I knew I had to have one more glimpse of Uriah. With a strangled cry, I ran and jerked the gate open. Heedless, I dashed up the path that led to the road to the fountain gate. Weaving through the throng of people going in the same direction, I ignored the shouts and curses sent after me as I bumped arms and legs in my reckless race. Just before I reached the gate, I tripped on a rock and fell headlong into the dusty, rocky road. My face in the dirt, I tried to catch my breath, spitting out grit as I gulped air.

"Bathsheba, are you all right?" It was Grandfather's voice, full of concern that reached me amongst the other startled voices around me.

I raised my head, and drew my scraped arms forward to lean my forehead against them. I ached all over, but knew nothing was broken.

"I – I think so," I stammered. I drew myself up to my knees.

Grandfather's hand gripped my forearm and he pulled me up with gentle strength. I stood swaying, his hand on my arm.

"You foolish girl," he scolded, "what did you think you were doing running up the hill that way? Do you want to break your neck?"

"I wanted to see Uriah one last time." I pulled my hair back, and wiped at the dirt on my face with my bruised and scraped hands.

"Ah yes, I thought I saw Rachel standing by the courtyard at the palace. She must have told you he left the palace grounds and was returning to Rabbah."

I nodded in mute agreement.

"He's gone, little one, you can see only the dust raised by his horse." He pointed out the gate.

I stumbled up to look out, oblivious to the people around us. In the distance, I saw the dust cloud that noted Uriah's passing.

I was too late to see his face. Too late to say goodbye. Too late.

"Come, girl, I'll walk you back to your house. You don't look like you'll make it home without some help." He took my arm and drew me away from the gate. I limped down the hill beside him, thankful for his surprisingly strong support.

"I can't believe a woman married over four years, should act like an unruly child," he grumbled. "And look at you, your face cut and dirty, with scrapes all over your hands and arms, and by your limp, I'm sure your feet must pain you as well."

I didn't try to stop his scolding. I was too numb with pain both inside and out. I wondered if such a fall could bring on a miscarriage. Even that thought brought no fear, no anxiety, no relief. . . nothing.

I kept my head down and let Grandfather lead me. After what seemed a long time, he stopped.

"Woman, your daughter has been most foolish," Grandfather said. "She was running up the hill and almost killed herself when she stumbled and fell."

I glanced up to see Mama at the gate, her face reflecting shock and concern. "Bathsheba, what have you done to yourself?"

"I was too late," I mourned. "I saw only the dust of his

passing."

"Thank you, my lord, for bringing her home. I'll take her now."

Mama's voice was gracious, her hand firm as she took my other arm.

"Rachel can get me a cup of wine and a raisin cake. I'll wait to be sure Bathsheba hasn't come to more harm than bruises, scrapes and maybe a sprained ankle," he said.

"As you wish," she said. "Come, dear one, let's see how badly you're hurt."

The basin of water was dirty and bloody after Mama wiped away the dirt, first from my face, then the rest of me with a soft cloth.

"Rachel, bring me the salve," she called. "Except for multiple scrapes and bruises, it seems you broke nothing."

"Please tell Grandfather I'll be fine. I don't want to face him again."

Rachel came into the room carrying the healing balm.

"Thank you," Mama said. She gently rubbed the ointment into all my cuts while I sat on the edge of the bed. "Now I'll go assure your grandfather you'll soon have only scabs as evidence to your rash behavior."

After Mama spoke to him, I watched him leave, grateful not to have to face him again.

"Your grandfather is thankful you have only small wounds to show for your great folly."

"I'm blessed the two of you were able to talk together today without animosity."

"With all our worries, your grandfather's cordial behavior was a small miracle, for which I am thankful. Before you rest, would you like something for the pain?"

"No, Mama, I can bear it. Truly, it's my heart that hurts the most, and there's no cure for it."

"Ah dear one, you're right. No cure, except, perhaps for prayer?"

"Then there's no cure, for I can find no words to pray"

Chapter 17

The next morning when I awoke, I wasn't sure what hurt more, my churning stomach or my bruised hands and knees. I reached for the bread I kept in a small container by my bed, and began taking small bites. Yet, it was the awareness of Uriah's absence that distressed me most. I ached with grief.

I'd only glimpsed him from a distance. But knowing he was in Jerusalem and not at Rabbah, had kept me from worrying about losing him on the battlefield. Now worry for Uriah was like a buzzing bee around my head.

As I got out of bed, I felt the scabs on my hands, knees and face tighten with pain. I gingerly touched my chin and groaned. All my scabs must make me look like a clumsy fool.

"How do you feel this morning?" Mama stood in the doorway, her face drawn in lines of deep concern.

"Like I'm nine again," I said, determined to make her smile. "Do you remember how I'd joined you and the other women to sing and welcome our victorious men home from war? I ran out ahead, leaping, I was sure, as gracefully as any gazelle, when I tripped on a stone and fell in an ungainly heap." I grinned remembering. "Papa saw my fall, and when he came home, he was all sympathy. But soon we were laughing with joy at his homecoming, and his humorous description of my less than graceful fall."

A radiant smile of remembrance lit her face. "He did say your strong, high voice was the one he heard first amongst the women in delightful song until it disappeared into a raven's screech. I think you looked much then as you do this morning. But though your scabs are ugly, they look to be healing well." She searched me closely. "Yes, I see no redness around them that would speak of infection, thank the Lord."

"I still have the scar on my knee from that fall. One time Uriah noted it and asked me how I'd gotten it. When I told him, he said he could still hear that screech among the singing, but hadn't known it was me. He laughed at my story."

"According to your grandfather, you made no cry when you fell yesterday, even if you were acting like a nine-year-old again."

"I was too numb with pain to cry out."

"I know, dear one, I know." She reached a hand to me. "Come, change your tunic and try and eat something before we go to worship."

"You think I should go looking like this?" I didn't want to go to the tent and see the king. Besides, I could only mouth the songs that brought me despair in the hearing. I hated the distance I felt from God. But I also grieved how all my prayers for mercy were met with silence.

Yet, if I remained here, would my mind not torment me? Already I feared what new scheme David might devise to free himself from me and my child. My stomach wrenched at the knowledge he must be busy even now on another plan to cover his sin.

"Bathsheba, you're suddenly ashen. What ails you, dear one?"

I couldn't voice my fears. "It's the babe, Mama. Perhaps, I'll try more bread." *Oh God, what will David do now?*

*   *   *

Six days of silence from the palace.

Had David forgotten me?

Yet, with each passing day, I'd grown more distraught. My outward wounds had healed, but I've been haunted by nightmares that leave me weak and frightened. The little energy I had has been sapped by oppressive heat. Nausea attacks me every morning, even ambushing me two of the last six afternoons.

I've tried to imagine what David might do. But I can't talk with Mama without being afflicted with a soul-deep fear. Yet, when I try to keep my fears within me, I only feel sicker.

"Mama, when will David send me word of his new plan? Do you think he has decided to wash his hands of me? I've spoken no word against him. Does he believe my silence will keep him safe?"

"Ah child," Mama said. She stopped kneading the dough to stare at me. "I have no answers."

"Before my belly rounds with his child, does he think I'll not accuse him of his sin? The law is clear: death by stoning. If I'm accused of adultery, I swear I'll not go to my death without accusing David before his people."

I paced the courtyard, my sandals scuffing the stones and throwing up dirt. I knew Mama watched me, and felt my desperation. "Remember when I fell into a stream and I almost drowned? Papa jumped in and rescued me, but I'll never forget how I tried to breathe under water and the shock of drawing in water and not air. I thrashed and twisted, trying to reach the surface to breathe, but felt myself continuing to sink to the bottom."

I stopped pacing and glanced over at her. "Poor Papa got kicked and scratched before his strong arms drew me close to him and we came to the surface. He dumped me on the grass face down and pushed all the water from me until I could take a choking breath. I can still hear his strong, calm voice saying; 'Courage, little one, you're safe now. Take small breaths and you'll be fine.'

"Mama, I feel like I'm drowning again under the weight of

David's silence. I don't know how much longer I can bear it."

I dropped to my knees and grabbed the stone quern. I crushed the grain and imagined it was David beneath the stone. The man who raped me. The king who left me feeling powerless, unclean, and desperate.

"Do you think David was shocked when he learned Uriah had never left the palace grounds to come home to me?" I looked up at her. "Was the king convicted of his own lack of honor when he discovered Uriah's integrity in not breaking his vow?"

Mama stood up and walked over to me. She slid down and slipped her arm around me and held me to her. "Dear one, calm yourself. I've never seen you like this."

"I've never been like this before. But I know if I hear nothing from David this day, I'll go to the palace and demand to speak to him myself."

* * *

I begged Mama to take Rachel to the marketplace to see if anyone there had any news of the war. Reluctant to leave me, she finally heeded my pleas and left. I sat under our tree to wait for our bread to bake when I heard a loud wail. Where was it coming from?

My heart beat with a loud, staccato rhythm. I watched our courtyard gate swing open. Grandfather staggered through, his face so ghostly white I couldn't distinguish his features from his snowy beard. His blue striped robe was rent and black ashes mixed with his white hair.

"Grandfather!" I yelled. I ran and knelt before him. *I know. Oh God, I know.* "Uriah is dead."

His grizzled head nodded. "Yes, little one, your husband was slain in battle."

I fell at his feet as all my nightmares coalesced into reality. This was David's solution. Uriah's death. *Of course, he let the Ammonites kill Uriah for him.*

"Bathsheba," Grandfather groaned as he leaned down to pat my head. "A messenger came to David from Joab. Our Uriah and others fought bravely against the enemy, but they perished in the fighting."

I keened beneath the weight of the truth. "No! Curse him! No!"

Suddenly, Grandfather's wiry arms were embracing my trembling body and holding me close. But there was no comfort from his warm presence, only darkness and pain and the sure knowledge of why there'd been no word from David. He'd been waiting for this news.

He'd had to wait six long days to get the news from Joab of Uriah's death.

With this insight, the cries of other grief-filled women penetrated the stillness around us. Nearby, Lillith's cry "Barak, my love! Barak!" filled me with even greater despair. Jerking myself free, I stood and ripped my tunic before falling prostrate on the ground. Grandfather rose up to stand before me.

"Dear God," I whimpered to myself. "How many faithful warriors died beside my Uriah? How many others did David sacrifice for his sin?" I scraped at the hard stones. "Oh, Lord, bury me beneath these rocks, too."

"Bathsheba, what are you mumbling?" he asked.

I couldn't repeat the blasphemous truth. I curled up into a ball, my arms over my ears, and tried to escape the cries of the women who'd lost husbands, sons and brothers because of me. I had bathed in my protected courtyard, unwittingly within the sight of a lustful king, and now, even as life grew within me, death encompassed me. My innocent husband was dead. I opened my mouth and let my loud cries of torment join my sisters in their grievous lament.

* * *

Someone shook me. "Stop wailing before you make yourself sick."

Mama's voice penetrated the wall of grief. I could not listen to her. *She doesn't know, she hasn't heard the news. Uriah is dead. My beloved husband is gone.*

"You must get up, dear one, and lie down on a bed."

My eyes were swollen shut. I brought my lips together on my last, hoarse wail.

"David had Uriah killed," I whispered.

"I know," she crooned softly. "But you'll live. You must live!"

I shook my head. "I'll die under a rain of stones, and the babe will die with me."

"Here, mistress, drink this." Rachel's voice seemed to come from a long distance.

"I'll help her drink, Rachel. Please check on Ahithophel? He's sitting in Uriah's chair where I found him when I returned from the market. He could use some wine."

"Yes, lady, I'll go get it for him."

"Good girl," she said. "Now, Bathsheba, I'll help you sit up. I fear once you're up, you'll be nauseous, but I brought your bowl."

"I'm too heavy to sit up. Mama, Uriah's dead body covers me. It's pushing me into the ground. Uriah knows the truth now, Mama, and he's calling me to come to him." I tried to take a deep breath, but I could only draw a short, shallow gasp. "Let me go. Let me die with Uriah."

"You're talking nonsense, daughter," her voice cracked above me like a whip. "I refuse to listen to such rubbish. Come, I'll help you sit up."

"We're too heavy. You'll see, even you won't be able to lift us."

"Uriah may be dead," she said, her voice ragged, "but he'd not want you to die, too. You will live, Bathsheba, and the child you carry will live as well, but first you must sit up. Now give me your hand, and let me help you."

"My hands are numb. All of me is numb." Deep sobs ripped through me again, shaking me from head to foot. "Please let me die."

"Didn't I want to die when I heard my Eliam was dead? But

as I found the will to live, so will you!"

"Mistress, there are women at the gate who want to come in and grieve with you," Rachel said, her voice low and urgent. "I told them to wait, that you were not well, but Mara is determined to see you."

"Bathsheba, Anna."

Ah, it was Mara's voice. Of course Mara would come here after she heard of my beloved's death. She'd covet one last time to shame me with my barrenness. One last time to gloat over me. Should I tell her I'm not barren?

"We heard the news and are here to mourn with you. Isn't it tragic Uriah died without a child, Bathsheba? Poor Anna, you've only an old man to care for you, and one who holds no love for you, either, I've heard. I'm sure your grandfather will find another husband for you, Bathsheba. One who has other wives and children, for he'll get no children out of you, will he?"

Harsh, dry laughter spewed from me. The fierce desire to tell her the truth grew strong within me. Should I tell her that I would have a child to comfort me: a king's child? I blindly reached for Mama's hand. I opened my eyes when I couldn't feel it and looked up. Mama stood straight and magnificent in her restrained grief and fury.

"You needn't worry, Mara," Mama's voice was flint. "Ahithophel will care for both of us. Is he not the king's trusted counselor, and were not both Eliam and Uriah two of David's renowned mighty warriors? I'm not worried for us. Not at all. But I do grieve the death of my son, and if you came only to gloat and not grieve, be gone."

Proud of my mother, I forced myself to stand so I could look Mara in the eye. But what I found was a mouth agape, bulging eyes, and her fat body shaking.

"Thank you, Mara," I said, "once again you live up to your name. . .'bitter.'"

Her round, fleshy face grew redder. "It's you who must be bitter, alone now with no child to—"

"Anna, Bathsheba." Sarai greeted us as she stepped forward, and around the large Mara. "I grieve with you, my friends, and I've brought you mourning bread." She handed it to Mama. "I'll lift my prayers to God for him to comfort and strengthen you."

"Thank you for your kindness," Mama said.

"Mara," Sarai said, turning to look at her, "as you didn't bring the traditional cup of consolation you said you'd bring, you should leave. I came to grieve with my friends, not speak cruel words that only add to their sorrow."

With amazement, I watched Mara snort, turn and waddle across the courtyard and out the gate. "Bless you, Sarai," I said.

Suddenly my body rebelled. Looking around me, I saw my bowl, leaned down, grabbed it and ran into my bedroom, where I retched.

"Poor Bathsheba," Sarai's words followed me. "I'm sure I'd be sick, too, if I'd just heard my husband had died."

Why did I now silently thank God she'd no idea it wasn't my grief, but my pregnancy that caused my distress?

Hearing a noise behind me, I turned to discover Grandfather's concerned gaze upon me. He was leaning forward in Uriah's chair next to the bed, a cup in his hand.

"I don't like this, little one," he said gruffly. "You're sick again. Surely the news of Uriah's death has made you ill, but it still concerns me."

In the courtyard I heard Mama wail out her grief, as Rachel and Sarai joined her. Setting aside the bowl, I knelt in front of my grandfather, put my head in his lap, wrapped my arms around his slender waist and moaned.

Sick of all the lies, I wondered if it was time to tell him the truth. Should he not know the source of my illness, and the truth of David's rape? How I'd dreamed of Uriah's death? But if the king had ordered Uriah's death to cover his sin, would he hesitate to arrange my grandfather's as well? *I must keep my silence.*

"Can I get you more wine, my lord?" Rachel asked from the

doorway.

I looked up to see Rachel. She looked so forlorn and grief stricken. She'd loved Uriah so much. I slipped my arms from Grandfather's waist, sat back on the rug, my knees pulled up, my head down upon them.

"Yes," Grandfather answered, "and perhaps some wine for Bathsheba? I don't like it she's still ill." Over my head, he handed her his empty cup.

"None of us like it that she's ill," Mama said. She stood in the doorway. "But I'm sure it's the shock of Uriah's death that has caused her to become sick again."

Had Mama suspected my desire to confide in Grandfather, and the fear that kept me silent? I watched her as she leaned down and grabbed my bowl before she left.

"How did Uriah die, Grandfather?" I had to ask him. "Did David say?"

"Yes, he told me the messenger explained how a strong enemy force came out through their gates, and as Uriah and his men fought them back into the city, a strong barrage of enemy arrows and stones cut them down." He swore loudly. "Joab's strategy was folly. He shouldn't have risked his men following the enemy to the very walls of the city when all know even women can kill men from there. Joab's never used such foolish strategy before." He slashed the air with his hand. "I told the king he should punish Joab for the loss of these men and remove him from his command. But David refused."

I put my hand to my shattered heart. Was I right? Had David ordered Joab to place Uriah where he'd be sure to die? It seemed the only explanation for Joab's deadly orders, leading to Uriah's, Barak's and how many others' deaths?

"You're right, my lord," Mama said from the doorway. "Those do appear to have been reckless orders. And I grieve Uriah's unnecessary death. 'The Lord gives and the Lord takes away, blessed be the name of the Lord.'"

She handed Grandfather a cup of wine, but I refused the cup

she offered me. I bowed my head and wept in anger more than grief.

"Uriah was a good and faithful husband to you, granddaughter, and a fine warrior." His voice was hoarse with emotion. "I was proud to call him grandson. But you're young and beautiful. I've no doubt I'll receive an offer for you once your seven days of mourning have ended."

I trembled at his words, raised my head and glared at him. "How can you so quickly dismiss Uriah's death and talk about marrying me off to another? Don't talk to me of husbands!" I shouted. "Can you not let me grieve my dead for even one day?"

I tried to stand, but my legs wouldn't support me, so I remained sitting. *Dear God, would David attempt to find me a husband?* The thought was a hot wind that blistered my mind. Would this be his new plan? Would he find a man who wouldn't mind being the father of a kingly bastard?

"We'll trust God with our lives and our futures," Mama said. "Won't we, my daughter?"

I glanced up to see her brown eyes radiating her grief and her resolve. My right hand settled on my stomach. It seemed even if my heart recoiled from the idea of another husband, my body wanted to defend the child in my womb. How could I betray Uriah's death by thinking more of this child than his murder?

"Your mother's right," Grandfather said, surprising us with his agreement. He leaned forward, and cupped my chin with his strong hand so he could see me more clearly. "God will supply you another husband, Bathsheba. Even though you're barren, I'm sure we can find a man who already has children by another wife." He cocked his head like a curious raven. "Yes, even overcome by grief, you're a beauty any man would desire, whether you give him children or not."

Hysterical laughter came bubbling out of me. I jerked out of his grip and rolled into a ball at his feet. My screaming mirth swiftly became deep sobs. *Curse him! He impregnates me, kills my husband and leaves me bereft."*

"Look at your daughter, woman, curled up like that, laughing and crying. She must have a demon," he accused.

"She needs no priest," Mama cried. "Can't you see she's crazed with grief? You shouldn't have told her you'd find her another husband. She needs time to grieve her beloved. There's nothing here but the shadow of death. Leave us."

"Yes, I'll leave."

Grandfather rose from the chair and stepped around me, as if afraid to touch me.

"I'll walk him to the gate and come back to you, dear one," Mama said.

I moved to sit up and rocked myself. A song from my childhood slipped from my lips:

"Let them be put to shame and dishonor
    who seek after my life.
Let them be turned back and confounded
    who devise evil against me. . .
You deliver the weak
    from those too strong for them,
the weak and needy from those who despoil them."

"How sad, my Lord and God," I sang, "that the evil I know and fear comes from the very man whom you comforted so often. Who will comfort me, Lord? Uriah is dead.

"Uriah is dead. . . David is alive. . . His child lives in me. . . I can see only death for us both. . . How can I bear to carry the child of my beloved's murderer?"

"By choosing to live," Mama answered from beside me. "And you will choose to live!"

I stopped rocking and singing. I lifted my head and stared at her. "Let me die, Mama. This child has brought me only sickness, pain and death."

"This child brings the promise of new life to you. Dear one," she pleaded as she dropped to her knees and wrapped me in her arms. "Your child is innocent of the blood of your husband. Even though he was conceived in sin, this babe needs your love, not your rejection."

"Mama, this babe is fatherless."

"No," she adamantly denied, squeezing me tightly against her. "He's a child of the king."

"He or she is a child of an adulterer."

"I believe God will intervene to bring you blessings and not curses," she declared. "Didn't he turn my life of sorrow and curses into one of joy and delight with my beloved Eliam? And he gave me new life with you, as well." She gently smoothed back my hair from my cheeks and cupped my face in her hands. "Bathsheba, our God is the Lord of life."

I stared into her dark eyes, misty with tears and shook my head free from her hands. I scooted away from her, pushing myself up with my back against the wall. "Everybody knows David is God's most trusted servant, right? He's even been called 'a man after God's own heart?' Yet, you and I know he had Uriah killed, Mama," I said. "Tell me, how can he be a 'man after God's own heart' and kill one of his own valiant men who's given him only loyalty and unselfish service all these years?"

"Perhaps it was fear, dear one. Fear of the truth, fear of men, and fear of discovery."

"Ah Mama, he should not just fear men, but fear women. . . one woman. Me," I declared. "I want only to rip his cold heart out of his kingly chest."

"Bathsheba, you know the Levitical law. God said we shall not take vengeance or bear a grudge against any of our people."

"He's also said adulterers will be stoned. Do you honestly think, even if anyone learns of his adultery, he'll be stoned? The anointed king?"

"It's pointless to argue with you when your grief is so fresh."

I bowed my head, exhaustion and sorrow drawing me into a place of hopeless surrender. "If I can't die, then let me rest."

"Yes, you rest. Wait here and I'll bring you something to

help you sleep without dreams."

"I don't fear my dreams," I rasped. "Only my nightmares. But why fear them any longer, Mama, when they've become my life? Truly, I'm a prophetess." A gurgle of wild laughter again choked me. "Now, I prophesy my death at the hands of Lilith, and all the others who lost husbands and sons with Uriah...."

"Stop it!" Mama gripped my shoulders and shook me, hard. "You will not blaspheme nor speak of such a thing again. Do you hear me?" she commanded.

"Oh, Mama, you are such a warrior-protector. But you could not stop Uriah's death and you will not be able to stop mine."

"No, I couldn't stop Uriah or Eliam's deaths, but I will not allow you to die because you lacked the courage to live." She leaned so close our foreheads touched, and her grasp was like the claws of a lioness. "You will do exactly as I tell you to do. You will remain silent while I go prepare a sleeping potion. If you refuse, I'll call Rachel in here. I know that as wild with grief as you are, you would not do or say anything to upset her. But we both know she'd be upset to think she had to watch you."

Suddenly, too full of grief to fight, I nodded my head. Besides, if my prophecy was true, death would find me, whether I slept this night or not.

Chapter 18

The sun's light and its unrelenting heat have scorched the earth, but I've lived only in darkness. Mama sent away most of the women who came to grieve my loss and theirs. She was afraid my wails of grief would turn to cries of murder, assuring my own death.

I've sat in the middle of our courtyard, dressed in the tunic I rent to show the depth of my grief, my head covered with ashes. I wanted to fast, as another demonstration of my deep sorrow, but Mama insisted I eat to nourish my child.

Grandfather has sent a servant to check up on me each day, but has avoided coming himself. *Is he now afraid of me?* Of course, he could be busy searching for a husband for me. One who won't mind a barren wife. . . who's pregnant.

Mama has seemed to be waiting for something, but I've been too sick at heart to question her. My beloved was murdered, and every day I've cursed David for his wickedness, and prayed for God to take his vengeance upon my enemy, the king.

I worked this morning to brush out new wool to prepare it for spinning. Somehow, the slow, deep strokes have helped to soothe my mind.

"Bathsheba, where are you? I have such news!" Grandfather's cheerful voice rang like cymbals through the courtyard.

I turned to the door and watched as he strode into the room. A wide smile on his face, he was dressed no longer for mourning, but for celebrating. He wore his best blue and white tunic, his hair and beard were clean and combed.

"My dear granddaughter, I arrive as the bearer of wondrous news," he gushed. "Come, put down your work, I must talk with you."

I glanced past him to see Mama standing behind him. Her whole face was alight with anticipation. What was going on?

I put aside the wool and sat with my legs crossed upon the mat, waiting.

With a grunt, he stood before me, his hands on his slim hips. "Bathsheba, I've just been with the king. He called me to him not to get advice, but to tell me he wants to take you as his wife. He asked me for your bride price." He smiled down at me, his body swaying. Would he dance in his glee?

"Woman, you'll be a wife of our king! He said he wanted to honor his valiant friend and warrior, Uriah, and what better way than by marrying his widow, so he might care for and protect you." He tilted his head. "Of course, I knew I must tell him you're barren, and have had no child by Uriah. But David assured me he believes God will bless you with a child because of how he's so abundantly blessed David's own life. In fact, the king's convinced your marriage to him will be blessed with many children."

I sucked in a breath, the truth of David's words struck into my very marrow. I had been barren with Uriah, yet, one time with David and my womb opened like a ripe fruit. And now he's told Grandfather he wanted to take me to wife? That he believed I'd bear him many children?

How dare he? Fury choked me. I knew if David were here and I had a weapon, I'd kill him. I jumped up to face Grandfather and tell him exactly what I thought about this offer.

"Don't look like that, Bathsheba, how could I not be honest with our king about your barrenness?" He rebuked me, misconstruing the source of my rage.

"Let me tell you what I think about your beloved king and his offer, Grandfather—"

"Ah Bathsheba, didn't I assure you our God would provide for you?" Mama interrupted. "And look how extravagantly he's answered our prayers? Won't Mara be eaten up with jealousy?" Mama violently shook her head at me from behind Grandfather.

I clearly understood I wasn't to reject David's offer. I stood rigid. My grief and rage intensified by her prohibition. I wanted to lash out at them both, but I gritted my teeth and said nothing. I took a slow, deep breath and forced myself to exhale.

Could I use my marriage to avenge myself on David? Only if I was ready to see Mama's and Grandfather's deaths. . . and my child's.

"So, David plans to claim his bastard?" I muttered under my breath.

"What did you call the king, granddaughter?" Grandfather barked, startled from his own thoughts by my shocking word.

"Bathsheba, watch what you call our good king," Mama rebuked me. "My lord, it's because she blames the king for Uriah's death that she speaks so. She's sure if the king had not stayed home from war, Uriah would have lived."

"I can understand her feelings. Didn't I think this, too?" Grandfather said, nodding his grizzled head. "But if Uriah must die in battle, how can we argue with God, who now gives her a king for her husband? David's shown great honor to me and to Bathsheba."

I laughed out loud, and held my stomach with the pain. Mama was right, if David hadn't stayed home, Uriah would be alive. But Grandfather can only see the false honor of his king.

"Ah, now you see the joy of his offer," Grandfather exulted. "Bathsheba, King David wants to marry you as soon as your week of mourning has ended."

"In three days?" I shook my head with adamant refusal. "No! I will not."

"Certainly, if the king thinks it best to marry you so soon, then you must do so," Mama affirmed. "I'm sure, daughter, you will be ready then."

"I want no husband, and especially not the king!" I exclaimed. "My husband has only been dead a few days!" I snapped my mouth shut on the words that almost followed: murdered by the orders of the very man you want me to marry!

"Of course you'll be ready in a few days," Grandfather said, ignoring my outburst. "Your mother's right. We know you grieve Uriah's death, don't we all? Yet, I'm sure if Uriah knew it was the king who offered to care for his beloved wife, he'd be thankful to him."

Mute in agony at his ignorant nonsense, I stared my rage at Mama.

"Bathsheba, your grandfather's right," she pleaded. "Uriah would want what is best for you. To be the wife of David is what's best, not only for you, but for all those whose lives are bound with yours."

Ah, she reminded me, again, of the babe I carried. David's child. The child that bound my destiny to David's as strongly as any umbilical cord. My stomach convulsed. She also reminded me of her life and Grandfather's.

"Bathsheba, I forgot to tell you the most extraordinary request David gave me," he said. "The king asks if there is any special gift he might give you beyond the bride price I required of him? Truly, the king seems anxious to please you."

David wanted to please me? I'd be pleased if he'd wed me and go to war and die. No, for the sake of all my family, I must agree to allow this man to become my husband in three days. *Lord in heaven, help me think! What do I ask from him?*

I looked over at Mama. Her mouth was lifted in a smile, but her eyes revealed her fear. What was she afraid of? Like an arrow to its mark, it struck me. She's afraid for her own life. Who will care for her when I'm safe in David's palace?

"Grandfather, the gift I desire is that this house will be given to my mother," I told him, "and he'll provide for all her needs. As I plan to take Rachel with me, Mama will need a handmaiden of her own. Yes, this is what I would ask of the king. Oh, and a manservant to protect her, as well." The request flowed straight from my heart to my mouth.

His face mottled beneath his beard. "You think I won't care for your mother?" he ranted. "You hold her in more value than you hold me? Why can't you request something for me? Do you think David would have married you if you weren't my granddaughter? It's not just because you're Uriah's widow, but David also wants to take you to wife to honor me as well, and align his house with ours."

With his words, I knew I could never tell him the truth. He thought David was honoring him by marrying me? Of course. Grandfather always held himself above all others; our family above all others. Under my breath I prayed he'd never learn how David had dishonored me while Uriah was at war, and Grandfather was busy about the king's business. He'd take my disgrace as a personal affront, and hate David with all the passion with which he now loved him.

"Mama, please leave us." I didn't want her to hear our conversation. I was determined to be honest with him, and knew he wouldn't like it. I watched her go before I spoke.

"Grandfather, I'm very concerned about Mama," I said. "After Papa's death, you gave their home in Hebron to your nephew, Abel," I reminded him. "So, I'd respectfully ask you how you plan to care for her?"

"Abel's wife, Hannah, could use help in their home now that their last daughter married. She'd be treated well."

"You'd force my mother to be a bondservant in the house that was once her own?"

"She deserves nothing more!" he hissed.

I stared him in the eye. "You dishonor your own son and your grandson, Uriah, with such a plan," I said with quiet force. "Both men recognized the worth of my mother, and treated her with the respect and love she deserves. She's now not only the widow of Eliam, David's mighty warrior, but the mother of the king's new bride. Yet, you'd treat her with no respect at all?"

"How dare you talk to me like this! I'm your grandfather—"

"And she's my mother, with only me to care for her," I replied. "So, my request of the king is that he honor my mother by giving her this house, a maidservant, a male servant and what monies she needs to care for herself and her household until she dies."

Grandfather frowned deeply. "I'll tell David your request," he snapped. "I'm sure he'll be happy to comply."

"Thank you, I knew I could trust you with this, whether you agreed with it or not," I said, thankful Mama hadn't heard our argument.

"Now, we should talk about your wedding celebration. David thought a week's celebration—"

"No. Forgive me for interrupting, but a week is too long," I said. "Israel is at war, and many other families are grieving the loss of sons and husbands."

"No, woman. A week's celebration would help them forget their sorrow, and embrace life once again, and it's our tradition."

"Can you so quickly forget your own grief, Grandfather?"

"How dare you show me such disrespect?" he shouted. "Do you think because the king wants you, I couldn't still beat you for such a show of rudeness?"

"Grandfather," I pleaded, "I grieve for Uriah. I know the king's desire to take me to wife is a great honor, but I have no peace about feasting for a week. Surely, our people will honor us more if we don't dishonor their own loved ones by celebrating for a week?"

"It's tradition." He stared at me for a long moment. "Harrumph," he grumbled. "I think you're wrong, but I'll ask the king. Whatever he chooses to do, we'll do."

"Yes, I suppose we will," I said. With sudden insight, I saw how my life had been personally ruled by the king for weeks now. In fact, ever since he called me to him.

"You mustn't worry about how you'll be treated in the court, Bathsheba. You'll not only be King David's wife, but you're my granddaughter as well, and Uriah's widow," he said. "For all these reasons, you'll do very well."

His words brought me no solace. Yet, for the first time in weeks, a sense of deep, inexplicable comfort stole through me, as if God himself breathed on me his "shalom."

"Thank you, Grandfather." I walked over and kissed him on the cheek. "I'm grateful for your willingness to express my concerns about the wedding to the king, as well as asking him to care for Mama's needs."

"Yes, well, I'll leave you now," he said. "You don't look well, and you must bathe, and wash away the ashes and leave off your rent garment. You're to be a wife of King David, and as such, you must prepare yourself. Once I return to the king to tell him you're ecstatic at his benevolent offer, I'm sure he'll send gifts to his new bride."

He rubbed his hands together, grinning. "Ah Bathsheba, after so much grief, it's good to plan a wedding. And think, granddaughter, when he marries you, I become not only his counselor, but his grandfather, too." He laughed aloud. "Hah, I might even call him 'grandson,' although not in the court, of course. But when I'm alone with him?" He gave me an exuberant hug and left humming, his stride long and confident.

I watched him go, wondering at the feeling of peace that touched my heart like a butterfly's kiss. Was God in this marriage? Could I trust him to somehow bring good out of all my grief? But my sorrow was so deep. I began to softly sing words that had so often comforted me in the past... David's words.

> "When the righteous cry for help, the Lord hears,
>   and rescues them from all their troubles.
> The Lord is near to the brokenhearted,
>   and saves the crushed in spirit.

Many are the afflictions of the righteous,
   but the Lord rescues them from them all.
He keeps all their bones;
   not one of them will be broken. . .
The Lord redeems the life of his servants;
   none of those who take refuge in him will be condemned."

"But is marrying David not condemning me to a bitter, polygamous marriage, Lord?"

Chapter 19

"Daughter," Mama said, walking into my bedchamber, "didn't I tell you God would provide?"

I looked into her beloved face, her eyes shining with confidence and love, and wondered how I'd live amid David's women without her to support and guide me. Yet, I'd known I couldn't ask her to share my pain by joining me in that foreign place, even if it would be possible. She needed no more pain in her life.

"Yes, you did, and you believed all along what I didn't want to believe. But, you also know I'm only doing this for the sake of the babe I'm carrying, and for you and Grandfather."

"Thank you. I don't know if I could live if you died, too."

"I know," I said.

"I sent Rachel on an errand to Sarai's when you asked to speak to your grandfather alone. I knew if he got angry, he'd say things she didn't need to hear."

She knew Grandfather so well. Yet, sadly, he knew her not at all, and refused to know her. "That was wise, although when she returns, I'm sure she'll be full of questions. Do you think I should ask her to come with me to the women's quarters?"

"Daughter, even if you're not delighted to join the women of David's court, I'm sure Rachel will be."

"Mama, this marriage brings me no joy. Yet, for the first time in weeks, I feel a peace. I can't explain it, other than to sense God is in this. But then, you know how I've grieved this babe's conception, and the deaths that followed from the knowledge of his life."

"Yes, I know, and I've grieved with you." She gently took my hand. "I'm thankful, dear one, you've found some peace. I have, as well, even though I don't know where I'll go."

I found my first smile. "Mama, you'll stay here in our home, and choose a new handmaiden and man servant who'll serve you here," I exclaimed. "I asked Grandfather to arrange this with the king, and he promised he'd do it. So you see, God has provided for you, too."

"How can this be? I know Uriah has no family but you, so wouldn't the house go to your grandfather?"

"I'm unsure of the law concerning Uriah's property, but however it might have been, the house will be yours. And when I can, I'll ask permission for you to come and visit me in David's palace." I drew her into my arms and hugged her tightly. "You must come see me often, Mama. It will be hard to live among his other wives and concubines knowing they'll resent me for being the new woman in David's life."

Mama squeezed me before she moved out of my arms. "I've no doubt you'll have your own rooms," she said. "Didn't we visit Abigail in her rooms that one time? Yet the women do share a common area and courtyard. Although some of his wives have their own homes."

"I'd think it would be better for me to have my own home, too. I fear the jealousy and suspicion of his other wives and concubines." I stopped, not wanting her to worry with me.

"You think they'll guess you're already pregnant?" she asked, aware of my anxieties. "I've thought of this as well. But you must be close to him in the palace. There you'll have your wedding week and soon discover your curse has been broken and your womb's been blessed with new life."

Nausea struck with her words. "The very idea of being with him makes me ill. How can I bear his touch after he raped me, and when I know he had my beloved murdered?"

Her eyes lit with conviction. "Daughter, David will expect you to come willingly to him when he's your husband. He'll expect your gratitude and obedience. You must submit to him with grace."

I trembled from head to foot. "With grace? It will be all I can do not to curse him to his face."

She took my hand, drew me down and sat with me on my bed. "Bathsheba, you know my history, and how God rescued me from the hands of the Philistines into the hands of David and his men. I've shared with you about your father's and my love, and the cost of it with your grandfather's unforgiveness." She smiled with a deep inner peace. "Yet, I've seen God's hand of redemption and mercy. Eliam and I had many good years together. God even opened my womb and gave us our greatest joy and delight, you!

"I know you hate David today for all he's done to you. For his betrayal of you as a woman and wife, and especially for arranging Uriah's death."

She put a gentle hand on my womb. "But now, you must think not only of your life, but your child's. For his sake, you must do all in your power to make peace with David. He first took you because he was attracted to your outward beauty. He doesn't know you have an inner radiance that's even greater, and how you're gifted with music and song, and can dance with more poise than any woman I know."

"Am I to sing for him? Dance for him?" I challenged. "I will never—"

"Ah, dear one." A sad smile touched her lips. "'Never' is such a harsh, unforgiving word, and it often comes back to haunt us when we find ourselves doing the very things we swore we'd 'never' do. David is the father of your child. Do you want your child to hate his father?"

With loving clarity, my father's face formed in my mind's eye. I saw him squatting down, arms outstretched, his deeply lined, bearded and sun-browned face alight with joy. He was waiting for me to run into his welcoming embrace when he'd returned home after another of our Israelite victories. I smelled again the strong, distinctive scent of man and leather, felt again the roughness of his beard against my cheek as he kissed me, and the strength of his arms around me. I heard his words of love, and joy in our reunion. He told me how he'd prayed for me each day, for my health and safety. With the memory, the tears came.

"You're remembering your father," Mama said, stroking my hair. "You know what it's like to have parents who love one another. A mother who encourages her child to be with her father and adore him."

"You ask too much of me," I said, and pulled away from her comforting touch.

"That may be, but I've given you things you must think about as you enter into this unwelcome marriage. You're to be the wife not only of our anointed king, but of a man whose sins have wounded you deeply. We both have seen the miracle of deep wounds healed, both physical and heart wounds. We've also seen great and small wounds become putrid, ultimately bringing death, even as an unforgiving heart brings death to relationships."

"Enough! I can't understand how you, who's shared my hatred and anger—"

"No, daughter," she adamantly denied, "I've never shared your hatred, only your anger. What he did to you was a terrible sin, and I've lamented the wrongs he committed. But David has been a friend to me and our family far too long for me to hate him. You didn't see him weep over Eliam's death, but I did, when he called me to the palace last year. And, you never saw him lead his men to rescue their captured wives and children." She looked deeply into my eyes, "I never told you about the Amalekite raid on David's town of Ziklag when David and our men were gone. Did Uriah or your father ever tell you that story?"

"Yes, Uriah once mentioned it, but gave no details. He said their battle with the Amalekites became insignificant after the news came of Israel's defeat by the Philistines, and the deaths of King Saul, Prince Jonathan, and so many of the men of Israel."

"My daughter, all the wives and children of David and his men are alive today because he pushed his tired soldiers to follow and rescue us. The raid of the Amalekites reminded me of the Philistine raid when I was a child. But although they torched our homes, burning them to the ground, they killed none of the old men, nor the women and children, but herded us like sheep away from our burning town," her eyes darkened with the memory.

"Our captors, after forcing us to travel night and day with only short breaks, had finally established a makeshift camp in a field. We were terrified, hungry, sick and exhausted. And, as we watched the men drink, we knew they'd soon be coming for us women. We feared not only for ourselves, but for the young babes if they cried too loudly while their mothers were being raped." She glanced at me, her face a mask of loathing.

"During our trek, they'd threatened Abigail and the other mothers who carried babes that they'd kill them and throw them out of the camp, 'fresh meat for the wild animals,' if they didn't stop their squalling. Abigail and I marched together and I helped to carry Kileab and sang softly to keep him quiet. Fear was our constant companion, even as we silently prayed to God for our deliverance. But we knew David and our men were with the Philistines, so we had no real hope of liberation.

"The tired sun hovered upon the horizon, as if to wait and light the way for David and his men. We saw them sprint over the hill, shouting and roaring like lions on a ravenous rampage. Outnumbered at least three to one, David and his warriors fought with the invincible strength given by our Lord of Hosts. Eliam, Uriah and others freed us and the other captives before the battle began. They led us away from the fight and soon left us with a small, protective force while they joined their brothers in battle."

Mama shook her head, her eyes radiant in awe. "They fought from dusk until evening of the following day. We heard the battle cries, but were on the other side of the hill, so could not see the battle. Amazingly, most of us slept during the fight, exhausted from our ordeal. But I'll never forget the triumphant shout that flowed over us like a wave of moving sound when the horn of victory was finally blown. Even as we heard it, the women and children joined our voices with our men's. We were free!"

Tears wet her cheeks, yet she was oblivious to them. "I swore on that day I'd love and follow David until God took the last breath from my body, and I'd honor him as king whether anyone else acknowledged him as the Lord's anointed one or not." Her resolute gaze met mine. "When you came home from the palace, ravished by the man who'd saved me twice from captivity and death, I felt anger burn through my veins that he'd abused you so. And I grieved with you when we heard of Uriah's death. But I also remembered how he'd saved both Eliam and Uriah more times than they could count, and I knew hate couldn't penetrate my vow to love David always, and it still can't."

"Even knowing David ordered Uriah's death after he showed himself too honorable to break his warrior's code and bed me on his leave?" I pressed. "Showing himself more honorable than his king?"

"Ah Bathsheba, you know I've always loved you more than anyone besides Eliam." Her eyes were filled with fierce conviction. "I believe if Uriah had returned to a pregnant wife, he'd never have condemned you for adultery, for he loved you too well. But his honor would have dictated he confront David to exact some kind of revenge, which could easily have led to his death, as well as yours and the babe's.

"Understand this. Now you'll live! And if God wills it, your babe with you. I'm thankful David has covered your dishonor by taking you to be his wife. Think, daughter, he's also the man who's taken the curse of barrenness from you."

"I can't believe what you're saying." My whole body shook. "It makes me wonder if you truly love me more than your savior, David."

"Dear one," she pleaded, taking my fisted hand from my lap. "I'm trying to tell you why I have hope. If you give yourself time, you may discover you can once again love David, if not as a husband, at least as your king and beloved musician."

"No!"

She stopped me, putting two fingers to my lips. "I know you once loved him as both king and composer. Now, whether you want to accept it or not, David is the father of your child and will soon be your husband. I believe if you can find it in your heart to forgive him, he may give you even more children, the children for which you've always prayed."

"Forgive David?" I scoffed. "You honestly believe I can forgive him?"

"Yes, I do," she said. "And be warned, if you continue to spew your bitterness, the other wives will wonder why you're not happy to be the king's bride. Dear one, if you nurture hatred, it's sure to grow and be the very thing to betray you and your child to David's other women, as well as your grandfather."

"I'm sure the women will understand I'm still grieving Uriah," I argued. "I can't believe you, who once showed me such understanding and sympathy, now lecture me on how I must think and feel."

She drew herself up and stood with rigid dignity. "As soon as we heard of Uriah's death, I knew David would marry you. I also knew you prayed he wouldn't. But I lived near the king for years and I know him. Now David wants only to cover his sin, and avoid the truth of his wrongdoing. I'm sure because he's marrying you, and giving you and your babe the protection of the King of Israel, he believes you'll welcome him with open arms. But before long, his sin will eat away at his soul, and he may yet avoid you, because you'll remind him of his transgressions against God and Uriah."

"I look forward to that day. Perhaps, I can do something to hasten it?"

She leaned over, put her hands on my shoulders and shook me, hard. "Listen, woman! David's relationship with the Lord has spanned all his long life. His passionate love for God has sustained him through great trials and hardships. The fact David forgot him, and took you to his bed, and used the Ammonites to kill Uriah won't be forgotten by God.

"Bathsheba," she pleaded, lifting my chin, she stared into my eyes. "David isn't Saul, who always had an excuse for his sin, or blamed others. When David is confronted with his sin, he's quick to repent. I saw this in Ziklag and Hebron, and heard of it from Abigail. She told me how she stopped David from murdering her husband and her people when she came to him with a peace offering. Another man would have ignored her, and still sought vengeance. However, David didn't, and because of this God was able to visit his own justice on Nabal, so that David ended up with a wise and beautiful wife and a wealthy estate."

I pushed her hand away, and added sarcastically, "And he's since taken many other wives and concubines, and now will have me, another beauty to add to his collection of lovely women. An honor I could live without."

"For the sake of your child, and for your own well-being, you must forgive."

"And have you forgiven your master, Mother, and his wives who wanted you dead?"

"Yes, years ago. For I came to understand how I'd never have agreed to be sold to the Philistine slavers without their plot to kill me, and thus, wouldn't have known your father and had his child.

"When you bring your babe to nurse at your breast, will you mix your mother's milk with the sweetness of forgiveness, or with the bitterness of your hatred?"

"Enough, Mother! I'll get water for my bath." I strode out of the bedchamber, shaking with the ferocity of my anger. Why couldn't she leave me alone? Didn't she believe I'd suffered enough? We're told to hate our enemies. David had proven himself my enemy.

Where was the peace I'd felt a short time ago? Had my fight with Mama destroyed it? It seemed so, for all I felt now was a wave of nausea.

Chapter 20

"I'll help you bathe, whether you want me to or not," Mama said.

I looked up from disrobing in the weaving room. "Thank you."

The way I felt, if she didn't help me, I couldn't bathe. I didn't have the strength on my own. Nausea threatened, and I shook from the aftershock of our fight. I'd never fought with my mother like this. First I disagreed with my grandfather, now Mama. David's sin was like a disease that infected all of us.

I stepped into the shallow bowl and she gently poured the warm water over me. I shivered, for as warm as it was, it still couldn't touch the cold despair of my heart.

"Forgive me, daughter, I shouldn't push you to feel what you can't right now," she apologized.

I closed my eyes against the pain in my head and the ache in my heart.

"I know it's much easier to hate those who hurt us, than to forgive, yes? But do you not realize that by hating David you'll only end up hurting yourself and your child?"

"Yes, I know." My head throbbed with pain and I lifted my arms and gently washed the ashes from my hair. The acrid, grey water dripped down my face and body.

Uriah, beloved, forgive me. I must marry David to protect the child you were so sure we would one day have together. I miss you so much. How can I go to David and welcome him into this body that abhors him? God, have mercy on me.

More water poured over me until it ran clean and pure. Oh, that I could be washed clean again, and could go back and take my mikvah in this room, never to be seen by David.

I ached with the reality that there was no going back.

"I'm sure David will send you gifts," Mama said. "Please, when his servants arrive, don't reject them or show displeasure. You must remember everything you say, every smile or frown will be reported back to the king. You're no longer just the wife of one of David's mighty men, but the soon-to-be bride of the King of Israel himself."

"I need no gifts from David. Hasn't he given me enough? He gave me both life and death."

"Come, dear one, don't let your heart become heavy once more. You look so pale, are you feeling nauseous again?"

"My head's pounding. My stomach's roiling. I've never fought with you like this."

Mama wrapped me in a cloth and in her arms. "You're my beloved daughter, and always will be. I'm sorry. I'll say nothing more to upset you."

*   *   *

Rachel opened the gate the next morning to greet the entourage of David's servants, each one bearing a different gift; a shimmering purple and white tunic, a necklace and bracelet of multicolored jewels and ripe fruits in a pottery bowl. Her enthusiasm seemed to please the servants, and as her squeals of glee rang out, my simple thanks were noted, too.

When they left, smiles of satisfaction wreathed their faces, and I knew David would hear their reports and be pleased. Would I tell him my true feelings about his gifts and this marriage once we wed? Did I dare?

"Oh, Lady, is this not the most beautiful tunic you've ever

seen? This purple coloring is brighter than any other color we've worked with." Rachel fingered the material of the tunic, a smile of wonder on her lips.

I wished I could match her excitement, but I couldn't, and I found only irritation at her enthusiasm.

"It is bright."

"Rachel, why don't you go and tell your friends about all the gifts King David's servants brought your lady?" Mama said. "Bathsheba and I can finish the row of weaving you and I were working on."

"Really, mistress? I can go?"

"Yes, little one. But be back in time to go to afternoon worship with us."

I stood next to Mama and watched Rachel run with the wind out our courtyard gate. "Bless you. I thank God for Rachel's innocent pleasure, but not her excited chatter."

"I know her joy in all of this has been hard on you."

"Yes." I slid to the hard but warm stones of our courtyard and crossed my legs. "What will I do at our marriage banquet when I have to eat all the rich foods they'll serve us?" I asked quietly, glancing up at her. "You know how I still can only eat mild foods, and even then, I'm sick, and often it's just the smell of food that makes me ill."

Mama grabbed a rug nearby and sat down beside me. "For most women, this malady leaves them between their twelfth and sixteenth week of pregnancy. You're almost eight weeks along, so you should be over this within the next four weeks, or sooner."

"Sooner would be a gift I'd gladly accept," I murmured.

She smiled. "I remember thinking the same thing when I was sick with you. And what was even more amazing was how well I felt once I was four months along. My appetite returned and I had more energy than I knew what to do with."

"I wish I felt like that right now." I glanced over at her. "Do you think Grandfather will be suspicious when he finds out I've been blessed by God and am pregnant so quickly?"

"No, I think he'll only be outrageous in his joyful boasting, and brag about David's prowess to everyone."

I stared at her and shook my head. "Mercy, I do believe you're right."

"Dear one, please, allow yourself a small measure of relief and joy with your marriage?"

"Mama, I know David is shielding me from stoning. But if there is any rumor that questions when I got pregnant, my reputation will be shredded like cloth caught by sharp thorns. Adulterers are not rewarded for their sin by marrying kings. Even if people suspect I had no choice but to submit to David, they'll still blame me. For is it not the nature of man to blame the woman for her rape?"

"Enough! Please, let's try to find some joy in all this."

"Truly, I'd prefer to speculate on my demise for adultery, than anticipate a wedding abhorrent to me."

"Dear one, no." She reached out and grasped my hand. "I've sadly come to recognize I'm not as brave as you, who has borne so much sorrow, and has still held to life with blessed tenacity."

"It's your grief, and sickness of body and heart which are speaking, not the daughter I raised and taught to be strong and loving."

I looked into her beloved and deeply distressed face. "Mama, it hurts just to think of leaving you here. I don't even know how often I'll be able to see you. I'm so afraid of my life in David's palace, living with all his women, and knowing I'll not have you near to talk to and comfort me."

She leaned over and kissed my lips. "Don't worry, I'm sure Abigail can arrange for me to visit you regularly."

Was she right? Could Abigail negotiate visits from Mama? Weariness stole over me like an uninvited guest.

"Let me rest. I feel so weary I can barely hold my head up."

She gently touched my cheek. "Trust God, dear one. I truly believe in his time, all will be well."

"I pray you're right."

I stood up and walked to my bedchamber. I didn't have the heart to crawl onto my bed, so I sat in Uriah's chair. As I sat, a song came to me:

"To you, O Lord, I call;
    my Rock, do not refuse to hear me.
For if you are silent to me,
    I shall be like those who go down to the pit.
Hear the voice of my supplication,
    as I cry to you for help. . . ."

I stopped, unable to go on. Even David's songs haunted me. Was there no escape from the man? No, for would I not marry him in two days? And it had been his seed that had rooted itself in my womb. . . this babe I've tried so hard not to love. *This babe I love.*

Chapter 21

God was merciful. I stood throughout our wedding ceremony and didn't faint from the heat or my grief, nor was I sick at the wedding banquet. In fact, I tasted enough of the rich foods to avoid all suspicion. Now David's servants have prepared me to go to the king for our wedding night. As they prepared me, it was as if I watched another woman being bathed, oiled, cosmetically beautified, and dressed in a sheer blue linen tunic.

For my wedding I had rebelliously adorned myself with Uriah's necklace and bracelets. For my wedding night I wore nothing but a sheer linen tunic and a circlet of silver upon my head. Had I not joined the ranks of David's queens?

"My lady, surely this was the most wonderful day of your life?" Rachel's question startled me back to an awareness of her. "I think you're the most beautiful of all David's wives."

"Don't say that too loudly, little one, or the servants of the other wives and concubines will make your life a misery."

I nodded at David's servants who'd helped prepare me. "You may go now," I said. They bowed and left me with Rachel in my new bedroom. Was I ready to join my new master in the bridal chamber? No.

I looked around my quarters and admitted the small, windowed room was adequate. It had a raised bed full of colorful pillows, a carved, cedar chest in the corner, a stand with a lamp, and a pallet for Rachel. There was a small table that held an assortment of perfumes, scented oils, creams, cosmetics and beautifully carved wooden boxes for my jewels.

Attached to the bedroom was another, smaller room with a beautiful rug, more multi-colored pillows, and a small table in the middle. Here I could entertain my mother and other women. But only men who were eunuchs were allowed near David's women, so my grandfather could not visit me.

"Aren't you excited, my lady?" Rachel chirped. "It was such an honor to witness your wedding. I'll remember this day for the rest of my life. Someday, if our God wills it, I'll tell my children I was at the wedding of King David and my beautiful mistress, Bathsheba."

"Lady, I've come to take you to your kingly husband," a voice announced outside my bedchamber.

Rachel grabbed my hand and kissed it. "Oh lady, perhaps if God is merciful, King David will give you the child you and your beloved Uriah never had."

Her innocent words acted like flaming arrows piercing my heart, and I burned with the heat and agony of it.

"Lady?" she whispered, her large eyes staring at me in distress.

I was mute from the intensity of the pain, but I gently touched her cheek and turned to leave.

Chilion, David's chief eunuch of the women's quarters, waited in my antechamber. I hesitated a moment as nausea rose within me. Had God's mercy deserted me? Swallowing, I walked out to meet Chilion. He bowed to me and led me out of my rooms. I followed him through the common room and to the door which led into the hallway that must lead to the bridal chamber. Would it be the same room where David had. . . where I'd first been taken?

Chilion led me up some stone stairs and down a cedar hallway. He stopped before an elaborately decorated door. Relief flowed through me when I didn't recognize the door, nor were there any guards close by.

Chilion knocked once.

"Come," David's deep voice commanded.

The eunuch nodded to me and opened the door. I knew I could show no fear to either man, so I straightened my back and walked into the room. The door shut behind me, reminding me of another door. Panic gripped me like a vice, and I wanted only to turn and run. David's overpowering perfume of cinnamon and other spices encompassed me. I suddenly remembered before whom I stood. I knelt and bowed my head to the floor, forcing the bile to my throat.

"Bathsheba, my beautiful bride, rise and come here."

As I slowly rose, I saw David was standing by a low table which was filled with bowls of fruit, bread, cheese and a golden pitcher with two matching goblets beside it. A large, ornately carved and raised bed lay behind him, with an array of colorful pillows.

Help me, Lord, it looks like the other bed.

He walked toward me, his hands outstretched. His strong scent permeated my senses, sweeping me back to my rape. Torrential fear swept over me as he grasped my hands, spurring my queasy stomach into open rebellion. With a choked cry, I wrenched my hands free, slid to my knees and retched at his feet.

"Mercy, woman," he exclaimed, stepping back. "What's wrong with you?"

Too miserable to answer, I heard him mutter under his breath, even as a bowl soon appeared in front of my face. "Here, if you must be sick, at least be sick in this."

I was.

After I finished, I shook with dry heaves. I heard him sigh deeply.

"Are you done?" he asked. His voice sounded more resigned than angry, which surprised me.

When I nodded the bowl disappeared.

"Stay where you are, and I'll get water and a cloth so you may wash."

I didn't expect his helpful attitude. He'd even held the bowl for me while I was sick. And now, he's going to serve me by bringing me water and cloths that I might clean myself? He's the King of Israel, with servants to do his bidding. Why didn't he call for one to help me?

"Here, take these and clean yourself."

He placed the bowl of water on the floor by my side, and put the cloth in my hand. I quickly wiped my face. The water was cool and refreshed me. Once I finished, I leaned over and cleaned the floor. I was afraid to look up at him to see his displeasure and anger.

"Was it the rich food that made you ill?" he asked. His voice sounded both curious and concerned.

I risked a glance up at him and was caught by the distress in his eyes, before I looked down again. "Yes, my king, it was that, but mostly it's the babe who declares his presence each day by making me sick."

A shocked silence greeted this truth. "I didn't think you might be sick with child." His tone was conciliatory.

"No, I was sure you wouldn't," I murmured, trying to keep the bitterness from my voice. I kept my eyes down so he wouldn't see my anger.

"So, this sickness comes upon you daily?"

"Yes, my king, each day, mostly in the mornings, but at other times as well. Truthfully, I'm never sure when I'll be sick." Could I actually talk David out of bedding me by the threat of nausea? That would be sweet revenge indeed.

"Bathsheba, this is our wedding night, and yet I find myself afraid to touch you for fear you may be sick again. As much as I desire you, my wife, I find myself loath to take this risk."

"And I wouldn't want to disgrace myself by being sick all over you, my lord," I lied. I kept my head down so he couldn't see my satisfaction at the thought of it.

"Nor would I want that," he promptly agreed. "Besides, no one needs to know we didn't lie with each other this night. It's not as if I need to affirm your virginity."

He couldn't be teasing me, could he? I looked up at him and noticed his hazel eyes were alight with humor, and he was grinning at me. Jesting was not something I'd expected from David, especially now. I wasn't sure how to respond. "No, my king," I said.

"Would you like some of the sweet wine I have here, or would that not agree with you?"

"Thank you, that would be helpful, but please, let me get it." I slowly rose from the floor. "You should not wait on me."

"Here, let me help you up." He gently grasped my arm to help me rise. "Bathsheba, I haven't been a king so long I don't know how to serve others. May I at least see your face?"

I raised my head and looked at him.

"I see you're uncomfortable having me help you, but you must remember, I'm now your husband, and as such, I'm concerned with your well-being."

It felt strange to hear such words from a rapist and murderer... would I ever be able to see him as the caring husband he claimed to be?

He led me to one of two chairs by the table. I saw it was totally unlike the one chair Uriah had left me. These were beautifully carved, with blue and red roped seats.

"Sit down. You'll be more comfortable sitting in this chair than on the rug."

I sat down and watched in consternation as he picked up the bowl and cloths and took them to the corner of the room where he'd left the other bowl I'd used. He came back and poured me a goblet of sweet wine from the pitcher and handed it to me. He then sat down across from me.

"I think it best I don't call the servants right now to come and get the bowls. I don't want the court gossips to spread the rumor I made my bride sick on our first night together."

I chose not to correct him. This was the second night we'd been together, and he'd made me more than sick the first night. I sipped the wine and watched a smile slowly appear on his deeply tanned and lined face. It peeked out between his full mustache and gray-streaked beard. I also noticed there was more gray in his copper beard than in his copper tinted hair.

Staring at him, the bittersweet memory of other times with this man swept over me with raw force. With startling recognition, I knew him again as the man from my childhood: the king who was also a family friend and confidant. The poet and musician with the all-consuming passion for worship of his God. . . who'd been grievously absent at our last meeting.

I placed the goblet back on the table as tears filled my eyes. I didn't try and stop them. They overflowed and ran down my cheeks, dripping onto the bodice of my wedding garment.

"Bathsheba, I was only teasing you." He quickly knelt before me, held my fisted hands.

I shook my head, but couldn't stop the silent tears streaming down my face. He pulled me up from the chair and lifted me into his arms.

I fought him then, silently writhing in his arms, but he tightened his grip. "Lady wife, I only seek to hold you, to comfort you."

His words slowed my struggle, could I trust him? He gently laid me down on the bed. The softness of the bed, the scent, the pillows around me, enfolded me into the terrifying cocoon of my nightmare. With fear-filled agility I shot up, scooted away from him and jumped off the other side of the bed. Dizziness caught me and I swayed on my feet.

"Sit down before you fall down, woman," he curtly ordered.

I glanced up. David stood across the bed from me, a ferocious frown marring his face. "Sit down! I promise I won't join you on the bed," he said. "Do you need another bowl?"

"No," I whispered as I sat back down on the bed.

"You remind me of a skittish lamb," he growled.

"And you remind me of a snarling wolf," I replied. My fear had dissipated as soon as he'd promised he wouldn't touch me.

His loud burst of laughter stunned me. I looked up to see him shaking his head, even as his merriment continued.

Watching him laugh was like experiencing a gentle spring rain soaking into dry, caked earth. Could Mama be right? Was it possible to forgive this man? This man wasn't a ravisher of married women, nor a killer of husbands. Who was he? The thought I might already be softening toward him literally made me nauseous.

He glanced over at me and suddenly sobered. "You look like you're going to be sick again." He sprinted to the table, dumped the fruit out, and rushed the carved wooden bowl over to me. "Here, use this."

I swallowed and fought the nausea as I grabbed the bowl.

"I remember Abigail was sick like you are with our Kileab. I was worried she might lose the child, she was so sick, but of course, she didn't. Not then, anyway."

I looked up to see his eyes fill with sorrow. Was he still grieving his son? I knew it had been over four years since Kileab had died.

"My family and I grieved with you and Abigail when you lost Kileab to that virulent fever," I murmured. "He was always kind to me when we were children in Hebron, even though he was older than I. My mother said he had Abigail's wisdom and humor, and your gifts of music and joy."

He gazed at me thoughtfully and I trembled at the awareness in his eyes. It was as if he were seeing me in a way he never had before. As he stared at me, respect filled his gaze.

I closed my eyes. I didn't want to empathize with his loss, and I didn't want to be swayed by his respect. I especially didn't want to feel compassion for him as a father who'd lost a beloved son, or as a man who'd known and experienced his own grief.

I glanced up to see him moving restlessly around the room. He stopped by a chest I hadn't noticed before. Unlike the one in my room, this cedar chest was carved with more intricate designs and inlaid wood on the top. With quick movements, he lifted the lid and picked up something wrapped in red linen. What was it? A gift he thought might please me?

Unwrapping it, he withdrew an exquisite lyre. I wasn't sure of the wood, but it held a golden sheen, and a lion's head was carved from the sounding box of the instrument. There was a moment of silence, before the air filled with the rich chords flowing from this unique lyre. Soon David's vibrant, melodious voice joined the instrument, creating a weaving of rich, harmonious music with luminous words I'd learned when just a babe.

> "The Lord is my shepherd, I shall not want.
>   He makes me lie down in green pastures;
> he leads me beside still waters;
>   he restores my soul.
> He leads me in right paths
>   for his name's sake.
> Even though I walk through the valley of the shadow of death
>   I fear no evil;
> for you are with me;
>   your rod and your staff –
> they comfort me. . . ."

The music was a soothing balm to my grieving soul. The nausea passed, and I put down the bowl. I was enfolded with weariness, and laid down on the edge of the bed. I curled myself around one of the pillows and held it tightly as the music wove in and around me. With a sigh of exhaustion, I closed my eyes.

Listening to David's song, all the times he'd visited our house and shared his gift of music haunted me, even as the comforting and well-remembered words invited me into a place of security and rest. I wanted to fight the lethargy that stole over me; didn't I need to be on my guard with this man? Yet, as his once beloved voice called me to trust in our faithful Lord, I yawned. I had to fight the invitation to trust this musician of my cherished memories; or did I?

Chapter 22

I awoke to the presence of a warm body wrapped around me, a calloused hand gently stroking my arm. "Uriah, beloved, you came home," I whispered, my eyes still closed as I enjoyed the warm closeness of his homecoming.

Abruptly the warmth fled with the body that rolled away from me. I opened my eyes. I was immediately struck with the foreign room and the awareness of where I lay. David's bed.

"First you vomit, then you fall asleep in the middle of my singing, and now you wake up and call me by the name of your dead husband," David roared. "If you planned to keep me out of your bed, you could choose no better ways."

I wanted badly to yell at him and defend myself. But his venomous accusations stirred my fragile stomach to violent life. I quickly slipped from the bed and grabbed the bowl I'd left on the floor just in time.

"So, even the sight of me makes you sick? Well, I can take care of that."

He stomped to the chair, pulled a tunic over his nakedness and sat and slipped on his sandals. He glared at me before he threw the door open, stormed out and pulled it shut.

I felt wretched, yet I was also thankful to hear his steps move down the corridor. I wanted no one to see my humiliation. No one to know how I'd awakened to believe I was in the arms of my husband.

"Oh, God," I groaned. "I did wake up in the arms of my husband, but not the husband I wanted. Not the husband who loved me. The husband who's dead." I curled up on the bed and fought my grief by cursing David.

Would David remove me from this room, if not his palace? Would he order his guards to throw me out of his rooms again? Or, divorce me as an adulteress, accusing me of being pregnant by another man? Would I defend myself or just allow him to have me stoned and welcome my own death?

Am I going crazy?

"Oh, God, I'm sick and weary of this life of turmoil and confusion."

Without any real hope of a reprieve from David, and because I didn't want the servants to know I was sick, I emptied the bowl into the chamber pot. Then I cleaned it and put the fruit back into it.

I drank a small amount of sweet wine, then washed my face. I would look my best for anyone who might come for me. I had just finished combing my hair when I heard more footsteps coming down the hall. Fear's cold hand gripped me, but I quickly shrugged it off. If David chose to kill me, I'd be free of this life of misery. Wouldn't that be better, anyway?

A knock sounded at the door. Would his guards knock if they were coming to arrest me?

"Come," I commanded. With my fear of death vanquished, I enjoyed a sense of power.

"Good morning, my lady."

A woman servant walked through the doorway, her white tunic accented with a blue sash. Another servant held the door open, then shut it behind her. The woman carried a tray with food. I breathed in the aroma of fresh bread while hunger stirred within me.

So, I'm to be fed and not banished. My king is merciful.

"My lady, the king ordered food for you to break your fast. His servant told us you'd be content with the simple fare of bread, cheese and milk. If you need anything else, you only need ask." She set the tray down, and bowed before lifting her eyes to mine. "May I serve you, lady?"

"Yes."

She poured me milk and cut the bread, putting it on a gold plate. "May I clean while you eat, my lady?"

I was thankful I'd cleaned up before her, leaving nothing to show how sick I'd been. "Yes, and please bring me more fresh water."

She bowed and did as I asked, but took her time. I was sure she noted the rumpled bed and my pale face. I wondered if she was in the pay of any of David's wives, or if she was curious for herself. Cynically, I suspected it was both. She took the chamber pot out, and handed it to the woman waiting and requested more water. Returning, she bowed to me again.

"Is there any other way I can serve you, my lady?" She stood with her head down.

"Yes, you can have my handmaiden, Rachel, brought to me," I said. I felt a strong sense I needed to take up my authority over her immediately. "I'll call you if I need anything else." I held my head high and watched her bow to me before she left.

When she was gone, I finished the milk, which was fresh and frothy and tasted delicious. Tearing off another piece of bread, I smiled at its goodness. David's baker was truly gifted.

So, was I to stay in this room all day? What was the etiquette of a new bride in David's household? Did he expect me to take my place with his other women at the tent of meeting? I didn't know, and I realized I didn't care.

Another knock sounded at the door. "Come."

Rachel opened the door, her face wreathed in smiles, and her arms held the tunic I'd worn for my wedding. "My lady, I was told you should be dressed in this again today, and I was to help you dress and prepare you to join the other wives for worship at the tent of meeting. They meet in the common room," she explained, "and we all walk over together."

She carefully helped me to dress and comb my hair. I felt weak from all my emotions and was thankful for her help. This would be the first time I'd join his other wives as one of them. Could I pretend to enjoy my new status as the king's wife? If I wanted to live, and wanted my babe to live without being cursed as illegitimate, could I do anything else?

"Come, child, let's go meet my husband's other women."

* * *

As Rachel and I entered the common area, I noted the hostile glances of many of the women before Abigail walked toward me, her face alight with welcome. Seeing my mother's good friend coming with outstretched arms to embrace me brought unexpected tears.

"Bathsheba, dear child," she cooed as she hugged me, and kissed both cheeks, "so you have joined me here in David's court in a very unexpected way. Although I must not call you a child, when you're clearly a woman of exquisite beauty."

She took my hand and led me over to a corner, positioning me so she blocked all views. "Wipe your eyes, child. Tears are not what's expected from a new bride who's just captured the affections of our king, even if you are a new widow."

I leaned over, as if to smooth my tunic and swiped at my tears. Straightening, I looked at her, amazed to see her unusual blue eyes filled with compassion. "Your mother, who's my great friend, came to visit and told me of your marriage to our lord and king," she whispered. "She pleaded with me to care for you as best I can in this foreign place. I assured her I'd protect you well from the jackals here, and introduce you to the more tame and domesticated cats."

She grinned, and deep dimples appeared in her round cheeks, making her look years younger, and quite beautiful. How had I missed seeing those dimples as a child, and how could I have ever thought her plain? Was it because I'd always compared her to my mother? Even as a girl, I knew my mother was a rare beauty, as she still was, even with the ravages of grief.

Abigail was dressed in a red tunic, her thick brown hair pulled back, and her face radiant with an inner peace and joy. I no longer wondered at the amazing story my mother told me of Abigail and David. And how she'd kept David from slaughtering her husband and people when she met him on the road with a large peace offering. She must've smiled deeply when she appealed to him for mercy, for her dimples would charm any man out of violence, and her vivid and unusual blue eyes would've captivated him with their beauty.

"Have I shocked you?" she asked. "I'm sorry. Truly, some of his women are kind."

"No, I was only wondering what you are?" I teased.

She stared at me a moment, her eyes alight with speculation, her head tilted to the side. "Hmm, I don't think the question is who I am, but who are you?"

"Why, I'm David's newest bride, of course." Bitterness bled into the humor I attempted.

"Ah, at another time we'll speak more about you." Her look promised more penetrating questions in the future. "For now we must go worship our God."

* * *

I paced the bridal chamber wondering if David would join me again or not. I'd been taken directly back here after going to worship. I hated the waiting. If David believed I'd purposefully thwarted him in his desire to bed his new wife, would he even allow me to join him at tonight's feast? As David had acceded to my request, this would be the second of our three days of celebration.

From the women's court, I'd seen David worship. Aware of the scrutiny of the women around me, I'd forced myself to smile and watch him with what must appear as perfect joy. For my child's sake, I had to convince everyone I was ecstatic with my marriage. As I stood in the court of women, surrounded with the distinct sights, sounds and scent of worship, I embraced the life of the child growing within me. I also knew to welcome his life, was to accept my own. However, I still felt sick at the thought of lying with David.

With a sigh, I sat on the bed. Exhaustion insistently pulled at me. I gave up and lay down. I wondered, would David be angry if he returned to find me asleep in his bed? Did I care? Mama had assured me both nausea and exhaustion were normal, but I still hated it. Had David watched Abigail tire easily, even as he'd seen her sick? What about his other wives?

When Mama first knew David, he'd only had two wives, Ahinoam and Abigail. Both came to Hebron with young sons, Ahinoam's Amnon only a few months older than Abigail's Kileab. Those few months had been the difference in whose son would be the heir to the throne of David. Yet, after watching Kileab grow into a musician and not a warrior, Abigail had told Mama how Kileab had been glad Amnon would be king, so he could give his time to his music.

I now knew David still grieved Kileab's passing. Had Abigail's son been David's only child to share his love and gifts for music and poetry? I knew Amnon and Absalom had no such talent.

Will our son be a warrior and leader or a musician and singer like me. . . and David?

I gasped at the thought and sat up. I'd never allowed myself to even think about what this child might be like. What kind of things would attract his attention in this violent, complex world.

"How is it I feel so strongly I'm carrying a son and not a daughter?" I questioned out loud. The answer shook me. I didn't believe God would have mercy on me by gifting me with a daughter, who could never inherit the throne. A daughter who'd never need to prove her legitimacy when she arrived into this world "too early."

I don't trust you, God of David, and my heart is rent in two.

"So, David," I said aloud, sliding off the bed to pace the

hated room. "Are you avoiding me? What will your court think when they see your lack of passion toward your new bride? Of course, I'm your eighth wife, and you have countless concubines as well. Does this explain why you're behaving like a bored old man?" I laughed contemptuously. "But if people are to believe I've been 'taken' with child so quickly, you should demonstrate some desire to join me in our marriage bed. Or, don't you care that you're putting me in the path of dangerous gossip?

"It's true I've no desire for you. Why should I? You were considerate last night only because you feared I'd retch all over your kingly person."

I stopped ranting and sat down in one of David's chairs. "Oh Lord, if there's to be any hope for me and my child, this child you're knitting together in my womb. . . this babe who might be warrior or musician, poet or dancer, or daughter. My child, who grows beneath my broken heart, please, bring my bridegroom back to me."

With sudden resolve, I went to David's chest and took out his lyre. If he'll not come and entertain me, I'll entertain myself. Boldly, I played David's beautiful and resonant instrument.

Chapter 23

"I remember your father playing that same song in your home in Hebron, with your mother singing it with him."

I looked up to find David staring at me by the door. Clearly, the music had kept me from hearing him enter. "Papa always loved Miriam's song of victory," I agreed.

"You sound well, wife, are you?" he asked. He walked over to the other chair and stood behind it.

"Better than this morning. Are you well, my king?"

"Better than this morning," he repeated, with a small smile. "Will you continue singing for me?" He pulled the chair back and sat in it.

Relieved to see him sit, and knowing I'd rather sing than lie with him, I began:

"I will sing to the Lord, for he has triumphed gloriously;
    horse and rider he has thrown into the sea.
The Lord is my strength and my might;
    he has become my salvation;
this is my God, and I will praise him,
    my father's God, and I will exalt him.
The Lord is a warrior; the Lord is his name. . .
    Who is like you, O Lord, among the gods?

Who is like you, majestic in holiness,
  awesome in splendor, doing wonders?"

"You have a full, passionate voice, though deeper than your mother's. I'd say it's more richly modulated than hers, as well," he complimented me.

I didn't want him to praise me. "I remember another time in our home in Hebron, I don't think I was more than three years old. You were sad about something, and my father, knowing how music could cheer you, handed you his lyre, and as you played, he and Mama began to sing with you. It did cheer you, and you left our home soon after, saying you needed to return to your kingly duties, although you would rather stay and sing."

"Your father was always a good friend to me. I grieved deeply when he died. After all our years of fighting together, I'd come to think him indestructible." He stared off, and shook his head. "So many of my friends have died fighting wars with me."

"And others have died fighting wars without you," I said, thinking of Uriah. I didn't have the courage to accuse him to his face of Uriah's death, but I could remind him of those who'd died while he was safe in Jerusalem.

His head snapped up and he stared at me, his eyes alert and watchful as he stood up and pushed the chair away. "You'd remind me of Uriah, here in our marriage chamber? After you already called out his name this morning? Aren't you afraid of me, woman? I've only to speak a word and you'd be exiled, or I could kill you myself."

I laid the lyre on the table and stood to face him. The blood roared through me like a raging river. "You think I fear death from you, my kingly husband?" I taunted. "The only reason I'm here with you and not dead already by my own choice is because of the babe you uncaringly planted when you raped me—"

"Silence, woman," he bellowed. "You dare to accuse your king?"

"No, I simply tell the truth, even to the king."

With two steps he was upon me, my neck between his thick, calloused hands. I closed my eyes, feeling the pressure of his hands grow painfully about my throat.

I didn't regret speaking the truth. Being a man, I was sure he'd convinced himself I'd wanted to be taken. He'd probably even persuaded himself I'd bathed in the courtyard to be seen by him. Men are so good at lying to themselves about women, especially women they lusted after.

At least he would kill me quickly.

Suddenly, the pressure lifted and his hands released me. I fell to the floor, weak and dizzy from lack of air. After a moment, I opened my eyes and stared up into his angry and bewildered gaze.

"You didn't attempt to fight me. I expected you to struggle and I would have immediately released you. Do you truly wish to die?"

I looked up at him. My eyes overflowed with more accursed tears. Furious at my weakness, I dried them with a back-handed swipe. "If living means submitting myself to you," I croaked, my voice wounded by his hands, "the man who made me an adulteress and ordered my husband's death, then yes, I'd rather die."

His eyes widened with shock at my words. Was he surprised at my accusation? Did he believe I didn't understand the convenience of Uriah's death?

"But what about the babe? Didn't you just say you chose to live because of it?"

"Yes!" I exclaimed. Irate with him and myself, I struggled up so I could stand and face him. Gulping air, I stepped to the table, grabbed a goblet, and poured some wine and drank. It soothed my throat enough to enable me to speak my heart to this man who was my husband.

"For over four years I begged God to give Uriah and me a child," I said, well remembering all my prayers. "I offered countless sacrifices to him, and confessed every sin I could remember, begging my mother to tell me if she could think of any others. She told me there were none.

"After that first year, I took all the remedies prescribed by family and friends, and still the curse of barrenness remained." With defiance, I stared at him and proclaimed, "Some women 'friends' encouraged me to worship the goddesses of our enemies, assuring me their fertility goddess would give me what our warrior God would not."

His eyes narrowed in accusation. I smiled at the irony of his readiness to condemn me for my supposed sin, even as I recounted his own. "Oh no, my king, I did not do it. My beloved stopped me, promising me that in God's good time, he would bless us with a child. Uriah often told me how we only had to wait, like Rachel and Jacob waited. I was still waiting when you observed me from your roof, for I was taking my mikvah.

"My tears blended with the purifying water when you commanded your men to come and take me into your presence. After you were done, and Benaiah left me at my gate, I was going to throw myself off a cliff when Mama stopped me. I reasoned I'd rather kill myself than be killed by stoning, once it was discovered I'd been with you." I stopped, my throat hoarse from my many words and the lingering pain of his grip. I took another drink.

"My guards know to discuss the king's business is to die a swift death."

I glanced up at him and laughed harshly at his credulity. "Someone could have seen me walking with them to your palace, my king. But it seems they didn't. So, the days passed, and my tears of shame and hatred dried, and my mother's words of hope and comfort eased me, and the pain of your betrayal lessened."

"You, woman will not. . ." he took a step toward me.

I put up my hand, and incredibly he closed his mouth on his words and stood in place. I lowered my hand to my womb. "Weeks later, my mother came to me, her face ravaged with fear and sorrow. She questioned me about my last menses." Shame lowered my voice and my eyes. "She asked me if I hadn't noticed changes in my body. Finally, she told me what I couldn't know, and never suspected—" I choked back a sob.

"You were with child," he finished for me, his voice no longer accusatory. "Was it your mother who told you to send me your message?"

I stared up at him and nodded, my throat aching from his wounds and my unshed tears.

"I've always respected your mother," he said. "I once told your father that Anna had more courage than many of my best warriors. With great pride, he agreed."

"It's taken all her courage to live without him this past year."

"You're very much like her."

I blinked, taken aback at the admiration gleaming in his eyes. It confused me.

"It's time for us to leave and worship God, again," he said, once more the king. "Afterwards, we'll celebrate our wedding with another banquet. Your grandfather has been enjoying himself immensely with his new role as grandfather to the king." He smiled at me a moment before it disappeared. "I don't know why he doesn't know you're carrying my child, but I'm thankful to you he doesn't."

I feared to tell him that if he'd killed my husband to keep him from the truth, how would I trust him not to kill my grandfather? Did I still believe he'd kill Grandfather or my mother? It would have been so easy for him to have killed me and just been done with me and his unwanted child. But instead, he'd listened to me.

Oh God, who is this man I've married? He raped me and killed my husband. He wanted to kill me. . . but he didn't. He's king of your nation, Israel. He has power second only to you.

He gave me life – my child's and now my own. . . .

"Bathsheba?"

"Why didn't you kill me? Why do you want me to live? I've told you I want nothing to do with you. You could easily bed another tonight, one who'll give you pleasure and joy."

With a swiftness that shocked me, he grabbed hold of my shoulders and shook me. "You, woman, will honor me as your husband and your king," he growled. "You'll go with the women to worship and join me at our wedding feast, where you'll show proper respect for me, and all will see how greatly you admire your king and husband. Later, I'll join you here in this room again and we'll have the wedding night we never had last night."

"If you touch me, I'll be sick," I threatened.

He shrugged. "Perhaps, wife, you'll make me sick and I'll retch on you."

"You mock me!" I cried.

"No," he said with quiet force, "perhaps I mock myself."

With those words, he turned and strode out of the room. I snatched the goblet from the table and hurled it at the closed door. It bounced off the door and fell to the floor. I stared at it and started laughing with uncontrolled mirth.

Gold doesn't break like pottery, but it does dent. Would he notice his beautiful goblet had been marred? Did I care? No.

Chapter 24

The banquet was loud with the many voices of the king's court raised to hear each other above all the other conversations. The aroma of all the different spices in the food, and perfumes worn by David's family and friends filled my senses. I fought the nausea by taking small breaths through my mouth. People were reclining around this, the king's table, as well as other tables set up below us.

My cheeks ached from my forced smiles. I knew David was right; for my sake, and my babe's, I had to convince everyone I was overjoyed to be a wife of King David. My grandfather, dressed in a richly embroidered blue tunic I hadn't seen before, leaned toward Mephibosheth. Clearly, he wanted to enjoy every comment made by Prince Jonathan's esteemed but crippled son. When I'd arrived in ceremonial splendor, David had welcomed me, and Grandfather had greeted me with kisses and such effusive praise for my beauty, I'd been embarrassed.

I looked past Grandfather and saw Absalom reclined on his other side. He was dressed in purple, his thick, long dark hair oiled. He glanced up and caught my eye. He leered at me and winked. I quickly turned from his gaze. I knew my cheeks blazed at the insult. As a child, and then as Uriah's wife, I'd always been too low to catch Absalom's notice. I wished I'd remained unnoticed.

"Are you well, wife?" David asked. He'd lowered his deep voice so only I could hear him, and his concern.

"I'm well, husband," I said, surprised by his apparent distress I might be ill again.

"Your cheeks turned a deep red, then you became pale and I thought you might be ill."

I couldn't tell him about his son's disrespect, so I gave him a different truth. "I'm not used to being at the king's table, or eating such rich food. However, it's good to see my grandfather enjoying himself."

"Your mother is at the end of another table below us. I've noticed she's been watching you closely throughout the meal." He leaned closer, whispered in my ear as a lover would. "She's probably concerned for your health as well."

I slowly smiled, as if he'd just fed me words of love and not worry. "Yes."

He smiled into my eyes. "I've watched you avoid the lamb, eating only the blandest of the foods on my table. Can I feed you some bread?"

"Can't I feed myself?" I asked and smiled back at him.

"Do you want people to suspect we aren't wildly enamored with each other?" he murmured as he stroked my bare arm.

"May I answer truthfully, my king?" I asked, allowing my lips to pout in a way Uriah once told me always made him want to kiss me. If David wanted to play games at his table, in front of his whole court, I'd play them. But not the way he'd expected.

His gaze sharpened and his hand left my arm. "I don't think I like what you call 'truth', woman."

I felt the change in the very air of the room as conversations stopped or quieted. His words were caught by those closest to us, and probably whispered to others. If I didn't want to be denounced now, before all these witnesses, I had to respond to his anger in a way that would coax him out of it.

Calling upon all the courage and wiles my mother had given

me, I leaned toward him with a seductive smile. With my finger, I lightly touched his chest. "My lord husband," I breathed, "the truth is I'm now your wife, and all of who I am is yours."

Staring into my eyes, I'm not sure what he saw, but it must have eased him. He took my hand, raised it to his lips and kissed my palm. "I think we've eaten enough of this banquet, haven't we, wife?" he asked loudly. "Perhaps it's time to partake of our own delicacies?" His eyes glowed down at me with promised violence, even as he smiled sensuously.

"Yes, my lord," I agreed. I knew any other answer would forfeit my life.

He leaped up from his place at the table and extended his hand to me. I took it and he pulled me up to stand beside him. He glanced around the room, and laughed with delight. "It's time for us to leave you. Please continue to enjoy the feast, as we will ours."

My cheeks flamed as I followed him out of the hall. The sound of raucous laughter billowed behind us. As we walked to our bridal chamber, he turned to grin down at me.

"You told me you're well, wife, so I don't expect you to get sick as soon as we reach our bridal room."

"And might I trust you are well, too?"

His startled gaze caught my eyes as he passed a guard in the hall. David allowed him to open the door for us, then close it.

I followed David into the room. With a soft curse, he spun around, put his hands on my shoulders, and drew me close. There was barely a hairsbreadth of space between us.

"I want a wedding night, Bathsheba," he said, his eyes searching mine. "I don't want to fight you with words or body. You're a puzzle to me, talking back to me when you know I could have you killed for such disrespect, and getting sick when I'd have you well. I understand it's the babe you carry who makes you ill, but did Uriah not slap your face to curb your tongue? Or give you a sound beating?"

I glowered up at him, and tried to step away. With what

sounded like a frustrated sigh, he let me go.

"My tongue, my king, has sharpened with my marriage to you. However, neither my father nor my husband were ever violent toward Mama or me. Uriah once told me if the Lord saw us as 'one flesh' why would he desire to hit himself? His view was that violence toward a wife only bred fear and pain in her, and ultimately more strife between them," I said, well remembering our discussion one winter evening after I told him of a friend's bruises.

"Uriah believed it unworthy for any man to use his strength to beat his wife instead of using it to protect her. And as a warrior, he found the very idea of beating a wife repugnant, although he knew many men who did, and boasted of it. He said he was happy to leave war and violence behind him to embrace peace and contentment at home with his wife."

David's eyes widened at my words, as if he'd never heard such an argument. I was sure he hadn't. "Truly, Uriah is the only man I've ever heard speak in such a way. But it brought me great comfort as his wife.

"May I ask you, my new husband, do you often beat your wives? It would help me to know this, so I might prepare for it in the future?" I glanced up to catch a look that reflected both anger and respect.

"Abigail is my only wife whom I've found to be both friend and lover. I surmise you and Uriah were such?" he asked gruffly.

His honesty encouraged me. "Yes."

"And even though you were barren, he took no other wife?"

My face warmed at his blunt question. Angry, I wanted to tell him exactly why Uriah took no other wife. But I knew I couldn't voice his view of David's family life. I shook my head. "He often told me I was the only woman he ever wanted or desired."

He reached out a hand and stunned me when he laid it firmly on my womb. "Yet, it's I and not Uriah who proved you to be fertile. Have you felt the stirring of life yet?"

"No," I said. I bit back the angry words I wanted to scream

at him in defense of my dead husband.

"I've felt babes in the wombs of my wives before," he said, suddenly smiling as he removed his hand. "I remember once, when Abigail was big with child and angry with me for something, I hugged her to me to comfort her and was shocked to feel the babe kick me, as if to say, 'let go of my mother.'"

He gave me a look that was both tender and a challenge. "Bathsheba, you're my wife and will soon be the mother of our child. Yes, I want you, but I'd protect you, too. I also desire you, and wish for you to desire me."

In both fascination and trepidation, I watched his countenance change to become, again, the all powerful king; his ruddy face fierce, his hazel eyes narrowed. "I tell you now, if you refuse me, I will take your advice and call another of my wives to me. However, if I do this, know you'll never be called to me again." He stared at me, his countenance a grim mask. "Do you think people will believe a long barren woman could be impregnated in one night?"

"Why not, it's the truth," I muttered. Shocked by my boldness, I slapped my hand over my mouth even as fear curled in my stomach.

"Don't you dare get sick on me again," he ordered, misinterpreting my gesture. With a deep sigh, he shook his head. "I truly don't know what to do with you, Bathsheba. As I said, you're unlike any of the other women in my life. At one moment, I want to love you passionately, and in another instant, I want to throttle you."

"I'm glad I'm different. You're not like Uriah nor my father, either, although I can see some similarities between you and my grandfather."

He stared at me and I could see in his eyes the battle between his anger and his humor at my temerity in answering him, again. Humor won out and he threw back his head and laughed uproariously. Watching him laugh, I felt such relief I smiled. Mirth welled up inside me. It had been so long since I'd laughed, could I allow myself to laugh with David?

I didn't realize David had stopped laughing. "You have a lovely smile, full of light and warmth. Do you know I've never seen you smile before this moment?"

"Of course you have," I said without thought. "I haven't stopped smiling this day, or yesterday."

"You're wrong, those were not true smiles, but a cheerful mask to hide behind."

I gaped at him in consternation. Afraid of David in a whole new way.

"Ah, now I've told you a truth you didn't like to hear. Sometimes, hearing the truth can be disturbing, can't it, wife?"

I swallowed, and nodded.

"Bathsheba, will you choose to be my wife, or will you choose to live your life without my protection or favor?" His hands were planted on his waist, as if he were getting ready to order his men to duty. "I'll have you willingly now, or if you choose to deny me, you'll live out your life without my acceptance or blessing, and I'll take our child to live with others once he's weaned."

I trembled at his words. He'd take my child and leave me bereft and alone?

He put his hands on my shoulders and looked deeply into my eyes. It was as if he wanted to gauge if his words had penetrated my understanding and stubbornness. "I'd advise you to agree, if not for yourself, then for the child you carry. The child God gave you from my seed."

He must have glimpsed my anger at his words, for his hands painfully gripped my shoulders, and the fierceness of his look caught my breath. I knew with a clarity born that instant that if I didn't submit to him now, he'd toss me out the door and have his guard take me to my room. And I'd never see David again, except from a distance, and within a few short years, lose my beloved child as well.

I bowed my head and slipped to my knees in supplication

and acquiescence. As I did this, he released his hands upon my shoulders. I stayed in this position of obeisance for long minutes. Would he accept me? Or had our conversation given him a disgust of me? Was he taking his time to enjoy my humble stance? I wanted to glance up at him, but I knew I didn't dare. I forced myself to remain silent at his feet.

"So, my new wife does know how to submit to her kingly husband." His hand appeared before me. "Bathsheba, my wife, take my hand, arise and come to me."

Remembering Mama's warnings, I took his hand.

Chapter 25

I tried not to disturb David as I slipped out of bed, grabbed a bowl from the table, and ran to the corner of the room. I placed the fruit on the floor and curled myself around the bowl, my back to the bed. My mind was full of conflict, and my soul grieved. I prayed I wouldn't be sick.

Although David had been all that was considerate as a lover, I couldn't escape the truth: I'd made love with the man who'd ordered my husband's death. I refused to cry and show more weakness than I already had at the reality of my position. I couldn't imagine bearing a child and having it stolen from me; I knew that would be a living death I couldn't endure.

"Oh God, I agreed to be his wife," I whispered.

"Yes, Bathsheba, you are truly my wife, now," David agreed from behind me.

I jerked in fright at the sound of his voice.

"Easy, wife," he soothed, even as he knelt down and put his arms around me, drawing me up against his warm chest.

I shook from the force of the sobs that swept over me at his gentle touch. With a sigh, he wrapped me more tightly to him. Did he sing over me, too?

When the wave of weeping subsided, I lay back against him, feeling bereft and spent.

"Bathsheba, are you well, or is your stomach queasy from all your crying?"

I queried my body and grabbed the bowl as my body convulsed with nausea. Gentle hands pulled my hair back from my face. When my body stopped shaking, he left me. I was shocked at my sense of loss.

"Here, wipe your face and give me that bowl."

I looked up to see him with a wet cloth. I gave him the bowl and took the cloth. He soon handed me a goblet. My hands shook as I put the cup to my lips. Rough hands surrounded my trembling grip and he helped me drink.

"I'm concerned this babe is leaving you with nothing to feed him or yourself."

The distress in his voice once again stunned me. "Mama told me she was sick the same way with me, but I came into this world strong and healthy with a cry that could penetrate rock."

He grinned. "I'm glad to hear it. Now, I'm going to lift you up and bring you back to the bed. No, don't tense like a skittish lamb again, I only want to hold you. Will you let me?"

I nodded my agreement.

He carefully lifted me, and held me close against him. He walked over to the bed and set me down, then joined me, again wrapping himself around me. His warmth seeped into me with amazing comfort. I wanted to resist, but I was too tired. And David was singing over me. I not only could hear him, but I could feel the vibration of his voice against my back. It was a love song for our Lord. Or was it a love song for me? No, it couldn't be for me.

* * *

"My lady, it's time to get up. Lady, please wake up."

Whose voice was calling me? I opened my eyes and looked around. Rachel stood at the foot of the bed, and wrung her hands. I looked around. The king was gone. Sometime after I fell back to sleep he'd slipped out of bed without awakening me. His consideration of me both touched me and. . . angered me. Why?

"I'm sorry, lady, but the king sent his servant to me so I could awaken you instead of someone you don't know," she said. "I've been calling you, but you wouldn't wake up. I didn't want to touch you, for you're the king's wife now, and I can't touch you."

"Rachel, child, it's all right," I said, slowly sitting up. "I wouldn't have minded if you had lightly touched me on the shoulder, as you've done in the past when Mama sent you."

"But you're now a part of the royal family and. . . ."

"I seem to still oversleep, right?"

"The king asked that you join the women to walk to the tabernacle for our worship."

"I'll do as he asks. I see you have my tunic. Good, you can also help me brush my hair."

"Yes, lady. And the king's servant said your mother has been asking if she might see you. King David graciously gave his permission for her to see you this afternoon."

"Thank you, Rachel that's indeed good of him." I hoped Rachel didn't hear the irony in my voice. Part of me rejoiced at the news, another part rebelled that I must now have David's permission to see my own mother. Would it always be so?

Tonight was the last feast of our wedding celebrations. I knew she wanted assurance I hadn't offended David so badly last night that I'd be thrown out of my rooms or given a sentence of death. Irrationally, I resented David because he treated me with compassion and care. It was as if he were purposefully trying to prove himself to be. . . what? A kind man, and not the abuser and murderer I'd called him? Truly, it was a miracle he hadn't killed me for my words.

* * *

After I'd returned from worshiping our Lord with David's women, David had joined me once again and taken a light meal with me before leaving to continue his "kingly" business. We'd said little, but I knew at least part of his reason for joining me was to make it appear he wanted to be with me every moment he could. How could I fight this kind of consideration? Yet, deep inside I knew I wanted to.

I rested on the bed when David's guards knocked on the door. Mama entered and I ran across the room to hug her tightly.

"Are you well, my daughter?" she asked when I released her. Her dark eyes searched my own, before wandering down my body. It was as if she could only read the truth by appraising the expression in my eyes, and the health of my body. When she saw I looked well, she nodded her awareness of my good health.

"I'm well enough, Mama," I assured her. "Although the Lord hasn't answered our prayers I'd stop being sick."

Her dark eyebrows knit over her bright, inquisitive eyes. "Have you been sick with David?"

I burst into loud laughter. "Ah Mama, yes, I've often been sick with David."

"And yet you laugh about it?" she asked. "Wasn't he upset?"

"Yes, he's been upset, to the point of wanting to strangle me," I half jested. "And he's also been patient and understanding." Tears welled in my eyes and with a small cry I launched myself back into her arms. She held me tightly until I was able to pull away, my tears abating.

"Ah, so the king hasn't been the man you expected, has he? He hasn't been the same man who used you that terrible night."

"Oh Mama, I'm so confused," I cried. "I want to hate him, how can I not hate the man who ordered the death of my beloved?"

"Yet, you've just said—"

"I know what I said." I walked away from her, picked a pillow off the bed and hugged it. "David's been angry and demanding, but he's also been tender and kind."

"Dear one, every man can be all of these things and more. You know this about men, you saw it in Uriah as well as your own father and grandfather."

"I don't want David's kindness and understanding." I threw the pillow across the room. "I don't want him holding me tenderly and singing over me until I fall asleep."

"David did this?" Mama asked. She caught my hand and forced me to stop and look at her.

"Yes!" I shook my hand free. "But he's also been violent and threatened to dismiss me, taking my babe with him, if I didn't give him the wedding night he demanded."

Mama slowly shook her head. "Bathsheba, he's been violent and threatened you, but he's also been kind? Has his kindness outweighed the threats?"

"I knew you'd defend him, haven't you always defended him?" I accused.

"I'm not defending him, dear one, I'm only trying to understand what you're telling me. Did he tenderly hold you and sing to you? Was this before or after his threats?"

"Both!" I snapped.

Mama stared at me and said nothing for a long moment. "I see we're not talking so much about David anymore, are we? It's you whom you despise. You who gave in to David's threats and kindness and gave him what he wanted. My poor daughter, can't you see you did the only thing you could do for your sake and the child's? Your life would have been a living death if he'd cast you out of his presence, and taken your child."

"I hate what I'm becoming," I exclaimed, making a fist with my hand. "How can I respond to his tenderness when it's only given so I might stop fighting him, or accusing him of the truth we both know?"

"I heard his comment at dinner last night, and sensed the simmering anger in him. I prayed you'd soften toward him. I cried out to God you'd give in and not fight him before all his court. If you'd humiliated him, you'd have forced him to reject you, and possibly have you killed."

"It seems your prayers were answered. For I did soften and tease, instead of accusing him before everyone of Uriah's death."

"Daughter, I know David," she said. "He could grow to love you, perhaps even more than his other wives, if you would only—"

"Shut my mouth and seduce him with my ripening body?" I touched my still flat stomach, the fullness of my breasts.

"And your loving heart and sharp mind, and gifts of music. If you were only willing to allow him to get to know all of who you are. Have you danced or sung for him?"

"I sang for him once, to keep him from taking me to bed. I won't ever dance for him."

"For you to dance, you'd need to feel better," she said, ignoring my words.

"Abigail has been very helpful to me. Thank you for visiting her and asking her to befriend me," I said, desperate to change the subject. "She greeted me warmly and has walked with me each time we go to the tabernacle. But surely you didn't tell her of my shame?"

"Of course not. Although I wouldn't be surprised if she didn't suspect something soon," Mama cautioned. "She's always been very wise to the ways of David and his court, and has often counseled him. In many ways, she's more discerning than your grandfather."

"How is that?" I asked, in disbelief.

"Your grandfather knows all in David's court, but he doesn't have access to David's women, in the women's quarters, or with his wives who live beyond the palace gates. Abigail has access to the secrets of the court as well as the secrets of the women."

"Hopefully, she doesn't know my secret, and never will."

"Don't be concerned I'll tell her the truth, dear one. But there may come a time when you feel led to do so, and if you are, do it," Mama said, taking my hand again. "The friendship we forged in Ziklag, especially when we were captured, has always remained strong. Then, when Kileab died, she shared I was the only woman she knew who truly grieved his death with her."

"How sad." I stared at her, stricken at her words.

"Her son was second in line to David's throne. With him gone, David's other sons were that much closer to the kingship.

She said his wives only pretended to grieve for David's sake."

"Has she found no friend among the other wives or concubines?"

"Not the wives. Ahinoam never forgave her for taking her place in David's affections when she became his third wife. And each of David's other wives lorded it over her when they arrived, sure they'd soon replace her in all of David's affections." She smiled with wry humor. "What they can't understand and despise her for, is even though she's beyond her childbearing years, David continues to call her to him. Although she told me it's often more for her counsel."

"Come, let's sit," Mama said. She pulled me to the chairs, and we sat across from one another. "David's treated Abigail with great love and kindness, and she's been his wife longer than anyone but Michal and Ahinoam, both of whom have their own homes. And Abigail is clearly still loved and trusted by our king."

"Are you sure Abigail isn't jealous David has taken me to wife?"

Mama smiled, one of her rare, radiantly happy smiles. "Ah dear one, she learned years ago to lay down any jealous feelings toward David's other wives and concubines. For she is most often the one whom the king calls to be his queen at many official functions. She's also his unofficial confidant and counselor. I believe of all David's women, he trusts Abigail the most. And, if you ever do desire to win David's favor, you'd be wise to seek Abigail's advice and counsel yourself."

"I can't imagine ever going to anyone but you for such advice," I replied caustically. "As it is I fear Abigail may see the truth and try to convince me to forgive him, even as you do."

She shrugged her shoulders. "Yes, Abigail could very well do just that. However, I think I've taken enough advantage of David's graciousness. I must go. I admit I was surprised David generously gave me permission to see you, but I think he must have wanted me to be assured of your well-being and, perhaps, encourage you to treat him well?"

"And of course this is exactly what you've done, right Mother?"

She hugged me tightly before leaning back to gaze intently into my eyes. "The Lord has given you life, Bathsheba, your own and your child's. You've seen David is more than the man who abused you. Please, dear one, be open to the man who, I believe, wants to make amends to you for the ways he's dishonored you. And also remember," she cautioned, "as king, your life and your child's is completely in his control."

"Have I not already acknowledged this?" I asked. "Do I not have to live with this fact every day?"

"Yes," she said. "And I pray you'll find it in your heart to forgive him and accept him as your God-given husband. For we both know if you do not, your life will be an unending misery."

Chapter 26

Mama's words echoed in my mind, and churned within my heart. I paced the room like a caged animal, trapped and angry. My eyes focused on the table where his lyre rested. I'd forgotten to put it back in his chest. Did David believe his songs would touch my heart more than his words? Would they?

I picked up his lyre and sat down with it in the chair. I admitted I was impressed by its exquisite craftsmanship. Had David made this instrument or had someone made it for him? Would I ever ask?

With fingers anxious to again play the eight strings, I gently stroked music from its supple body. With wonder, my ears were seduced by the lovely sound, and as I experimented with different notes, I recognized that without my volition my hands found the notes of David's lament for Saul and Jonathan.

However, as my heart picked up the music, my mind formed new words to the song. Words woven to create my own lament for Uriah.

> Your glory, O Israel, lies slain
> upon the rocky hills of Rabbah.
> How the mighty have fallen!
> It has been proclaimed in Rabbah,

> On the streets, the daughters of Ammon rejoice and exult
> for Uriah, David's mighty warrior
> lies dead outside their gates.
> In the hills of Jerusalem
> let there be no dew or rain upon you,
> nor voices heard rejoicing.
> For there the shield of the mighty was defiled
> the sword of Uriah was betrayed.
> Uriah, my beloved husband,
> In life we were not divided
> In death, separated by the order of a friend,
> and the bow of an enemy.
> O daughters of Israel, weep over Uriah
> mighty warrior, faithful servant
> Killed for steadfast honor.
> How the mighty have fallen in the midst of battle.
> Uriah lies slain against the city gate
> I grieve for you, my husband.
> Greatly beloved were you to me.
> Your love to me was wonderful,
> passing the love of a king.
> How the mighty have fallen
> and the weapons of war profaned!

Tears burned behind my eyes. I heard a sound, and turned. David slipped out the door. My heart sped with fear. How long had he been in the room? Had he heard the whole lament? Yet, this time he'd done nothing to alert me he'd returned to our bridal chamber.

What would he have said to me? Especially if he did hear how I'd transformed his very personal lament into one as grief-filled and personal for me. . . and accusing? Now would he send his guards to take me back to my own quarters, or have me killed? Our last feast to celebrate our wedding was tonight. Would I join with him once more in our marriage celebration or would he go in and give excuses for my absence?

"Oh, Abba, you know David has continued to be a revelation to me since our wedding. Yet, ultimately it's you who holds my life and my babe's in your hand. I'm your servant, do with me as you will."

*   *   *

I didn't see David again until I was called into his presence at the feast. My heart raced, as I didn't know what to expect. Hadn't this new husband of mine been contradicting as well as affirming my opinions of him at each new encounter? As I took my place beside him, he nodded his greeting and smiled. As his mask was clearly in place, I donned my own and smiled back.

To those around us, he appeared to be all that was generous and loving. However, his words were few. And behind his eyes, I could feel the force of his thoughts, like a hammer that pounded rhythmically upon my highly strung nerves. What was he planning?

Date cakes and other sweetmeats had been brought out when he gave me a smile that seemed to hold a silent threat within it. "Bathsheba, I've already come to delight in the many gifts you've brought to me as my wife," he announced, to much knowing laughter. "Yet, one gift I'd have you share with those here tonight. This afternoon, you sang 'the Song of the Bow' in a way I'd never heard it sung before. Won't you share it as your gift to our guests this last night of our wedding celebrations? I've even had my own lyre brought in for you to play."

He raised his hands and a servant immediately came and set his lyre in them. He handed it to me, his face a perfect facade of joyous anticipation. "Truly, wife, with all we've shared the last two days, I'm sure you'd enjoy playing for us. Giving our family and guests your special rendering of the lament I wrote for Saul and Jonathan so many years ago."

I stared at him in silent alarm as he handed me the lyre. Surely, he couldn't want me to sing my lament for Uriah to these people? Or had he not heard it all and recognized it as an indictment of him? Far in the depths of his eyes, was that pain I saw, before they lit with challenge?

So, he was testing me? Would I share my own pain and loss with these people, revealing the truth of Uriah's death, and David's guilt? Incredibly, he was giving me the power to speak the truth through my music. I forced myself to smile as I glanced around the room. Abigail had called some of David's women jackals. If they were jackals, many of the men in this room were ravening wolves. I took the lyre from his hands and silently prayed to the Lord, even as my trembling fingers began to strum the strings.

I prayed in silence, and with amazing clarity of mind and heart, I knew I couldn't sing Uriah's lament to these people. I'd created the song in memory of my beloved husband and sung it to my God. I'd never intended to share it with anyone, not David, and certainly not his family and courtiers. And more importantly, I knew I couldn't take this kind of revenge on David.

So, what did I play? "The Song of the Bow," but not as David or the others knew it, but as I'd experimented with it years ago by changing the key and tempo. In that way it had become less a lament and more an acclamation of the lives of Saul and Jonathan. Uriah had loved it, and insisted I always sing it that way, for it helped him remember Jonathan with joy instead of sorrow.

I closed my eyes and played David's instrument. This time I sang his words to my music. I didn't want to see anyone's face, especially not David's, until he knew how I'd chosen to answer his dare.

> Your glory, O Israel, lies slain upon your high places!
>   How the mighty have fallen!
> Tell it not in Gath, proclaim it not in the streets of Ashkelon;
>   or the daughters of the Philistines will rejoice,
> the daughters of the uncircumcised will exult...."

Finally, I opened my eyes to look at David. I was shaken to see both respect and appreciation on his face. He bowed his head to me and gave me a smile full of wonder. When I nodded back to him, it was as if I'd given him an unspoken invitation, and his deep, brilliant voice joined mine. With an inner joy I didn't understand, I listened to the blending and weaving of our voices as they rose and fell, filling the room with a kind of splendor that almost took my breath away.

When we closed our lips on the last word, I held the note for a moment longer on the lyre, then lifted my hands. Loud exclamations of praise immediately filled the room, and amidst all the voices, I caught David's quiet "thank you." I didn't trust myself to look at him, as I quickly handed back his lyre.

"Now, my lord husband, I'd ask you to sing us a song," I said. I found myself frightened by the depth and complexity of the feelings our duet had stirred within me.

Others shouted their encouragement to him, yet he didn't answer. Curious he didn't begin right away to sing and play, I looked up to find his eyes riveted on my face.

"How can I sing alone when I've finally found a woman who not only writes music, but whose voice blends and compliments my own so beautifully? And, wonder of wonders, she's my wife?" he praised. "What should we sing next, my musical bride? Do you have a favorite, or would you allow me to choose?"

I swallowed my trepidation and said, "Please, my lord, you choose and I'll join you."

Leaning over to me, as if to give me his request, he asked, "Are you well, wife, or should I give you leave to go? I don't want you sickening before these people."

I gave him a reassuring smile. "Yes, I'm well."

He leaned back with a broad smile. "My lady wife agrees we should sing the victory song of Miriam."

This announcement was met with loud praise.

He took up the lyre and, nodding to me, we began to sing. As we sang together, my voice naturally intertwining and blending with his, I remembered the many times my parents had sung with David. Music had always seemed a precious and integral part of their deep and abiding friendship with one another. Would it become that for David and me, too?

As our song came to an end, and he finished with an added flourish of notes on his lyre, my heart trembled in recognition. David and my shared love of music might be the most dangerous weapon against the walls around my wounded heart. I felt the blood drain from my head at this startling revelation. Suddenly, I felt dizzy and vulnerable.

He glanced over at me and his jubilant smile fled, replaced by a look of concern. Then his smile returned, the smile that fit his mask. He handed his lyre to the nearby servant before David jumped up, turned and slowly drew me up beside him.

"Dear family and friends, we'll again leave you to enjoy your evening, while we enjoy ours. We thank you for helping us celebrate our wedding."

I wrapped a smile on my face, and prayed I didn't look as sick as I felt.

He took my hand and slipped it onto his arm as he walked beside me, instead of having me walk behind him, as was usual. "I can see you're again feeling unwell. I'll have us back to the privacy of our own chamber in just a few minutes."

I don't know why I was surprised he should so easily discern my discomfort. If I could have continued singing with him, I would have. I didn't want to be alone with him again. And yet, the more we mingled our voices in song, the more I felt that subtle bond with him which I deeply feared. What a wretched, sick woman I was, full of confusion and pain.

David walked silently beside me, as his guards followed us down the hallway and up the stairs. Weariness joined the nausea I felt. All I wanted to do was crawl into my own bed, curl up and try to sleep.

A servant was there to open the door to our bridal chamber. Instead of going in first, David shocked me and the servant by ushering me in ahead of him. When the door shut behind us, I slowly walked over to one of the chairs by the table and sat down.

"Would you like some wine?" David asked in an anxious voice.

"Thank you, but no, my lord." I felt an awkwardness that made me angry with myself and him. Why must he be so kind?

He poured wine for himself and sat down across from me. "I think you're confused about what you feel about me, right?"

Startled, I glanced across at him. What should I say?

"I didn't know I was testing you until I heard myself encouraging you to sing your lament for Uriah."

"I saw the challenge in your eyes."

"When I walked down the hall this afternoon, I heard you again playing my lyre, and was even more impressed by your talent. I also remembered how Eliam used to boast to us about your gift of music and I appreciated the truth of his claim. But, because I didn't want to disturb you with my presence, I silently entered, for I was sure you'd stop if you noted my entrance."

He cocked his head to the side, as if asking if this were true. I nodded my assent. "Yes, I thought so. I stood silently leaning against the door, and soon became aware that the lyrics of my song were changing as I listened." He stopped, as if to go on was painful. Taking a long drink from his goblet, he glanced over at me. I saw the anguish in his eyes. "Uriah would have been proud of the song you wrote for him."

His voice was deep with emotions I couldn't and didn't want to identify. I didn't know if I should respond or not, yet, his words unexpectedly comforted me. "Thank you," I murmured.

"I can see you're feeling sick and tired, wife. Go to bed and sleep. I know it's not been an easy day for you, and you and the babe need your rest." His eyes caught mine and I was moved by the tenderness I saw in them. "I'll join you to sleep later."

I nodded, filled with deep relief at his words. I think he recognized it, for a regretful smile flitted across his lips. I rose and, within a short time, slipped quietly into bed. Glancing back, I saw him staring at the dented goblet in his hands. I couldn't help smiling; did he guess who dented it?

Grabbing a pillow, I curled around it and tried to relax. I knew David had just promised me he'd not disturb me with any sexual demands this night. As thankful as I was, I trembled at the unwelcome insight that if David continued to treat me with such tenderness and compassion, I might not only forgive him, but also care for him.

Was David right? Would Uriah have been proud of my lament for him? Had David known my husband so well?

I punched the pillow. *Oh God, I know you call upon us to forgive, but how can I? Yet, I catch glimpses of the man I loved and respected. The wise and kind king I once knew. But is he not also the man who ordered my beloved's death?*

Chapter 27

I plucked at the strings of David's lyre as I awaited him in our bridal chamber. It was the seventh night of our marriage. Would he stay with me for more days and nights? I don't know. Do I want him to? No. Yet, his kindness and music were proving to be effective weapons against my anger and bitterness.

However, even as I've learned to be a wife to David, I've grieved my loss of Uriah. Uriah was an unusual man in how he treated me as a wife. He not only gave me honor, but he'd also abstained from all violence. In fact, he'd allowed me to voice my concerns in ways I knew most other wives could not. I now wondered if he'd learned this from my father, who was the most gentle and kindest husband I'd ever seen.

With David I felt none of the freedom I had with Uriah. However, what we did share was our passion for music. Rachel had brought me my lyre, and although it was not of the quality of David's, we were still able to enjoy playing together. David was definitely the better musician, but as I played with him, I learned and often followed him so closely, he'd laughed aloud with delight.

Together we sang many of his poems for worship I'd learned as a girl. I could tell David enjoyed blending his voice with mine, even as I played my lyre, often in counterpoint to his. But I never shared with him anymore of the poems or music I'd written, and I spoke none of my thoughts or feelings. I decided I'd share his music with him, and his bed, but I had little desire for him to know me in any other way.

And each day as I joined his women at the tent, and concentrated on the worship, I found a little more comfort. David had left me alone during a part of each day as he'd dealt with kingdom business, but each evening he'd joined me in our bridal chamber after worship. There, I've submitted to his lovemaking, but my heart has not been in it, as it always had been with Uriah.

After worship this morning, I surprised myself with the realization that I no longer hated David for his assault on me. I wasn't sure what had changed inside me or how, but the rabid hatred had dissipated. However, what also became clear was that I couldn't forgive him for ordering Uriah's death. His murder was cruel and unnecessary. I'd convinced myself that David could have found another way to bring Uriah home to me, a way that still allowed him to honor his oath.

I sat strumming my lyre, and felt the depth of my grief welling up inside me.

"You're playing my lament again, wife, but you're not singing."

I looked up to see David standing just inside the door, staring at me, his eyes questioning. "I was pondering something in my heart and didn't realize I was playing your lament."

"Well, I'd like you to play something less mournful on this." He smiled broadly, his whole face alight with joy.

From behind him, he brought forward a gift wrapped in purple linen. Walking over to me, he took my lyre from my hands and put the gift in my lap. "Here, this is for you. Open it."

I glanced up at him, and down at the gift. From the shape and weight of it, as well as his words, I knew what it must be. My hands shook as I unwrapped the soft linen and drew out an exquisite lyre, whose sound box was extended with wondrous detail into the likeness of a lamb's head. I was awed by the lavishness of David's gift, but also sorrowful because the shape of the lyre was a reminder of Uriah's pet name for me.

"I sense both joy and grief in you wife," David said. "When I'd only wanted to bring you joy."

"It's a wondrous gift, my lord, and I thank you."

David's arch look spoke of frustrated acceptance, and he shrugged his broad shoulders. "Play me a song, and see how you like it."

The lightness of it was a delight, and even as I began to pluck the strings, I could tell a master craftsman had made this instrument. It didn't surprise me it was already tuned. I glanced up to see David watching me with the anticipation of a boy with his first toy. I gave him a tremulous smile. He smiled back at me with satisfaction.

A song came to mind I hadn't played in years, and as my fingers skipped and strummed the strings, the words sprang from my lips:

Wildflowers bloom with fierce abandon
    upon the verdant hills,
Inspiring songs from my full heart
    as beauty draws me near
I dance my way along the path
    and sing my praise to God
Delighting in the wonder
    of life again renewed.
O Spring you come and call to me
    to hope in life's blessed dream
And father will bring home to me
    the promised man to wed
Who'll love his precious daughter
    and cleave to her through life
Enjoying all the fruits of marriage,
    home and children dear. . . .

The discordant note I ended with seemed to echo around the chamber, even as David walked over to me and lightly touched the tears that had, again, formed a stream down my cheeks. I'd forgotten those last verses until they flowed out of my mouth and straight into my aching heart. I couldn't finish the song.

"I think you wrote this, and haven't played it in many years?" he asked gently.

I nodded.

He put his hand under my chin and lifted my face up, searching my tear-filled eyes. "Your gifts in music astound me, wife. Somehow, I feel sure you've written many other songs, but I don't believe you're up to playing anymore." His hand left my chin and rested on my shoulder.

Again, I nodded. It was as if grief consumed my voice as soon as I stopped singing.

"I'm glad you like your gift."

Taking a deep breath, I let it out and brushed the tears from my face. "I thank you, again, for honoring me with a gift you knew would bring me great pleasure." I heard the formality in my voice, and hoped he wouldn't take offense.

Lifting the instrument from my lap, he began to play a quick, lilting tune I didn't recognize. "I was given this instrument when I first became king in Jerusalem," he said, his face both thoughtful and somber, in counterpoint to his music. "The artisan thought I'd enjoy the 'lamb' motif, which I did, and also hoped I'd give him more business once I played his beautiful instrument, which I did." He smiled in remembrance.

Slowly, the tune changed, became more a lament. "When Kileab was about ten years of age and showed such promise on the lyre, I decided he should have this instrument. By then, the same craftsman who made this 'lamb' had created for me the 'lion' you've enjoyed playing." His sigh was echoed on the lyre. "I knew my son would appreciate the instrument not only for its perfect tone, but also because it had been mine."

He looked down at me, his face furrowed with the deep

sorrow of his loss. "We used to play together for hours, as you and I have done these past days. Our playing reminded me of my 'lamb.' You see, after his death, I put this lyre away, never thinking I'd take it out again."

He stopped playing and carefully put the lyre back on my lap. "When I learned how you liked my son, and how you grieved his loss, well, it somehow seemed right that you should have Kileab's lyre." His eyes grew bright with unshed tears. "Somehow, I was sure he'd agree you should have it."

I found myself grieving with David for the son he'd loved and still missed. I felt guilty that although I'd understood Abigail's great grief over the loss of her only child with David, I'd never imagined David would still grieve. Especially as he had so many other sons and daughters. Clearly, I had much to learn about my new husband.

"I have one more request," he said, his voice deep and somehow, unsure. "Please, Bathsheba, when you play this lyre, will you promise to think well of me?"

I stared intently up at David. His face still reflected deep grief. Was his sorrow still only for his son, or also for me and my loss of Uriah?

Then my heart raced with sudden insight. He, the king, had said "please." Surely this was a word far from his normal vocabulary. Could he, in this way, be telling me he was sorry?

"Is this really that hard of a request, wife?" The words were almost a jest, but his voice vibrated with deep emotion.

"I will try, David," I promised, trying out his name for the first time, testing his sincerity.

"Thank you."

He took the lyre from my lap, rewrapped it in the linen cloth, and placed it on the table. He took my hand and drew me up into his embrace. With great tenderness, he stood silently holding me. And then he took me to his bed.

* * *

Nightmares chased me through the dark hours and startled me awake early the next morning. I lay in bed, my heart racing with fear. What was the dream? I reached for it, but although the dream escaped me, the terror lingered. Restless, I got up.

"Sick again, wife?" David's drowsy voice found me.

I didn't answer, but poured myself some sweet wine and drank it. I softly padded back toward the bed, the light from a small lamp in a corner guiding my way. I felt chilled and wanted David to warm me. I stopped in mid-step and shivered. How could I so quickly have come to seek David for his physical heat and comfort, even as I'd so often done with Uriah?

"Bathsheba, come back to bed, the morning air is cold."

I picked up my tunic at the foot of the bed, shrugged into it, and folded my arms to draw in more warmth.

"Bathsheba?"

"I'm going to try some of the bread I keep here in a covered bowl." I walked back to the table. "Nibbling bread often helps settle my stomach."

I tore off a piece of bread and slowly chewed it. I sensed David somehow knew my desire for food was more an excuse not to return to his bed than a need to eat. Or do I think this because I feel guilty for lying to him? No! I don't need to feel any guilt when it comes to David.

I gnawed another piece of bread and swallowed it. I didn't hear his silent approach, but felt the heat of him even before he enfolded me into his strong embrace, my back to his front. A part of me wanted to lean back into him. The stubborn part of me resisted for a moment, but then I leaned into him.

"You're trembling, come back to bed and I'll warm you," he coaxed.

As he held me, I could feel he was ready to do more than warm me, and a spark of resentment rose within. "Thank you, my lord, but I need to finish this bread, unless you want to risk me being sick?"

He abruptly released me. "When are you going to be well

again?" he demanded, turning me by the shoulders so I faced him, his hands remained heavy upon me.

His apparent anger shocked me. Had he sensed my resentment and now responded to it? "My mother told me this sickness often lasts through the third or fourth month," I answered honestly, "and some women remain ill during their whole pregnancy."

He released me, and grunted his acknowledgement. "And how far along are you now?"

I wanted to ask him why he couldn't remember this, but instead I forced myself to calmly answer. "I'm eight weeks along."

"So, you could have more weeks of this?" he looked pained, then thoughtful.

"Yes, my lord husband." I felt an inner exultation at the way the conversation was going. Surely, he'd not want to continue to awaken to a sick woman when he might enjoy morning sport with a wife or concubine hungry for his attentions?

"This is our eighth day together, after spending seven nights together. Surely, when we announce the blessing of a coming child, people will remember this week we had together and see how the Lord has taken the curse of barrenness from you with our marriage."

"If no one suspects my illness doesn't come from the 'curse' being lifted much earlier," I muttered.

He gripped my shoulders again and shook me. "I am the king," he growled. "Gossip will not touch you if I forbid it."

I stared up into hazel eyes that sparked with anger. Could he see my disbelief?

"You don't believe me?" he raved. "How dare you? I married you to protect you and the babe and I'll do this. I won't let any spiteful gossip or accusations harm you. I will—"

"Come to live with me in your harem?" I challenged, infuriated with his apparent ignorance. "Do you truly believe your other wives and concubines won't suspect my sickness is from a too early pregnancy? Will you banish all your women if they come to gossip about the new wife who already has symptoms of being with child?"

"You think to mock me? I could kill you for such insolence."

"Consider and answer me, O Lord, my God!" I sang.
"Give light to my eyes, or I will sleep the sleep of death,
and my enemy will say 'I have prevailed':
and foes will rejoice because I am shaken."

His grip loosened and his arms fell to his sides. He shook his head, even as he stared at me. I couldn't read his expression. With a voice filled with a kind of angry joy, he finished.

"But I trusted in your steadfast love;
my heart shall rejoice in your salvation.
I will sing to the Lord,
because He has dealt bountifully with me."

"Bathsheba, you use my own words to rebuke me in a voice that reaches to the depths of my heart. Have you often sung the first verses of this song I wrote?"

My grieving heart filled my voice, and I sang David's words which had become my own:

"How long, O Lord? Will you forget me forever?
How long will you hide your face from me?
How long must I bear pain in my soul,
and have sorrow in my heart all day long?
How long shall my enemy be exalted over me?"

"I'm not your enemy," he ground out, distress wrinkling his brow.

"Do friends threaten death?" I asked quietly.

"I'm not your friend; I'm your husband and your king," he proclaimed passionately.

"Ah, forgive me." I smiled wryly. "I forgot it's husbands and kings who threaten death to their wives."

"You are impossible, woman, and your tongue is as sharp as a priest's knife."

"'I will keep a muzzle on my mouth as long as the wicked are in my presence.'"

David's ruddy face grew much redder. In fact, his whole body glowed with rage. I gazed at him and stepped back as his fisted hand rose slowly at his side.

Oh Lord, I didn't put a muzzle on my mouth soon enough. Surely this time he'll strike me down, or strangle me until I'm truly dead.

Suddenly, my knees buckled beneath me, and I fell prostrate on the floor at his feet. Above me, I heard David's harsh breathing, felt him working the reins of his anger. Did I want to die? I must, for I'd never talked to Uriah as I'd talked and sung to David. Yet, if I did wish to die, why did I fall at his feet and why have I remained silent?

"How have you lived so long with such a mouth?" he exploded. "If I'd struck you as I was tempted to do, your jaw would have been broken and you would have died slowly in silence, unable to speak, sing or eat."

I shuddered at his words. I felt very small and very vulnerable. Clearly, the Lord had finally muzzled me to save me from David's killing rage. Had he also buckled my knees?

"Bathsheba, I'll call you to me again when I know I can be in your presence without wanting to strangle you." The breath from his long exhale touched my bowed head. "Take the lyre I gave you, and go back to your room in the women's quarters. But until I leave, don't move."

David's enraged steps shook the floor. He loudly muttered as he got dressed, and the louder his curses, the more I felt as if I couldn't breathe. With a groan, I pulled myself up to a kneeling position. The footsteps stopped.

"I told you to remain on your face," he thundered.

I kept my head down, and quietly replied. "Forgive me, my king, I was beginning to feel sick again, as I could not catch a breath. I thought it would be better to move than to—"

"Yes, I understand. Fine, kneel, but don't get up or say another word." He sat to put on his sandals. "I can't even get out of this cursed room without you sickening on me again," he complained loudly. "If I didn't know about baby sickness from my first wives, I'd think you were doing this just to spite me."

His strident words had the unusual effect of calming me. I risked a sideways glance. He was trying to fasten his sandal, but it wouldn't cooperate.

He growled. "Here, you, wife, come and fasten this for me."

I didn't dare stand up, but hobbled over on my knees. With an agility I didn't know I had, I quickly fastened the clasps on both sandals. He stood up. I waited for him to walk away, but he continued to stand in front of my bowed head.

I felt his large hand move through my hair, lifting it, sifting it through his fingers. "No other woman has hair as beautiful as yours, Bathsheba. Nor a mouth like yours. Except Michal."

Her name hung like a weight between us, even as he tightened his grip painfully on my hair. "Be well, Bathsheba. When I call you to me again, I trust you will be well, and your mouth will be muzzled." His hand left my hair and he strode out of the room. I heard the door open and shut behind him.

Slowly I stood up. Michal. Mama had once told me about David and Michal. How Michal had asked her father, King Saul, to be wed to David out of her love for him. She'd even saved his life, but after he left the court and became a renegade, she'd been married off to Paltiel, a man loyal to Saul.

Mama said it wasn't until David sought to unify Israel's tribes again that he'd required her to be returned to him as part of his kingdom dealings with her father's general, Abner. She'd then been forced to leave her beloved Paltiel to be returned to David at Hebron, a political pawn and now one of many wives. Later, in Jerusalem, it was said how in her bitterness at her diminished status, Michal had cursed David for his uninhibited dancing before the Lord's ark and his people. After her rebuke, I knew David had sent her away from him.

"Did David mention Michal as a warning to me? He told me 'when I call you to me again,' which means he will see me again, doesn't it?" I asked myself.

"Lord, it's as if there are two Davids living in this one man. The powerful and ruthless king, and the compassionate and loving poet/musician." I sighed deeply. "Lord, I hate how my emotions run rampant over my good sense. And I hate how conflicted I feel toward David. He said he was not my enemy. These last few days he's acted more like a friend than an enemy. No, to be honest, he acted more like a lover than a friend," I grumbled. "No, more like a husband," I conceded. I felt the admission like a fist to my gut.

Chapter 28

Her face lit with an innocent smile, Rachel arrived to accompany me back to the women's quarters within an hour of David's angry departure. "Chilion told me to come and help you prepare to return to our rooms, my lady," Rachel said as she entered.

"Did he?" I asked, as I wondered what the protocol was for a new bride once she'd been expelled from the bridal chamber. Had my week with David been normal, or did he usually spend more time exclusively with his bride? Whatever, I dreaded to return to my small rooms in the forced confinement of the women's quarters. Yet, whether I wanted to be or not, I was now one of David's many women.

After he'd left, I'd washed my face with cold water, dressed in my bridal tunic, and made up my face to look as beautiful as I could. I'd rejoin David's women looking like a radiant bride, not a sorrowing widow. Although I felt more like Uriah's widow than David's bride, especially after his angry dismissal.

"As you can see, I'm ready to leave here and return with you to our rooms." I forced a happy note to my voice. I suddenly wondered if she ached to return to Mama and our old home as much as I did.

But I was thankful for Rachel. I'd become sick thinking

about facing David's women alone. Rachel was still a child, but she was someone I knew and loved. And though I couldn't confide in her, we could still find things to do together. Rachel carried the basket with my possessions, and I carried my new lyre, as well as my old one. I didn't want a servant to carry my instruments.

I strode out of the room where I'd become wife to King David, determined to have no regrets. So much had transpired in this room. It had witnessed violence and grief, as well as kindness and wondrous music. Soon it would be occupied by another of David's wives or concubines. One who wasn't sick with child, and who'd pleasure him in ways I had no desire to.

Who would it be? I laughed softly as I realized I was ignorant of the names of most of David's younger wives, and all his concubines. Yes, I'd seen a number of them as I walked with the women to the tent of meeting, but I had few names to put with the faces. However, I'd soon know them all, not just by name, but by face and character.

I found no joy in the thought. With Uriah, I awaited his return joyously, whether from meetings or training or war. Now, I had no choice but to await David's summons. He had taken away all my choices weeks ago. Even as he'd taken my honor, and then my husband.

Yet, he'd also given me the promise of new life. And when he married me, he'd attempted to give me back my honor. If I'd had a choice, I would have chosen Uriah's life over this child's.

I'd had no choice.

* * *

As Rachel and I followed a guard down the hallway and the stairs to the women's quarters, I heard the dissonant voices of the women. However, as soon as we entered the common room, their voices simmered down to a low buzz. I hugged the lyres more closely to my body, as I glanced around the room. To my chagrin, I was the recipient of their avid looks of glee. Was spending a week with the king after being wed considered too short a time?

I nodded toward the women and said, "Shalom."

Not seeing Abigail among them, I felt the lack of her comforting presence. The heat trapped in the room, with the various perfumes of the women, was overpowering. I took a deep breath through my mouth to still my suddenly queasy stomach.

Deriding laughter erupted from some of the women, and I understood why Abigail had called them "jackals." They sounded just like them.

"So, David's new wife has joined his other wives so soon," one of the women mocked me. "Surely, being a widow, you'd know how to please a husband so he might keep his new bride by his side longer than a week?"

Many of the other women snickered at her barb.

My face heated. I wanted to scream just why I was glad to be reprieved from his company, but couldn't. However, I could speak part of the truth. Straightening my back, and lifting my head, I stared at my tormenter.

"Obviously, you've never known the privilege of being the sole wife of one of David's mighty warriors," I declared. "Uriah was a husband any woman would have been proud to call her own. The fact I'm now a wife of the king may be a great honor, but it doesn't compare to the position I held as beloved and *only* wife to my dead husband."

Her full, lovely mouth contorted into a scornful line as her eyes became slits of contempt. "Are you so stupid, woman, you don't know that to speak such things could be called treason?"

I gazed back at her, determined no fear would show on my face. She had a lovely, olive-complexion, and thick, straight brown hair, with a curvaceous figure. "If you already feel the need to try and get rid of me by reporting what I said as treason, I can't stop you." I grinned at her, reckless in my grief. "But might that be seen by our king as a desperate act to put yourself back into his good graces?"

She gasped, and I knew my guess had hit the truth. She'd

sounded like an imprudent woman, and she was.

"Jezebel, she's right," another woman cautioned her.

"Yes, she is right," Abigail said, walking out of her room off the common area. "I really would keep her comments to yourself, Jezebel. I know you're distressed David hasn't called you back to him since you gave him a son two years ago, but I'd advise you not to take your anger toward David out on Bathsheba."

She stared at Abigail, as her face grew red. "Who's this old hag to give me advice?" she jeered. "You can't give our king anymore sons, and your only son was cursed by God and died young."

Her hateful words were rain on a stone roof, as proved by Abigail's deeply dimpled and radiant smile. "And yet, the king continues to call me to him, as he has even now. I was just adorning myself to meet our king, which is why I wasn't with you to welcome Bathsheba to her new home among us."

I think I was as shocked as the other women to learn David had called her to him. Yet, I found myself comforted by his choice.

With a nod to the others, Abigail gripped my upper arm and led me to my room. "After a full week with our virile king, I can see Bathsheba is tired," she said. "I'll see her back to her rooms before I go to join our king."

Abigail led me straight back into my bed chamber, telling Rachel to close the door that led to my quarters behind us.

"Do you want to stay alive, woman, or do you desire an early death?" she demanded in a low, angry voice, as she released my arm. "I can't protect you from the jackals if you foolishly give yourself to them to attack and feed on."

"I only spoke the truth."

"A truth that could easily lead to you losing your life," she snapped. "Do you really want to follow Uriah into death?"

"I don't know what I want," I whispered, bowing my head. It was true. Confusion had become my constant and bewildering companion. I could feel her staring at me and glanced up.

"I must go to the king, but I want you to promise me you'll stay in your rooms and not go out with the other women, not even to eat, until I return. Rachel can serve you, filling a plate when the meals are brought to the common room."

My stomach rebelled within me at her rebuke and words of caution. Was I also upset because I was afraid of what David might tell her? Or what he'd do with her? No, there was no jealousy, only fear of what David might say. I caught her grin.

"Yes, I must admit I was surprised to receive David's summons so quickly upon your dismissal. You're a mystery, Bathsheba, and your words to the women today make you even more so. I'll check on you when I return. But first, promise me you'll stay here, except to go to afternoon worship. Then, you and Rachel can follow the others."

"I promise. Do you really think I want to face that pack of jackals again?" I grimaced.

"Good." She kissed me on the cheek and glided out of my rooms. Rachel closed the door behind her.

As soon as she left, all the emotions of the day seemed to settle in my stomach, upsetting it once again. With a cry of dismay, I dropped the lyres on the bed, and grabbed the nearby bowl.

"Lady, how can I help you?" Rachel cried, running into the room.

Once I began to feel better, I stood up and glanced over at her. Poor child, she looked so concerned and afraid. "It's all right, Rachel, the food I ate with David must have been too rich for me, but I'm fine now. I'll just lie down and rest for awhile. Abigail is right," I said with a smile, "my kingly husband did wear me out."

"Yes, lady, I'll clean up for you."

I removed the lyres from the bed and placed them on the chest of cedar. With a groan of weary despair, I laid down and closed my eyes. Uriah's beloved face rose before me. It felt like years and not months since I last lay with my husband. No, it had been hours since I lay with him.

David.

My stomach cramped. "Please, Lord, let me rest and not be sick again. I'm so disheartened and tired. How will I survive among so many rabid, jealous women?"

Uproarious laughter burst into my inner sanctum from the women's area. Were they planning something to make me feel even more unwelcome? Did I care? Laying a hand on my womb, I realized for the child's sake, I cared.

* * *

When I awoke, I saw the low lying sun from my window. I'd slept much longer than I'd expected, but I felt better for it. I slowly sat up, not wanting to disturb my stomach again, put my feet on the floor and stood. Good, I didn't feel dizzy, but I was uncomfortably hot.

"Lady, are you awake?" Rachel asked, coming to the open door into the bedchamber, she smiled at me.

"Yes, Rachel. You were very quiet while I slept."

"I didn't want to do anything to awaken you, so I just sat here and softly sang to myself," she admitted shyly. "I also thanked the Lord for Lady Abigail. She was most helpful to you today. Truly, I feared for you with the other wives and concubines."

Her comment prompted a question. "How have you gotten along with them while you were here and I was with David?"

"When I first arrived, I felt like a rabbit chased by foxes," she admitted. "The other handmaidens grabbed me and kept asking me questions about you. Some of their questions were very rude, and I was so angry, I cried and ran back to our rooms." She heaved a shaky sigh. "Lady Abigail's maidservant, Naomi, found me in your room crying, and she took my hand and brought me back to Lady Abigail. They invited me to join them in her room with her and her other maidservants during the day, but I came back to my pallet here at night."

"I'm so sorry, Rachel, I never should have brought you here with me. Perhaps I should send you back to my mother?"

"No," she said, but there was little conviction in her voice.

"Rachel?"

"My lady, your mother warned me I'd probably be pounced upon and asked many questions, and I was to tell them that I don't gossip about you."

"Mama advised you about this, did she? I wish she'd given me more advice," I admitted.

"I think she believed Lady Abigail could advise you better."

Her perceptive comment touched me. "You're right, and in fact she already has."

"Yes, I've thanked our Lord many times for giving us such good friends in Deborah, Naomi and their lady."

"What is that in the basket at your feet?"

"I've been restringing beads into a necklace Lady Abigail asked me to string. May I finish it?"

"Yes, of course."

As I watched her with the beads, I wondered why David summoned Abigail to him. Was it to lie with her, or to ask for her counsel, or perhaps, both? I knew Abigail loved David, probably very much as Mama had loved Papa . . . as I had loved Uriah.

Have David and Abigail been together longer than my parents? I wasn't sure, but I knew for many of those years, Abigail only had to share David with Ahinoam. It wasn't until David became king, and needed to make more alliances, that he'd taken more wives. But most of his concubines were different. Mama said many of them were women he'd seen, desired and had brought to him to relieve his own lust, not to help establish alliances.

I'd been brought to him for this same purpose, but circumstances forced him to give me more honor and status than a concubine. Yes, my pregnancy had forced David to marry the daughter of his friend, granddaughter to his counselor, and wife of the mighty warrior whose death he'd arranged.

And now, before God and man, I am his wife.

I heard a bell sound and knew it must be time to go to

afternoon worship. I prayed I might find some peace at the tabernacle, but I felt little hope of it.

Chapter 29

I was thankful for the small window in my bedroom, which made the heat more bearable after we returned to my room from worshiping at the tent. Although it was set high in the cedar wall, if I stood on tiptoe, I could catch a glimpse of the sky, so I didn't feel quite so caged in.

When the evening meal was delivered by servants to the common room, Rachel went out and brought us back fresh bread, fruit and some lamb. Once we'd finished, and I knew the food had settled in my stomach, I asked Rachel to open the door into the women's common area. With the air from my window, and that which came from the women's courtyard, located beyond two open doorways, it created a small, welcome breeze.

The courtyard beckoned me to its lush and cool beauty, but I resisted, because of my promise to Abigail. As I sat in my anteroom, I thought about my week with David, and how it had subtly changed my view of him, especially as we shared our music. I no longer feared him, but I also didn't desire him as a woman would her beloved. All day, whenever I thought about David, it was as if my mind were enveloped by a fog of confusion. I wanted to ignore him, and occupy my mind with something else, but I sensed his presence everywhere.

"Lady, I noticed you have another instrument. Will you show

it to me and, perhaps, play it?" Rachel asked.

"That's a good idea," I said. Thankful for her request, I stood up and walked back into my bedchamber. I lifted the lyre from the chest and returned to sit by her. I unwrapped it and held it out for Rachel to see.

"Look, it's shaped like a lamb's head! I've never seen such an instrument," Rachel exclaimed in awe.

"The king gave it to me after he recognized how much I loved playing my lyre." With a smile, I showed her the artistry of the craftsman, before I began to lightly strum the chords. Being in a smaller room, the fullness of its sound was muted, but it still reverberated with a clarity of tone that penetrated every corner.

"Oh, lady, this is truly a royal gift the king has given you," Rachel exclaimed, grinning with unbridled joy.

"Yes, it is." I didn't have the heart to sing, but played a soft lament that left Rachel in tears, and me in tempered grief, but no tears. Had I finally shed them all?

I'd forgotten our door was open, and hearing a sound, I looked up to find a small boy looking at me. His large, hazel eyes were very like his father's, but his face and lips had the shape and coloring of his mother, and her hair color. . . Jezebel.

Reaching out a small, inquisitive hand, he took a few steps toward me. Smiling at him, I began playing a simple dance tune to coax him nearer. Suddenly his mother was behind him. Without a word, she swooped him up into her arms and carried him away, throwing a hateful look at me over her shoulder. My heart wrenched at the sudden loss of his innocent presence.

"I'll close the door," Rachel said.

"Yes, we wouldn't want to corrupt the king's children with my music, would we?" How could these women already hate me when I'd done nothing to them, but marry their husband? Would their children learn to hate me, too? I knew well how hatred of others was taught and caught, but not naturally present in young children.

Mama's words suddenly echoed in my mind and took root

in my heart. If I hated David, my child would learn it from me, and hate his father, too. Even as I knew these children's mothers would probably teach them to hate and avoid me. His wives would do it out of jealousy and fear. I saw how I'd teach my child to hate his father because of unforgiveness and anger.

Could I live with myself if I did this to my own child? Children mimicked their elders and, by doing so, continued the cycle of hate instead of encouraging appreciation, gratitude and love. Did I want to do to my child what I believed these women were doing to theirs?

"I'm quite tired," I said. "I think I'll go to bed."

"As you wish, my lady, may I help you with anything?"

"No, Rachel, please stay here until you're ready to join me on your pallet. Go ahead and light the lamp and work on Abigail's necklace if you'd like."

"Thank you, lady."

As I prepared for bed, I realized it was the first night of many I'd spend in this room. The thought depressed me, yet I knew I was thankful I wasn't with David. How sad, here I was a newly married widow who wished to be back home with her mother. Would David ever allow me a home as Ahinoam had and other of his wives? Or would I live in this forced captivity like a caged bird for the rest of my life?

I had so many questions. Would Abigail be able to answer them, or would I have to ask David when he decided to call me back to him? I hated not knowing the details of my life that I had taken for granted with Uriah.

I slipped onto the bed and lay awake as my mind spun thoughts like I was used to spinning wool. Would my own child play with the other children here? I'd had such a carefree and active youth, as I grew up in Hebron. I'd played with the other children there, even some of David's. I'd thrown rocks with the boys, and played with stick dolls, and sang and danced with the girls.

My child would have only the children here to play with.

And his playground would be the women's common area, our rooms and the secluded courtyard, at least for the first years of his life. If the women held to their hatred of me, it must poison their children and their view of him. Wouldn't my hatred of David infect my own child? Mercy, I was barely two months along, and I still felt strongly I was carrying a boy, and already pictured him playing with David's other children.

Seeing Jezebel's sweet little boy, and knowing how quickly seven months could pass, must be prompting these thoughts. Also, now that I no longer feared stoning, I had the freedom to think about this life growing within me without fear of his death, nor my own.

I heard Rachel as she quietly entered our bed chamber. I pretended I was asleep by modulating my breathing. I listened as she settled herself. She soon fell asleep, but my confused and tormented thoughts kept me awake long into the night.

* * *

In the morning after I'd eaten and knew I wouldn't be sick, I wondered if I should break my promise to Abigail and venture out of our room to join the other women. After a good sleep, facing them didn't feel like as great an ordeal as it had yesterday. Besides, sometime I would have to be with them without Abigail's comforting protection.

Yet, I'd promised her, and surely she'd be back soon. Or would she? I had no knowledge of the protocol of life in David's harem. Would Abigail teach me about my new life? Could she tell me if David usually spent more than one night with a wife or concubine? How many wives and concubines did he actually have? *Do I really want to know?* And, what about the wives who were in their own homes: if he desired them, did he summon them to himself or did he go to them in their own homes?

No matter how I felt about David's women, our lives would always be woven together in one way or another. Our children shared the same father, and our lives were controlled by the same man. David might not live with us in the same quarters, but his presence was definitely felt by all.

I stood in my open doorway and watched the children play with each other, their mothers talking while they played.

With a sweep of her tunic, Abigail strolled into the common room. "Shalom, my sisters," she greeted us. She looked toward my room, and seeing me, smiled. She walked over and drew my arm into the crook of her own. "Bathsheba," she murmured softly, so the other women couldn't hear, "we've much to discuss once we return from worshiping our compassionate and all-powerful God."

I stared at her glowing face, and tried to read her meaning in her words. I couldn't and found that worried me.

"Come, we can't be late and incur the displeasure of our God or our king." She nodded at the other women and drew me to the head of them all. With me firmly attached to her side, Abigail led us out of our quarters.

As we walked, guards I hadn't noticed before followed closely behind us, even as others moved in to lead us once we were in the palace courtyard. In sudden fear, I stared at them. Would I recognize any of them from the night I was brought to David? I sighed in relief, when I recognized no one.

The walk to the tent of meeting from David's palace was not long, but for some reason, today it felt much longer, the road dustier, the heat more oppressive. When we entered the women's court and Abigail swept up to take her place in front of every woman there, I felt more exposed than ever before, and wanted only to unlink my arm from hers and run to the back of this flock of women. But I knew this was not only impossible, but it would also draw the very attention to me I didn't want.

I couldn't concentrate on the worship. I was too conscious of Abigail's animated presence beside me. She worshiped the Lord fully, with all her body, soul and heart. The way I used to worship him, but could no longer. At one point, I glanced over at the men and was startled to see David staring our way. I looked away and closed my eyes. I wanted to shut out any awareness of him I could. I grimaced at my stupid naivety. Whether I could see him or not, he obviously could clearly see me.

As the heat weighed me down, I prayed I'd be able to keep standing, and not wilt like a plucked flower and slide to the ground.

"Only a few more minutes," Abigail murmured.

I startled like a fawn. Could she read my mind?

"I heard your sigh, and your body just swayed against me," she whispered. "You're so tired and distracted, you didn't even notice when you leaned into me."

Her words restored my backbone, and I pulled myself erect. When it was time to leave, I stepped away as Abigail reached for my arm. I didn't mind walking with her, but I refused to appear weak, and unable to return to the palace without her help.

With a pang of longing, I caught a glimpse of Mama as she disappeared around a corner in the company of another woman. Was it Sarai? It might have been, but as I only saw her back, I wasn't sure. Had she found a new maidservant? I longed to go home to her.

"Come, we need to leave," Abigail said, "David's other women have already left the court and our rear guard is awaiting us."

With a nod of acknowledgement, I walked with Abigail back to the palace, feeling like a caged bird with clipped wings. But unlike the mindless bird, I knew I'd never again have the freedom I'd experienced as the beloved wife of Uriah the Hittite.

* * *

I entered the common room with Abigail to see Jezebel and a few of the other women playing with their young children, and then my gaze was caught by a lovely young woman who was nursing her tiny baby.

"That's Rebekah," Abigail said. "She's one of David's concubines, and right now, little Leah is David's youngest child."

My heart skipped at the inflection of Abigail's voice on the words "right now."

"Come, I know you're weary and need to rest," she said. "We'll talk once you've eaten something and napped. I think standing so long in the heat wore you out."

I flushed. How did she know all this? She reminded me of Mama. "Will I see you in a few hours?"

"Send Rachel to me after you've rested, and we'll talk."

I nodded, turned and walked away from her. The curious looks on the faces of many of the women I passed on my way to my rooms told me they wondered about Abigail's interest in me as well. Yet, it seemed they were more inquisitive than I about Abigail's desire to talk with me. I entered our room, grabbed a piece of fruit and sat down.

"Come, Rachel, sit with me while we eat and tell me about your week here," I said. "I think it has been worse for you than you've yet shared."

She poured sweet wine for me. "Oh lady, so many of these servants sound like Mara, always critical and questioning and making up terrible lies about you because they know you're barren."

"Dear Rachel, I'm so sorry you've had to listen to them. I'm sure they're only mimicking what their ladies are saying." I took the wine and slowly sipped it.

"What do you think your mother is doing right now? Do you think she's found another handmaiden?"

"Are you very homesick for your old home?" I watched her as she fought to put a smile on her face. But, like a sudden spring squall, tears swept into her eyes and down to her trembling lips. I wrapped her in my arms and let her cry, feeling as homesick as she.

Chapter 30

Abigail came to my room alone. "I asked Rachel to remain with Naomi. What I need to say to you, she shouldn't hear," Abigail said. "Although if you're up to walking a bit, I think we might have more privacy strolling in the courtyard than staying in your room."

"I'd like that." A walk outside, even in the enclosed courtyard, would be a welcome change.

"Most of the women nap during this time of day, which is why this is my favorite time to be in our courtyard." She smiled at me. "You napped while we had our mid-day meal and now we can be alone. Come, there's a small bench in the far corner that's shaded by a date palm. It's my special place."

I followed her into the courtyard and marveled at the trees and bushes that were cultivated here in this small space. Looking around, I was surprised to see a room off the court which had the tools for weaving. In another corner of this space was an oven and a small millstone.

"Yes, we don't have to live idle lives here if we don't want to," Abigail said, watching me closely as if to read my face. "Even though we're fed from David's abundant table, and given clothes made by some of the best weavers in the land, some women enjoy making their own bread and weaving and sewing their own cloth."

I nodded, acknowledging her information, but didn't comment.

"Come, sit here beside me. We'll talk in soft voices, and I'll watch to be sure we're not interrupted."

I sat down on the stone bench next to this woman who was my mother's friend and the king's favorite wife. Her lovely face appeared friendly and open, yet there was something. . . my heart quickened at the look in her eyes.

"Bathsheba, David called me to him to talk about you," she said. She touched an earring at her right ear before she reached for my hands and gripped them tightly. "Little one, David told me about calling you to him after watching you perform your mikvah. He confided how you, who've been barren these four years with Uriah, are now pregnant with his child."

I stared at her, shocked into silence by David's confession. I also saw a deep sadness reflected in her eyes. How could David have confided in her so quickly? Why would he even tell her of my shame?

"After being with you for your bridal week, he realized how your persistent nausea might make your condition obvious to his other wives and concubines here in the women's quarters. He proposed I take you with me to my former home in Carmel."

She looked back at me, as if waiting for a response. I was too angry to speak. I jerked my hands from hers and fisted them in my lap.

"I heard what you told the other women. You clearly loved Uriah deeply. I also saw how unhappy you were when you first came here. Of course, I know no one refuses our king what he wants, but I did wonder if you felt more than grief."

"You're most astute, lady," I murmured sarcastically. "David may have told you part of the truth, but he didn't tell you all of it. Do you know he forced himself on me?"

"Quiet, woman, unless you want all to know your secret," she warned me. "No, I didn't know this, and it truly grieves me to hear it. I am sorry, Bathsheba, sorry for you, your child and for David."

"You forgot to include Uriah, Abigail. We can't forget my beloved, for he's the one who paid the greatest price for David's lust. He paid with his life," I spat. "Of course, David used the arrows of the Ammonites to do it, clever king that he is."

Abigail's eyes grew wide, and tears pooled like blue sapphires in her eyes. "Ah, I had wondered about the convenience of his death so soon before your wedding." She brushed under her eyes with her fingertips and shook her head. "I doubt you know this, but David and I've been married for over twenty years, Bathsheba. I've lived with him in great deprivation, and immense wealth. I bore him a beloved son, lived through the death of our son from a fever when he was only eighteen years old, and have loved David always. And although I grieve with you for what he's done to you and Uriah, my love for him remains unchanged."

"You sound like my mother. She, too, has grieved with me, but also affirmed her love for King David. It appears you both have a history with the king that extends him grace even for his worst sins."

"So, Anna, too, refuses to hate David for his sins against you?" She patted her heart. "I've always felt we were more sisters than friends, and now I see how right I've always been to believe this way." She leaned over and touched my cheek, capturing a tear I'd not known I'd cried. "Little one, if you'll allow me, I'll tell you some of my story?"

I nodded my head, my emotions too much in turmoil to say anything.

"My first husband's name was 'Nabal' and he lived up to his name 'fool' all too well. I came to him when I was barely thirteen. His reputation was not the best, for he was known as an arrogant and wealthy man. He had excellent servants who served him well, but it was out of fear and not respect. He'd also been married to three other wives, who'd all died before me, one quite suspiciously.

"He never fathered a child by me, his other wives, nor the women servants he forced to his bed. I won't go into all the sad details of my life with Nabal," she said quietly, "but I will say my life with David has been far better than all my years with Nabal."

"With such a husband as Nabal, I can see how it would be. But I sense you're trying to tell me even more with this story?"

"Bathsheba, not all wives with one husband have lived lovingly with them, and I've also discovered, in over forty years of life, that when a woman doesn't bear children, it isn't always the fault or sin of the woman."

"So, are you asking me to be thankful for David's abuse, and blame my barrenness on Uriah and not myself?"

"No, I—"

"You must think me very naive if you believe I never understood the incredible gift I had in my loving and understanding husband," I replied curtly. "As to why I never had children with Uriah, but am impregnated in one violent act with David, only God can answer that mystery." I worked to keep my voice low.

"When your mother came here to talk with me, she told me about Uriah's return to Jerusalem, and that he'd never come home after consulting with the king, but stayed on the palace grounds because of his vow of holy war."

I took a ragged breath, and fought the tears I refused to shed before her. "Did Mama tell you how she came here to the palace to see Uriah, and pleaded with him to come home, receiving the wrath of both Uriah and my grandfather for doing so?"

"No, she didn't," she said. "But Ahithophel has despised your mother since he first learned of her, and Uriah would have forgiven your mother anything. He loved her like a younger sister, and always treated her with the utmost respect."

Her words spoke of a history between my husband and my mother I'd never considered, although she had finally told me about her past. "I think you must have stories of my mother, father and husband I've never heard before."

"Yes, of both your husbands, Bathsheba. We all survived events that can only be described as miraculous acts of God, as well as humorous and tragic episodes, just like so many others have experienced, including you."

I gazed at her, thinking about what she'd just shared. "Abigail, David must have called you to him to do more than talk about me...."

"Oh, yes, he did." Her mischievous grin and dimples made me hear my own words in a totally different way. I felt my face redden and turned away from her delighted laughter. "Dear girl, I see why you've been the joy of your parents and Uriah, and why David has already formed a tender and protective spot for you in his heart."

I didn't believe her statement about David and turned back to stare at her. Was she teasing me or telling the truth?

"He told me he gave you Kileab's lyre, and you have a rare gift of music. He'd never have given you such a treasured present if you hadn't found a place in his heart."

"For myself, I want no place in his heart, or in his life, although I'll fight for the place of my child in both his life and heart."

"So that's how it is, is it? How sad." She paused and stared at me a moment. "However, it does explain even more to me." She shrugged her shoulders. "Now, to return to David's concern for you. For years he's allowed me to return to my old home in Carmel as a rest from my work here with his wives and children, and for me to spend time with old friends, and check on our property and the work there."

"You still have a home in Carmel?"

"Yes, you see when we married, David inherited Nabal's property and servants. What he didn't know, until after we were wed, was that for years I'd performed the duties of steward of our property. Even Nabal didn't know this, as my trusted servants hid this from him," she told me, her voice subdued.

"It was these same servants who saved our lives. They were the ones who came to tell me how Nabal had ridiculed and denounced David's emissaries and sent them away without extending any form of hospitality." She stared down at her open hands, before glancing back at me. "If they hadn't come to me, and I hadn't immediately prepared a small caravan of food and drink and met David and his men on the road, I fear my story would have been very different. But I had wise servants who knew I'd extend hospitality my husband never would."

She smiled at me with radiant joy. "Yes, David's and my first meeting was quite auspicious. Anyway, out of David's concern for you, he suggested that this year I should take you with me for the month I'll be in Carmel. He knows the place well, for there were times he'd escape from Hebron with me and Kileab and join us there. He also understands my love for the place, although I never loved the husband who came with it." She took my hand again in hers.

"Bathsheba, when David shared with me his concern for you and this idea, I immediately agreed with him. By joining me in Carmel, I'll enjoy the pleasure of your company, and it will give you a month away from any rumors or suspicions that might arise from your persistent nausea."

"David suggested this?" I exclaimed, amazed. "He truly is willing to give me a reprieve from living in this perilous cage of women to travel with you to Carmel?"

"Yes," she said. "He also told me you made it clear to him you're still grieving the death of Uriah. He understands your sorrow, and, I believe, grieves Uriah's death with you."

"That I can't believe," I told her, incredulity raising my voice.

"Well, whether you believe it or not, isn't important," she said quietly. "What's true is he's willing for you to join me in Carmel for the next month. Then, when you return sick, everyone will believe that during your wedding week he broke the curse of your barrenness and the Lord has blessed your marriage with a child."

"Ah, so this is just another of David's strategies to cover his sin," I retorted.

"No, woman, it is not. Hear me well, Bathsheba, what your husband, David is doing is protecting you and the babe," she reproved. "David and I discussed giving you your own home, but he knew to do this would only bring greater scrutiny. For only those of his older wives have been given their own homes, and those who have older children. His wives and concubines with no children, or young children, have always remained in the harem."

"And you, Abigail, why have you remained here?" I asked, curious to know.

She shrugged her shoulders and a reflective smile touched her lips. "I had my own home with Kileab. But after he was gone, David saw how my grief consumed me. As he understood how I felt, he asked me if I might want to return to the women's quarters where I'd be closer to him. In this way I could more easily join him as Queen for many of his official functions, as well as help him with the many problems created by his young women and their children." A look of deep contentment stole into her vivid blue eyes. "I know I've called them jackals and cats, but most of the children are a delight to me, and I see them as the grandchildren I'll never have, and some of his women, especially his concubines, have become like daughters to me."

Her honesty destroyed my defenses. "You and my mother are the most incredible women I know." I looked at her, awed by her resilience, compassion and love.

"Thank you. I consider it an honor to be placed beside your mother in your respect. So, will you come with me?" she asked. Her lovely face was lined with what appeared to be concern and anticipation.

"Yes, I'll come with you. But I think you may have more to tell me?"

"You are a perceptive young woman," Abigail admitted with

a slight grimace. "I was going to tell you once we got to Carmel, but I'll tell you now. David mentioned you'd made him quite angry, and when you return, he wants your promise you'll treat him with the respect and honor he deserves."

Anger burned through me. I wanted to blurt out just how I'd angered him when I heard a slight noise. I looked to see a small girl dancing toward us on tiptoes, her head full of curly light brown hair, her face alight with joy. "We have company," I warned Abigail softly, thankful for the interruption.

She looked up and gave the little girl a smile full of welcome. Opening her arms, the child ran into them. After giving her a warm hug, Abigail put her on her lap.

With great animation, the child chattered so rapidly, I could barely understand her. However, Abigail obviously caught every word, or at least was nodding as if she had.

"Ruth, I want you to meet Lady Bathsheba," Abigail introduced us when the child finished her monologue.

Reaching out her hand, she touched my hair and a random curl slipped around her finger. She giggled. "How did you do that? Your hair caught my finger."

"It likes to curl all over, even around fingers." I smiled at her, and as she grinned back at me, my stomach turned. Her smile was so much like her father's.

"Ruth, I think Hannah is looking for you, why don't you go and find her?" The child looked up and around, jumped off Abigail's lap and ran toward the smiling woman standing by the door. Hannah appeared to be in her mid-twenties, with straight black hair and a tall, spare frame. She caught up Ruth and twirled her around. I loved hearing Ruth's childish laughter.

Still watching the child, Abigail said, "Her mother was one of David's concubines. She died giving birth to this precious little one. David named her for his great-grandmother." She turned to me. "I had just learned from my steward in Carmel that Hannah had lost both her husband and her babe to a fever. When I asked her to come help with Ruth, she immediately made the trip. She saw my invitation to nurse and care for Ruth as God's way of comforting her in her grief."

"And you will take me to Carmel so I might be comforted?" I asked.

"Yes, I suppose I will."

"Ruth's grin is very like her father's."

"From all that you've said about David, I'm surprised you recognized the resemblance in their smiles."

Glancing around to be sure no one else was near, I answered her in quiet intensity. "David raped me and killed my husband. He also impregnated and married me. He has shown me brutal strength, and tender kindness." My heart was racing, and I gulped a breath. "Growing up, he was my warrior-king and poet-musician, as well as a good and faithful friend of my family. Throughout my life, I saw him as the man most like God, and loved him with the same adoration I gave in worship to our God."

Abigail's hand gripped my own. I looked at her. Tears streamed down her cheeks. "Oh, Bathsheba," she whispered. "I'm so sorry."

"You now tell me David is demanding my respect when I return from Carmel, and Mama has told me I must forgive David, or I'll be a disobedient daughter to her and to the Lord, as well as being miserable for the rest of my life." I closed my eyes to the threatening tears. "She still loves David as king and savior, because of the times he rescued her, and how he honored my father, and supported their marriage."

I turned and stared intently into Abigail's compassionate gaze. "In the days and nights I had with David, I saw glimpses of the man I once revered, but I also experienced the power and anger of the king who cruelly raped me and ordered my husband's death. I would like to go away with you, Abigail. I'd like to get out of Jerusalem and find a place I might seek the Lord who has shown me mercy by removing my cursed barrenness, and grief in the way he did it. Perhaps, if I can find God again, he may help me find the way to forgive David."

Abigail didn't say a word, but wrapped me in her comforting arms. As I rested my head against her shoulder, the thought struck that David himself had probably been embraced by Abigail just last night. What a paradox—she can soothe both my tormentor and me.

* * *

Before we left for Carmel, I sent Rachel back to Mama. Abigail and I agreed she was too young to be subjected to the often cruel life of a maidservant within the women's quarters. We also discussed how Rachel's innocence might work against me if she made any remark to anyone about my recent sickness.

Naomi was sent to speak with Mama, who agreed with us, and was delighted to take Rachel as her own handmaiden. It was hard to watch Rachel leave, but I knew I had little time to miss Rachel's comforting presence before we left the next day.

Chapter 31

It was early morning, and the sun had just made its bright appearance when Abigail and I stood ready to leave. We were on the side of the palace closest to our quarters, surrounded by a contingent of David's palace guards. Because of the war, David had decided he'd send more soldiers to protect us. I watched as four strongly built men walked toward us carrying the poles of our litter. They placed it on the ground so we might easily enter it. I'd never traveled in such a conveyance before, and I found the idea somewhat intimidating.

Before we stepped into the litter, Grandfather surprised me by rushing around the corner of the palace. Out of breath, he smiled at me with obvious delight.

"Shalom, my granddaughter," he wheezed. "Your kingly husband told me I might see you before you were taken from me for so long." He kissed me and caught me in a strong hug. "Are you well, Bathsheba?"

"I am well," I said. Smelling his familiar, lightly perfumed scent and feeling his slight frame against me brought a bittersweet longing for my former life when he could visit me regularly.

He released me and bowed to Abigail. "Thank you, lady, for honoring my granddaughter by taking her with you to your home."

"It's my pleasure to do it, Ahithophel," she replied graciously. "I've always loved my dearest friend Anna's daughter as if she were my own blood kin."

I watched Abigail, and got the impression she'd used her words to goad grandfather. I inwardly smiled.

"You're all that is kind, my lady." His frown belied his words.

"We must be off and take advantage of the coolness of the morning," Abigail said. "I'm sure you understand our need to leave now."

"Yes, of course." Grandfather bowed again.

Impulsively, I walked over and hugged him once again, then followed Abigail into the litter. Deborah closed the curtains, the litter was lifted up smoothly and we were off to Carmel. We were surrounded by David's guards, some on horseback and some on foot, as well as an array of servants and pack animals.

"It was good to see Grandfather," I said quietly, aware we were carried by men who could easily overhear our conversation. "I haven't seen him since our last wedding banquet."

"Your grandfather has reveled in the attention he's gotten because of your royal status," Abigail said with a clear note of sarcasm.

I sighed. "I know. He thinks David wed me to honor him."

"Really? Then let's hope he never finds out the truth."

* * *

The arid heat of the sun soon penetrated the confines of our litter, and because of the curtains, there was no air circulating in the enclosed space. Abigail's good humor and stories diverted me, and the pillows were quite comfortable. But the undulating movement of our ride, combined with the heat and humid air, made me sick within a few miles outside Jerusalem.

"Abigail, I must get out," I said.

Abigail had them stop alongside the road while I ran out and was sick behind some rocks. Abigail's maidservant, Naomi, cared for me.

I returned to Abigail, who'd chosen to stand outside the litter while I was indisposed. I whispered. "Abigail, if I stay in that land boat I'll be sick most of the day. Could you please ask the Captain if I might use one of the donkeys to travel on? I'd even be willing to share Naomi's with her."

"I know exactly what to do." She gave me a sympathetic smile.

In only a few minutes Deborah joined her in the litter and I was lifted onto her maidservant's donkey. We were soon on our way again. As we rode, David's guards watched the rugged, rocky terrain for all the possible hiding places of enemies or bandits. But as David gave us forty of his best guardsmen, I felt no fear as we traversed rocky roads that followed hills and deep ravines, with myriad hiding places, and little vegetation.

We spent the night in a large, dry cave. I didn't even see it until we rode off the main road and wound our way right up to the opening. Abigail told me it was one that David and his rebels had found years before. The women stayed within the cave while guards were posted at the entrance, and David's soldiers camped below us. I fell asleep listening to Abigail's excited descriptions of her beloved home.

*   *   *

Traveling the second day, Abigail purposefully kept the curtains open so she could talk with me as I rode beside her on my donkey. It was late afternoon when her face lit up with recognition. "We're getting close, Bathsheba, as soon as we get around these rocks, you'll be able to see it."

Riding around a large outcropping of multi-colored rocks, I looked down into a valley to see a large sprawling stone structure surrounded by what looked like a small village. As we rode closer, people poured out of each of the buildings and began to run up the hill to greet us.

"My lady! Queen Abigail!" shouted her people as we rode toward the main house.

"We've been awaiting your arrival, lady." A tall, stately man with silver hair and a face marked by a wise, calm countenance, walked up and helped her down from the litter.

David's men immediately surrounded him. "Captain," Abigail said with clear authority, "this is my steward, Josiah, and he would not think of harming me or Bathsheba."

The men stepped back and I quickly slipped off the donkey before one of the guards tried to help me.

"Josiah, this is Lady Bathsheba, new wife to King David and widow of his mighty warrior, Uriah. I'm sure you remember Uriah from years past?"

Josiah bowed to me. "We had not heard of Uriah's death, lady, we were honored to serve him here before. We're honored to serve you now as wife to King David, may he live forever."

I nodded to him. "Thank you, Josiah."

I noticed as he stood erect from his bow, he glanced over at Abigail with a look that held many questions, but she only smiled, her dimples in full splendor. "Come," she said to me, "I'll show you your room and let you rest before we partake of our meal. I know you're tired."

We entered a large courtyard surrounded by rooms. I followed her down a partly enclosed hallway with a fitted stone floor. She stopped at the open door to a room that held a raised bed, a small table with a lamp and red and blue embroidered pillows on the floor. Another door opened up into a small, enclosed, stone courtyard. Amazingly, it had a palm tree and small bushes, as well as a stone and wood bench. I had no doubt this had once been Kileab's room.

On our ride, Abigail had told me how much Kileab had loved coming with her to Carmel. He'd never enjoyed the competition and political games of David's sons, but loved the peace and quiet of this home, where he could practice his music and write his songs.

Still a proud mother, she shared how she believed Kileab had been most like the pastoral and musical young David. She confided how close David and Kileab had become, sharing their love of music, dancing, and worship of their Lord. How often in Carmel they'd sat under the stars together late at night, marveling at the beauty of God's bright canopy.

As I had listened to her, I'd heard the deep notes of her grief which resonated in her voice, and reminded me of what I'd heard in David's reminisces of Kileab as well.

"Was this Kileab's room?" I asked.

Abigail's smile was tempered by her luminous, misty eyes. "Yes, I thought if David believed you were worthy of his lyre, I'd give you the room and courtyard where he wrote so much of his music."

Her generosity of heart was profound. I gave her a long hug, before kissing her cheeks. "I don't understand why you're being so good to me."

She stepped out of my arms and gazed at me, her face serious. "You're my closest friend's daughter, and more than that, you remind me of a younger Abigail, who overcame great trials and grief to become the beloved wife of a king. Now rest, for your sake and the babe's." She turned and walked away. I watched her go and wondered if I would find the peace I needed here or if I'd only leave at the end of the month more tormented.

* * *

Within two days in Carmel, I realized Abigail came to work. However, she expected me to rest, enjoy my music, and allow myself time to adjust to a new life without the fear of someone discovering my pregnancy, or of being called to David. Truly, being with her in her home was an extraordinary gift.

On my third morning there, Naomi, Abigail's maidservant who'd come from Jerusalem with us, arrived at my room carrying a tray with warm bread and pomegranate juice.

"When Lady Abigail was carrying Kileab she said she always felt better when she ate bread and drank juice the first thing in the morning. It seemed to help calm her stomach, and she asked me to bring you these to see if you might feel better eating them as well."

"Thank you," I said, even as my stomach grumbled in hunger,

and not, thankfully, as a precursor to being sick.

"The Lady also thought you'd appreciate having me as your maidservant while you're here. So, after you eat, I thought I could bring you some water to wash, and help you with your hair and to dress?"

I smiled at her. "It's obvious that Lady Abigail is determined to indulge me with her most gracious hospitality. I'd be most appreciative of your help, Naomi."

She bowed before she looked up and gave me a lovely smile. "I told my Lady that I've never seen hair like yours. I'd love to see what ways I might attempt to adorn it."

I laughed as I pulled my fingers through my curls. "My mother would tell you there's no taming this mane, as I inherited the same hair as she has. We have both agreed if there were a way to straighten all these wild curls, we'd be glad of it, but we've never found such a cure."

Naomi's large brown eyes lit with humor. "Well, if nothing else, we can braid it."

"I'd appreciate your help to do just that."

* * *

Abigail told me I was free to walk the hills around her home, although one of the four of David's guards who'd been left at Abigail's always followed me closely. After my first jaunt, Abigail had explained that although we didn't need to fear bandits around her home, we did need to fear some of the wild animals that roamed nearby, attracted by the sheep that grazed in the hills surrounding us.

Abigail and I soon established our own routines; we'd break our fast, then take a walk together in the morning. After our walk, we'd spend a time of worship to our God with her community. Then, she'd join Josiah and others as they went over the records, or discussed problems, leaving me free to do whatever I wanted. We'd then take our evening meal together upon the roof of the house, where a soft breeze often cooled us, and we'd talk as we watched the nightly display of stars, moon and sky, often awed into silence by their translucent beauty.

I continued to feel nauseous, but as Naomi made sure I ate bread both in the mornings and some at night before I slept, I rejoiced in the fact I was sick less often.

As Abigail went about her day, questioning the men and women about their jobs, meeting with old friends, and discussing recommendations for improvements, I entertained myself.

As the days passed, I napped, played Kileab's lyre, and sometimes sang or even danced. When I felt guilty at being so lazy, I went to the weaving room, where I was welcomed by the women to help them, or I'd go with Naomi to take a turn grinding the grain or kneading the dough for our evening meals. I realized I hadn't been so carefree since I'd been a young child in Hebron. Yet, I still struggled with deep grief and anger over David's decision to have Uriah killed.

* * *

We'd been in Carmel for almost two weeks when I was sitting in what I'd come to consider my courtyard, fingering the lyre that rested in my lap. I was frustrated, as words skipped inside my head like fractious children who refused to be caught. And my music was only a jumble of notes, lacking harmony or melody.

"It sounds like a mixture of lament and frenetic dance."

I glanced up to see Abigail standing in the doorway watching me.

"David didn't have to order Uriah killed," I exploded, all my sorrow and pain bubbling to the surface. "He could've ordered him back to the palace, back to train his tribal troops or join his personal guard with Benaiah." I put down the lyre and stood up to face her. "Did you know it was Benaiah and another guard I didn't recognize who brought me to David that night? Benaiah who led me home after David raped me, and abandoned me outside our gate? I'd just turned to run away and throw myself off a cliff when Mama opened the gate and drew me inside."

I paced the small courtyard. Her silence was like a prod to

me, so I spewed out the words which had simmered inside me for days. "I forgave him the rape, the sin against me, the sin that's led to this child grasping life within the womb I thought dead. Is he not a king with the power to take what he wants? He took me, the child of his dead friend; the wife of his faithful comrade in arms, the beauty he spied while taking her mikvah."

I stopped and stared at her. "Do you ever wonder what would've happened if you hadn't been told your husband insulted David's men? How things might've been different if you hadn't met David on the road with your extravagant peace offering? Can you imagine what it would've been like to have David and his men running down these hills like ravening wolves, ravaging through this peaceful valley, killing all your men and raping you and your women?"

She closed her eyes and bowed her head. Her hand came to rest upon the wooden door, as if to hold her up.

"How can I forgive the king for killing Uriah?" As she looked at me I saw the question in her eyes. "No, it wasn't David's hand that killed him, but I'm sure it was his orders. The irony of his death still haunts me," I said bitterly. "Before Uriah left for Rabbah, he told me he was a warrior who knew the best strategies to stay alive. And what strategy did he use as an example? He never fought too close to an enemy wall. Where did he die, Abigail?" I taunted. "He died next to their wall, shot down with his closest comrades by enemy arrows, ordered to fight there by Joab.

"We both know Joab is a crafty strategist in battle. I knew he'd never willingly send his men that close to the wall unless he was ordered to do it by someone with more authority than his own. David's the only man who has that authority. Tell me, Abigail, could you have forgiven David if he'd killed your husband and all your men and raped you and your women?"

"But he didn't do it, Bathsheba," she cried. "God used me to stop him."

I gasped, bent over, and fell to my knees. "So, why didn't

he stop David from killing Uriah?" I wailed. "Why didn't God send my beloved home to me and bed me so David's sin would be covered and my husband would still live?"

"Oh little one, I don't know." She sadly shook her head.

"God, you sent Abigail to stop David and protect him from seeking vengeance and having the bloodguilt for Nabal and her people on his hands. Why, Lord, why didn't you let David listen to my entreaties not to touch me?" I groaned. "And why didn't you let Uriah listen to Mama when she implored him to come home to me? Why didn't you make him listen like you made David listen to Abigail?"

"Bathsheba, please, you'll make yourself sick. Come, let me help you."

"Leave me," I demanded.

"Think of your babe."

"I can think only of my dead husband. Leave me alone." I heard her sandals scrape against the stones as she turned, took a few steps, stopped. Her footsteps came back and I felt her slip down to sit beside me.

"Anna pleaded with Uriah to come home to you and he didn't come?" Abigail asked. "He should have known Anna well enough to know she'd never beg unless it was critical for him to come home. Foolish man, he held his honor as more important than his wife."

Startled and angry at her words, I jumped up. "He'd taken a vow of holy war not to come home to his wife until we'd won the victory over the Ammonites... How dare you call him foolish for being even more honorable than his king, who chose to stay home when the ark and his men went to war!"

"Calm yourself, little one, I meant no disrespect to Uriah." She stood up, grabbed my hand, and led me over to the bench. I reluctantly sat down beside her. "I know you're hurting, and I wish I had answers that would somehow bring you the peace you so crave." She gently patted my hand.

"And it is true, David could have called him up from war to

train our tribal warriors, but do you think Uriah wouldn't have become suspicious, when his wife had all the signs of pregnancy so precipitously after his homecoming? Of course he would have. And from what I know of you, you couldn't have kept the truth from him, right?"

I trembled with my desire to shout my denial. I couldn't.

"Of course I'm right," she said. "So, understanding *my* husband, I can see how David's strategy was really quite expediently simple. Let Uriah die heroically in battle, and marry his secretly pregnant, grieving widow, so she's well-cared for and his secret is protected."

I stared at her in rapt horror.

"Don't look at me like that," she snapped. "I haven't lived with David for over twenty years without coming to know the man very well. Oh, David, you tried to cover up one grievous sin with another even more egregious, and then you ended up with a sick and sorrowful woman who's intelligent enough to figure it all out and hate you for it."

"And you love him," I accused.

"You, little one, had only four years with Uriah and loved him dearly. I've had many more years with David. . . ."

"But he's taken other women, including me."

"And, years ago, nursed me when I was sick unto death, praying and singing over me day and night. He also spent hours with Kileab teaching him how to play the lyre, ride a horse, and use the weapons of war. David fasted and prayed for Kileab's life, and then sat by his bed when he lay dying. After we lost our son, he held me in his arms for days, and wept with me, and loved me well."

She looked up and smiled winsomely, "I'll tell you a secret. Every time we're together David praises me for being the most beautiful and intelligent of all his women, and tells me he treasures me as both wife and friend. That is high tribute indeed from a man who's always greatly valued friendship."

I chose not to disagree with her, although I wanted to say he didn't value his friendship with Uriah highly enough. But I'd come to cherish her friendship, and didn't want to anger her.

"David also allows me to come here each year for a month so I can have a respite from his court and helping care for his younger women and their children. Many of whom, as I've told you, have become more like my own daughters and grandchildren."

"I don't understand how you can accept them in this way," I admitted, shaking my head.

"No, and if you choose not to forgive David you never will understand," she said, without rancor or judgment.

I leaned back and silently gazed at her.

Her blue eyes were clear and convicting. "I know in God's word he talks about marriage being between one man and one woman. And there are many marriages, like yours to Uriah, and your parents, where this was the norm. But in our land, we also have accepted the custom of multiple wives, as Abraham and Jacob experienced.

"When David decided to take other women to his bed, I knew I had a choice. I could continue to love and accept him as he was, or hate him for displacing me with others. I knew if I hated him, I'd become a bitter, lonely old woman with no joy in my life. I chose, Bathsheba, to keep loving him and accept his other women, even if I could not always like them.

"I befriended Michal when Abner brought her back to David in Hebron," she said quietly. "I comforted her in her grief at being forced to leave Paltiel, whom she'd grown to love. I spent hours talking to her about how David had been forced to change through years of hardship, and told her how I'd come to be his wife."

Abigail's eyes suddenly focused on me. "Michal could never forgive David for abandoning her, and taking other wives. I tried to convince her to release her bitterness, but she felt justified in her anger, and stopped talking to me. After she publicly denounced David for dancing with such wild abandon before the ark, David removed her from his palace and found a house for her far from him. To this day, he's never entered that house or seen her outside it. Bathsheba, I know if Michal had chosen to forgive David, she'd not now be living a life of bitter barrenness and grief."

She stood up and looked down at me. "We've been here two weeks. You've two weeks left to decide if you want to live in bitterness, or live in forgiveness. Do you want to be like Michal? Or like me? David allowed you this time with me specifically to come back to him as a respectful wife, if not a loving one."

"I can act very respectfully to him and still not forgive him," I said. But I heard the lack of conviction in my voice.

She laughed with quick humor. "Little one, your face is much too expressive, beside which you have a tongue you've not yet learned to rein in. The other news I must tell you is that two days after your return from here, David will announce your pregnancy to his court. He'll rejoice in how the Lord has removed the curse of barrenness with the blessing of a fruitful womb. He'll then wisely call you back to his bridal chamber, to show everyone his delight in you and your news. And he'll emphasize your time away with me was his way of honoring you. And he has honored you by giving you this time, Bathsheba," she said with adamant conviction.

"Knowing all he's done, how can I ever respect him?"

She leaned over, gripped my shoulders with her hands and stared intently into my face. "With God's help, you will forgive him," she said. "So your child will know the father Kileab knew and loved, and you'll come to honor, if not love, a man who can be the most gentle, kind and loving of husbands, as well as the most demanding and cruel, depending on how you treat him. You, woman," she exhorted as she lightly shook me, "would do well to learn to approach him in a way that elicits his gentle and kind side. You're both gifted musicians. If you're wise, Bathsheba, you'll use your music to woo David, not alienate him." She abruptly released me and stood erect and queenly before me.

"I'll leave you with one more thought. Would Uriah want you to hate David or forgive him? We both know Uriah loved David as his king, his fellow warrior, and as an older, trusted brother. You were the wife of his heart, with whom he could never have children. The two people he most loved are now together and expecting a child."

I opened my mouth to dispute her, but she put a finger to my lips. "Yes, how you came together was wrong and tragic. But we serve a God who can give a faithful man and woman, Abraham and Sarah, a son at ninety and a hundred years old. And make Joseph, a Hebrew slave in the foreign nation of Egypt, the most powerful man in the kingdom to save his family from extinction. David could come to love you, Bathsheba." She grinned at me with disarming candor. "I know this because you truly are very much like me, although I've never had your gift in music."

"Abigail—"

"I'm praying our good and loving God will be with you, and you'll discover his goodness in allowing your lament to become a song of rejoicing. David wrote his own song about how God turned his mourning into dancing, and took off his sackcloth and clothed him with joy. I'll leave you to think about how our Lord might help you to do this if you'd let him."

I watched her walk away, my heart battered, and a prayer for help on my lips. I thought of Michal, and how David had compared me to her our last day together.

"God, I do understand Michal's bitterness. Will I let bitterness consume me or find the cure in choosing to forgive as Abigail chose to do?"

Chapter 32

During most of the next two weeks, I wrestled with what Abigail had said to me by taking long walks alone in the early morning, and playing my lyre. I couldn't escape David's songs, and the one that kept coming back to me I ended up singing each day for the comfort it brought to me:

"Be merciful to me, O God, be merciful to me,
    for in you my soul takes refuge;
in the shadow of your wings I will take refuge,
    until the destroying storms pass by.
I cry to God Most High,
    to God who fulfills his purpose for me.
He will send from heaven and save me,
    he will put to shame those who trample on me.
God will send forth his steadfast love and his faithfulness."

I also went to weave with the women, showing them some of the patterns my mother had learned while a slave in Philistia that she'd never shown Abigail.

"Lady Bathsheba, will you come and show me again how you work the pattern you showed us yesterday?"

With a nod, I stood and worked with the thread so that Tamar could follow the way it was woven through the other colors to create a pattern Mama had shown me years before.

"Please, might you do it a little more slowly?" Tamar asked. "I can't follow your hands, they move so quickly."

I sighed, recognizing the little patience I had with her. It seemed that my inner discord made me less than agreeable to those around me, and even though I was conscious of it, I couldn't seem to help it. "I'm sorry, Tamar, I'll try to go more slowly."

"It's alright, Lady, I'm often a slow learner."

"And I'm a very impatient teacher," I admitted, as I showed her again how to weave the pattern.

Naomi walked into the weaving room, her tall, lithe form and understanding smile a welcome sight to me. "Come, Lady Bathsheba, you've worked hard enough at weaving this morning. I've found some beads that I believe you'll enjoy using with the necklace we've been stringing. I have all the beads set up under the palm tree in the courtyard, where we can work under its shade. We'll see how the new beads look with the others we've used so far."

I gratefully followed Naomi out of the room, sure that the women were as thankful as I was at my departure.

* * *

Discontent and restless the night before we were to return to Jerusalem, I decided to climb up on the large boulder I'd seen soon after I'd arrived. It was the perfect place from which to stare up at the brilliance of the night sky. Might I finally find the serenity I sought in the dark beauty of this night?

"You still have found no peace," Abigail said quietly.

I looked down to see her standing by the rock. "No."

"The women have appreciated your help, but not your irritability."

I noted the wry humor in her voice and laughed sheepishly. "I'm sorry; but when I came to see how my inner turmoil didn't lend itself to be a help to them, I did stop visiting."

"Bathsheba, walking so far and working so hard won't help you find our God or his solace. Have you thought you might just sit, wait and listen? I've often felt a gentle 'touch' of the Lord when I'm just sitting quietly in the courtyard, or looking up at the evening sky, on a night like this one, where the stars glow so brightly you feel you could take a shepherd's crook and capture one.

"Little one, you remind me of a sheep that's determined to wander into the wilderness where it's dangerous and there's little to eat or drink, when the rest of the flock is content to stay close to water, grass and their shepherd," she laughed softly.

"I suppose you couldn't resist using such a picture," I commented dryly, "living amongst all these sheep and being married to a man who spent years as a shepherd."

"David and I used to exchange stories about the antics of sheep, and how they were very like many people we've known, including ourselves at times."

"I'm truly grateful for the time I've spent here with you and your people, and I wanted to find God's peace...."

"And I believe he's ready to gift it to you," Abigail said, clearly exasperated.

"But it's not that easy," I argued. "Besides, I sense God wants to make an exchange, not give me a gift."

"An exchange?" she asked, sounding puzzled.

"Yes, my hate for his peace. But I don't know if I'm ready to do this."

"You'd cling to your hatred when you could experience God's peace and love?"

I lifted up my body and removed the small pebble which uncomfortably pressed into my bottom. Sitting back down, I laughed with sudden insight.

"What, my morose friend laughs?"

"Abigail, I just removed a stone from under me that's been an irritation since I sat down on this boulder," I said. "Because it felt small, and caused little discomfort to begin with, I left it.

However, as I've sat here talking to you, it became so painful, I had to remove it. As I sat back down, I felt the Lord whisper that this pebble is like my hatred, I can live with it, but it'll only become more painful, until I either remove it, or choose to live my life with the agony."

"Bless the Lord," she cried. "Now, why don't you give me that pebble that represents your hate? I'll get rid of it for you, and we'll trust God to exchange it for his peace."

It sounded so simple, but it didn't feel simple. I opened my hand and stared down at the small, smooth stone. "Abigail, this stone is smooth! But when it was under me, it felt so much larger, and I was sure it had ragged edges because of the way it bit into my skin."

"Bathsheba, are you going to give me that pesky pebble or not?"

"I'm coming." Gripping this symbol of my hatred, I carefully slid off the boulder. "Give me your hand," I said. The night was full of starlight and a crescent moon, so I could see her as she held it out to me, palm up. My hand shook as I dropped the stone into her palm.

With a shout of triumph, Abigail curled her fingers around it, drew her hand back and threw it away. "Praise God for small stones and stubborn women," she exulted. She grabbed me, and exuberantly hugged me. Her warm embrace was a blessed benediction of love.

"Just tell me, when you praised God for stubborn women, were you talking about me or you?" I asked.

"I was praising God for both of us stubborn women."

Our loud laughter startled a star right out of the sky, and we stood in wonder as we watched its glowing trail streak down toward the earth.

* * *

The next morning, as Naomi left with the last of my things, Abigail strode into the room after her.

"How would you like to keep Naomi as your maidservant?"

she asked, her voice full of joyful anticipation.

Surprising me once again, I stared at her in open-mouthed wonder. "But she's been with you for years."

"Yes, so she knows all the politics of the women's quarters and how to keep the secrets of her mistress. She's also wise, and has a good sense of humor, of which you'll have need."

"But, I'm sure she wouldn't want to leave you, would she?"

"Bathsheba, I asked her to serve you for this month and told her why. Because she's been my faithful servant and companion for so many years, I also allowed her the choice to continue with you or come back to me once we reached Jerusalem. She told me this morning she'd be pleased to remain with you when we returned."

"Truly, she wants to stay with me?" Naomi's acceptance of me as her new mistress filled me with unexpected joy. From my first encounters with her, I'd been aware of her quiet strength and wisdom, and was constantly amazed at how well she seemed to anticipate my needs.

Abigail grinned. "Yes, she does, and because I'm also a wise and far-seeing woman, I arranged for two of my loyal servants here, to come back with me to Jerusalem to serve me there. So, my dear, I'll still have the help I need, and you'll be blessed with a handmaiden who can help you avoid the pitfalls that are sure to be thrown your way in the coming weeks and years."

"You, my lady, are all that is kind and generous." I bowed low to her, wanting her to see how much I honored her.

Her sparkling laughter rang with pure delight through the room. "Thank you, my lady," she chimed. "Now, we must return to our kingly husband, who knows we'll be arriving back tomorrow, as I sent a messenger ahead of us yesterday to tell him. When we return, you'll send him word of your great joy. How, while you've been gone, you discovered your curse has been lifted and God has opened your womb to David's seed."

"Can't you send him this news?"

"No, it must come from you," she said, adamant.

I felt myself wilt, even as the hated nausea swept over me. "Don't you dare get sick again," she commanded regally. Her command didn't stop my stomach's loud rebellion.

* * *

After two days of a long, but uneventful ride, Abigail and I returned to the women's quarters. As soon as we entered the common room, I felt the jealousy of the women like a hot wave of rancid air. No one said a word to me, although many of the women greeted Abigail warmly and asked how her time at her old home had gone.

They'd just finished their evening meal, and the smell of spicy lamb swept my stomach into immediate distress. Nodding to the women, I hurriedly walked to my room. Naomi, understanding my condition, followed me with my travel bags, and shut the door after us. I grabbed a bowl and was sick, thankful the bout of nausea didn't last long. With silent efficiency, Naomi cleaned up after me.

"I see someone left fresh bread and sweet wine here for you, my lady, would you like to try to eat something or just go to bed?" Concern laced her voice.

"The trip has worn me out, Naomi. I think I'd like you to help me wipe the dust off from the ride. Afterwards, I'll try to eat something before going to bed."

"That sounds wise, lady."

While she prepared my bath, I looked around the room. It didn't seem to have changed since I'd been gone, but I saw the beauty of the simple room in a way I hadn't before. It was as if my eyes were open to appreciate the carvings in the small table, and the red/gold sheen of the cedar chest for the first time. Was being able to enjoy my small home a taste of the benefits of my new attitude toward David?

Yes, I'd given my hatred of David to God, but I knew that to learn to trust David and show him honor was not going to be easy. I'd need God's constant help.

On the way back to Jerusalem, Abigail had taken delight in

telling me stories about a younger, more charismatic and daring David, who'd been clearly adored by his new wife. In David, Abigail had found an escape from marriage to a man who'd treated her and their servants with an abusive control which had left them in continual fear of beating, if not worse. What I couldn't tell Abigail was how I felt our lives had been lived in reverse: my marriage to Uriah had been the delight, while my marriage to David was more like her experience with Nabal.

As I slipped into bed, I knew the first thing I would have to do in the morning was send David another scroll telling him I was pregnant. However, this time he'd respond to the news with apparent joy, and probably declare some kind of celebration. What irony, with my last missive to him he'd ordered Uriah's return to Jerusalem, and then his death in battle.

"God, help me," I whispered. "My memories pick at my resolutions like hungry vultures."

Chapter 33

Returning to Jerusalem didn't agree with me. I awoke sick and filled with anxiety. I feared I wouldn't be able to live out my resolve to forgive David and enjoy his company. What would I do if he said something that stirred up my anger again? Would it stir up my hate once more, too?

My hand trembled as I wrote the necessary news, sealed it and gave the scroll to Naomi to give to Chilion. I knew he'd give it to David personally.

Abigail came by when it was time to join the other women to worship our God. Taking one look at my pale face, she shook her head. "I can see you're not well. I'm sorry, Bathsheba. Do you think you have the strength to come with us to worship?"

"I'll find the strength, lady," I vowed.

Although I still felt queasy, I was thankful to be able to get out of my "cage." After the freedom of living in Carmel for the last month, coming back to the women's quarters felt like forced confinement, and it made me thankful for our twice daily trips to worship.

"Did you write to David?" Abigail asked as we walked behind the other women.

"Yes."

After being gone for a month, and all that had happened

during that time, I wondered if coming back to the tent of meeting would feel different. Standing in the women's court next to Abigail, I closed my eyes as I listened to the priestly choir weave their melodious adulation to our God. The music lifted my spirit, and for a timeless moment, I felt surrounded and immersed in the peace of God. As I took a deep breath and slowly exhaled, it was as if one of God's angels flew by and touched my face with gentle wings of silent benediction. Cleansing tears came.

"Bathsheba, it's time to return to our quarters," Abigail said.

I felt dazed, and opened my eyes to find her staring at me, her look more curious than concerned. "Yes, all right," I stammered.

As I followed her out of the court I became aware of some of the women looking at me strangely, and whispering to one another. But God's peace was still so tangibly present I felt no concern. Once we returned to our quarters, Abigail ignored the other women and quickly swept me into her rooms, her maidservant Mary closed the door behind us.

I found her rooms different from what I remembered. First, they seemed bigger. Upon entering, she had a room much larger than the small outer room I had, and assumed the other women had as well. Off of it were three other rooms, all constructed from cedar wood and stone. Her bedchamber was in the middle, with no window, but she had a raised bed bigger than my own and covered with brightly colored and embroidered pillows. In the room on the right side of her bedchamber I saw Deborah carding wool to prepare for weaving. This room had a window which gave wonderful light for her work.

In the room on the other side of the bedchamber, again there was no window, and her two new handmaidens from Carmel, Mary and Eve, were standing in the doorway, as if awaiting Abigail's orders. They both were older women, with graying hair, Mary taller than the smaller, rounder Eve.

"I've always loved to weave," Abigail said, seeing my interest. "Your mother taught me many patterns I'd never known before, although you taught my women some Anna had never shown me. But it was our mutual love for weaving that became the catalyst for our long and loving friendship."

"Mama is the most gifted weaver I know." I said with pride. "I've never matched her ability."

"Ah, but she's never had your gifts in music."

"That's true, isn't it? It seems God gives all of us different gifts."

"You appear to be feeling better, which is good, as I've invited another guest to eat with us."

"Really? Will she join us soon?" I was surprised she was expecting another woman. Who could it be? I didn't want to appear rude by asking.

"Yes," Abigail said.

A small tap on her door signaled her other guest had arrived. Eve opened it and as I watched, Mama walked into the room. With a cry of joy, I ran and embraced her. It felt like it had been years instead of a month since I'd last seen her. "Mama, it's so good to see you."

"Ah, dear one, I've missed you so much," she crooned. She wrapped her arms around me, and gently rocked me as if I were still her small child. "Abigail told me about your time in Carmel, and how much you needed me right now. She knows it will be hard for you to adjust to being here in David's harem again."

"She's been so good to me," I whispered.

"Come, tell me all about Carmel," she said. Gently extricating herself, she stared at me with loving intensity, as if to read my face and heart. "You do look better." She glanced over at Abigail. "Did she give you much trouble, my friend?"

"No more than we suspected she would," Abigail teased. "Come, eat with us, our food is ready and I'm quite famished.

We all sat down on pillows around the low table and for the first time in a long while, I enjoyed eating and talking. I decided it had to be because Mama was with me again.

"Rachel's doing so well," Mama said, "and is very thankful to be back in a place she knows, and with me, whom she can trust. It was good of you to see her unhappiness and send her back to me, daughter. We're both enjoying each other's company once again." She took a bite of cheese and nodded toward me. "Abigail tells me tomorrow David will call you back to the bridal chamber, and arrange to tell the court your news. Are you ready to be with him again?"

"I don't have a choice, Mama," I said with quiet dignity. "My first two weeks at Carmel, it was almost as if I was back to the time I was a young woman before I married Uriah. It was a blessed gift to be away from Jerusalem and the palace, yet David lived with me each day. He was like a shadow that dims a corner of the sun, not enough to stop it from shining or giving warmth, but enough to mar its radiance."

"But Abigail told me you've stopped hating David."

I bit my lip. "Yes, but it doesn't mean I trust or love him," I said, pulling my fingers through my hair. "Only that I've chosen not to hate him, and to work at making the best of the life I must live with him."

"I'm sure David would give you permission to come visit me, wouldn't he, Abigail?"

"I'm sorry, Anna," she said, glancing at Mama, "but it's rare for a wife to be allowed that kind of freedom. Especially when she's carrying a royal child. If it hadn't been David's idea for Bathsheba to come with me to Carmel, I don't think I could have convinced him of the wisdom of it."

"I knew this must be how it is here, for remember how you wanted Abigail to visit us once, and she couldn't?" I said. "But it does make me feel like some exotic, caged bird."

"An exotic, singing bird," Mama teased. "But as long as I can come and visit you, I'll not complain."

"I suppose I shouldn't grumble, either. Especially as I promised Abigail I'd really try to rein in my tongue and my temper."

Mama nodded. "Daughter, both Abigail and I have learned how bitterness and hatred invite a sickness of the soul that refuses healing, even as love and forgiveness embrace health and life."

I stared at her, absorbing her words. "May God help me to embrace your wisdom."

"Yes," she agreed.

* * *

After returning from the tent of meeting the next morning, I was called to David. Chilion gave me the order as soon as I returned with Abigail and the other women. Naomi prepared me, dressing me in a blue tunic with gold thread the women of Carmel had given me the morning I'd left them. She braided my hair in a new way and helped with my cosmetics. She also slipped on the beaded necklace and bracelet we'd made together at Carmel. It matched my tunic so well, I knew she must have consulted the women who'd created it.

"Thank you, Naomi. I feel more prepared to face my king than I ever have before."

"I will pray for you."

I followed Chilion out of the common room. A guard led me up the stairs and down the hall to the bridal chamber. As I walked it came to me that this chamber was not just the "bridal" chamber, but the room where David met his wives and concubines to have relations with them. Living in the palace, I'd come to recognize it was much closer to the women's quarters than the bedchamber I'd been taken to when David had. . . when he'd taken me the first time. David must have two bed chambers. I prayed I'd never see the other again.

In some fear, I clutched Kileab's lyre to my chest. Just before I'd left my rooms, I'd grabbed the lyre, hoping our time together might be alleviated with the balm of music. I'd felt closest to David when we shared our music, and I knew I needed some kind of buffer for our time together this day. I had little desire to offer up my body to him for his pleasure. The fact he'd expect it, sent both my heart and stomach into rebellion.

The guard stopped, knocked lightly on the door and opened it. With an outward calm and inward panic, I walked past him into the room, and heard the door shut behind me. Glancing up, I saw David. He sat somber and regal in his chair by the table, facing the door. His position immediately communicated to me his desire to act the all-powerful king and not the forgiving husband. So be it.

I took two steps away from the door before I knelt down, put the covered lyre beside me and prostrated myself at his feet.

Silence reigned in the room. My heart beat with a measured rhythm. I knew David tested me, and was thankful my stomach had chosen not to revolt. A fly landed on my arm and walked up it, tickling me. David's strong perfume permeated the air around me.

"You may rise, woman," David commanded.

There was no joy or welcome in his words, but I was thankful to stand up again. I kept my head down, to show my respect. Besides, I didn't want to see the antagonism I heard in his voice reflected in his face. I left the lyre on the floor. I would not touch it unless given permission to do so.

"Are you well yet, wife?" he asked abruptly.

I glanced over at him. He stared at me, his eyes sharp, his strong hands gripped the sides of the chair, as if he would rise. "I'm better, my king," I answered truthfully, "but not well yet. The babe still sickens me at times, although not as often as before."

"You look better. I wonder, is it because you had a month away from me or my wives?"

How do I answer this question? "Thank you for allowing me to go with Queen Abigail to Carmel. It was a gift for which I'm most grateful to you." I bowed to him.

"Ah, such a very diplomatic answer, that says nothing." He cocked his head and stared at me with hostile intensity. "I heard you couldn't abide riding in the litter like the royalty you are now," he chided. "That you rode, like Abigail's handmaids, on a donkey."

I felt my face heat under his critical eye, but remained silent under the lash of his reprimand. Had one of his guards told him this?

"You've nothing to say? Not even another polite response?"

I bit my lip as I wondered how to respond. Sarcasm warred with humor. "I thought it better to ride a donkey than to demonstrate poor manners by retching all over Abigail and the royal litter." I gave him a small smile.

I watched David's ruddy, bearded face as he fought his own battle. . . to laugh or reprimand me for my gross honesty. Thankfully, laughter won, and he jumped out of the chair and caught me in a painfully strong embrace, while he continued to laugh loudly.

"Ah, Bathsheba, I've missed you," he said, his voice filled with an affection I'd never imagined I'd hear from him. "I would have called you back to me within a few days if you hadn't been in Carmel with Abigail. Just to sing with me, as I know to do anything else would probably have brought on more nausea. True? And is this not why you brought Kileab's lyre? So we might enjoy our music if not share our bodies?"

At his acceptance of the truth, my body slowly relaxed against him in relief, even as my arms lifted from my sides to slip around his waist. David was, again, the endearing man of my childhood, and the considerate lover. "Thank you," I whispered against his hard chest.

I felt him kiss the top of my head. "You seem to elicit both tenderness and spite from me, wife, and I admit I'd rather be tender with you, for both our sakes."

"And the babe's," I added.

"Yes, this babe whom we can now acknowledge and proclaim has removed the curse of barrenness from you, so you can be seen as blessed in the eyes of God and man." Gently releasing me from his embrace, he stared down into my eyes.

I wanted to take exception to his words, but couldn't decide why. I also knew that to do so would destroy the fragile goodwill we had discovered. An amity I needed to build upon, not tear apart. "Have you announced our news to my grandfather and to the court?"

"No, after thinking about it, I decided I wanted it to appear you shared this news with me privately today, here in this room, as we were celebrating your return to me from Carmel," he said. "I'll share the news with everyone tomorrow."

"I'm thankful to you for this consideration. You've been more than kind to me. First by sending me with Abigail, then giving me a day to recover from my journey, and now in inviting me to be with you here, demonstrating your care of me to everyone."

"Bathsheba, are you praising me?" His eyes sparkled with humor.

A slow smile of wonder drew up my lips. "Yes, my kingly husband, I believe I am."

"Good, every husband needs the praise of his wife."

When I went to open my mouth to correct him with "wives," it was as if God put a muzzle on my mouth, even as a song rose to my lips. I quickly took up the lyre, unwrapped it, and let my fingers blithely dance over the strings as I accompanied myself.

"O God, you are my God, I seek you,
    my soul thirsts for you;
my flesh faints for you,
    as in a dry and weary land where there is no water.
So I have looked upon you in the sanctuary,
    beholding your power and glory. . ."

David picked up his instrument from beside his chair and sang and played back to me the next verses:

"Because your steadfast love is better than life,
    my lips will praise you. . . ."

Together our voices and lyres blended and harmonized through the rest of the song, before David began another hymn, and as that one ended, I began another. With an effervescent joy he sat in his chair and I on the floor, facing each other, and singing until our voices were hoarse and our fingers sore. When the last note faded into the humid air, we stared at each other, even as we took a deep breath and exhaled in unison.

"It's as if my music lives in you as deeply as it does in me," he whispered in awe. "And I feel God's pleasure as we sing his praises."

I shook my head in quick denial, even as my heart beat with the truth of it.

He reached out his hand and gently touched my cheek. "Please, Bathsheba, don't deny the reality or the beauty of this gift."

Laying down the lyre, I bowed my head and trembled as I caught my breath on a sob. David gently lifted me into his lap, where he held me close while I silently wept. I was both astounded and terrified at the truth of his words. Somehow, as we worshiped together with our music, I felt God's peace. Yet, my heart still resisted surrendering any more of myself to this man I didn't want to trust or care for.

Chapter 34

I slipped quietly out of bed and was reaching for the fruit bowl on the table, to again empty it for my use, when I heard a soft chuckle, and the empty bowl appeared in front of me.

"I wondered if you would need this again," David said.

Startled, I glanced up. David was fully dressed and sat in his chair by the table. He shook his head at me, and sympathy shone in his eyes.

"Thank you," I gasped before I grabbed the bowl, turned and was sick.

When I'd finished, he handed me a cloth and took the bowl. "I wasn't sure you were being honest with me about still having this sickness," he admitted. "Clearly, you were telling the truth. And I'm sorry you're still ill."

"As am I," I said. "So, today you'll tell everyone I'm pregnant?"

"Yes." David patted the chair beside his, even as he sat down again. "Come, sit. Do you want to try and eat anything?"

"No, not yet," I said, but I sat down across from him. Sitting together at the table seemed almost natural, yet it wasn't. Would he talk to me?

"Everyone, but especially your grandfather, will be surprised by our news. He'll be overjoyed. Did he not warn me there'd be no children from our marriage because of your cursed barrenness? Yet, I told him I believed God would bless our union with children." David laughed in delight. Glancing over at me, his laughter stopped and he frowned. "Ah, I can see from your angry expression your grandfather must've told you about his warnings to me?"

"Yes, he did," I said, remembering it well. "He also told me of your boast. It was all I could do not to scream at him that my 'curse' had been lifted already, but not the way I'd ever asked for or wanted." I felt the old anger rise within me, as bitterness burned like acid in my throat.

"Bathsheba." David leaned over and grabbed my fisted hand from my lap and held it within his warm one. "Don't be angry. I shouldn't have mentioned this."

"No, it brings back memories I've been trying hard to forget." I worked to keep my turbulent emotions bound, so they wouldn't erupt all over him. "During my time with Abigail in Carmel I came to understand my need to release my anger and forgive. But I admit at this moment, my grief is overcoming my good intentions. Please, go and share the news with the court, and leave me to prepare to face your other women."

David stared at me, and I glimpsed more pain than anger in his eyes. Could he see the helpless rage in mine? "I'll send for your handmaiden to come so she can return with you to the women's quarters. There, Abigail can help and support you when you make your announcement."

His hand left my fist and I felt him rise, but I lowered my eyes as I couldn't look at him. My body shook.

A finger lightly touched my cheek, and he was gone. The door closed quietly behind him.

If only he hadn't mentioned my grandfather... or his arrogant boast to him. If only he'd shown some remorse for his actions, instead of his careless words, would I have been so angry?

Lord in heaven, how do I return to the women and pretend to be joyful with my news? Your peace is gone, swallowed up by my anger.

* * *

After David left, I walked around the room, swearing I wouldn't cry another angry tear. But they escaped my eyes to burn a path down my cheeks. What was taking Naomi so long to come for me? Had David forgotten to call her? Should I leave the room and trust the guard would let me return to the women's quarters? Or, could I just walk down the hall in the opposite direction, find my way out a palace door and escape? The idea became an extraordinary temptation. I was thinking through the possibilities of it when there was a slight knock on the door.

"Come" I said. The door opened and I was shocked to see Abigail glide into the room. She had a dimpled smile on her face that melted into a look of concern as soon as the door shut behind her.

"Ah, no wonder David asked for me to come to you, you look wretched. So, little one, tell me what happened between you two this time?"

"He said something that made me very angry," I told her.

"David sent me word you needed me. Of course, I told no one, not even Deborah where I was going. However, tell me what happened and then we'll wash your face and I'll help you with some cosmetics so no one will guess you've wasted time weeping. For what woman would weep after she shared with her kingly husband the miraculous news of her curse being swallowed up by the blessing of new life?"

Her words were like a sharp slap to my face. I stared at her, but I couldn't be offended. "You're right, of course, aren't you always?"

"Don't give me that look," she replied. "I've told you what you have to do, and you continue to ignore my advice. Thank God David has shown you sympathy and not anger. He must care for you deeply for him to send for me." She shook her head in obvious disappointment. "Bathsheba, if you don't want to play into the hands of David's enemies, and yes, he does have them here in his court, you'll do as you promised your mother and me and accept your life here.

"Little one, I've never seen David respond to a woman the way he has to you. Even in his words to me, I could feel his pain at the fact he'd hurt you again. He's the king, yet with you he acts like a distraught lover."

"Yesterday we shared our music with such delight," I said. "Today, he reminded me of something which had been especially painful and, well, the grief and anger rolled over me like an unstoppable wave."

"No emotion is unstoppable. You may feel anger but you shouldn't express it, especially to your king and husband."

"You're right," I said, determined not to allow my hurt to show. I couldn't believe she had no sympathy for me at all. Again, only with David was she concerned.

She gazed at me a moment and then had the effrontery to laugh in my face. "Oh Bathsheba, do you truly believe I can't see the anger swirl around your face like smoke about a fire? I've told you before you aren't a good liar. But, my dear, the longer you're around the court, the better you'll get at hiding your feelings. If not, you simply won't survive, and you know I want you not only to survive, but thrive in David's court." She took my hand and led me over to the chair. "Sit, and I'll act your handmaiden and use these wonderful cosmetics to erase all trace of your tears and tantrums. Then we'll join the other women, who will, I'm sure, already have heard the news of your pregnancy."

"How could they hear so quickly?" I asked, shocked.

"All of us have our sources for news, and the coming birth of a royal child is always significant. Especially when it's also from David's newest bride; a woman who was known to be cursed by God with barrenness."

"So, now I'll be even more envied and hated by his other wives and concubines?"

"Not all of them," she teased. "I don't envy you, nor do I

hate you."

She smiled at me, her dimples deeply evident, and my heart lifted. "I've no idea why David would ever have wanted another wife once he had you," I told her truthfully. "You have more intelligence, boldness, wisdom and kindness than anyone I've ever known."

For a moment her inner brightness dimmed, then flickered again into radiant life. "Marriage to kings, my lady, usually has more to do with politics than sentiment. I married and loved David while he was still a rebel leader in the desert, and King Saul was determined to hold onto his kingdom for himself and his sons. You've married a king who rarely thinks about the rebel he used to be, for he's too busy protecting his own kingdom from his many enemies. Which reminds me, I hear the war continues well, which is always good news."

"Since Uriah's death, I've felt no need to keep up with the war," I admitted. "Abigail, do you miss your rebel leader?"

She looked past me, a wistful expression on her lovely face. "Ah Bathsheba, David will always be my rebel leader, as well as my warrior husband, my poet lover, my brave savior and worthy king." She laughed softly, "He's also my rude, unreasonable, sometimes cruel and arrogant husband and friend. David is all these things and more. And if you're truly blessed, you'll come to know him at least a little bit as I do, and be thankful for knowing him and being a part of his life."

"Perhaps, but I can say right now I'm thankful I know you. And I do praise God I'm a part of your life."

At my words, she swept me into a tight hug. Did I want to know David as she did?

* * *

Abigail arranged to enter the women's quarters a half hour before me. She decided if we walked in together, it would be clear she'd been with me, and she didn't want this to be known. She also wanted to gauge how much had been said about me and my pregnancy, and the mood of David's other women. We agreed when I entered, if she smiled at me, it would signify the women accepted my news with some amount of grace. But if I walked in to see her shake her head, the women were less than pleased at my news, and I was to be cautious in how I greeted them.

I entered the room, my lyre clutched tightly to my chest. It was as if I'd stumbled into a hive of bees, the buzz of voices rose and fell around the room, until all eyes were upon me. Then the noise modulated into a low hum. Abigail shook her head. I drew a quick breath, thankful to be forewarned.

"So, the new bride will also be a new mother," Jezebel announced. She stood and faced me, her eyes hard, her face set in arrogant lines. "How good of our God to remove your curse and quicken life in your womb, Bathsheba. It seems all you needed was a kingly husband with great prowess impregnating his many wives. Is it not a pity you weren't David's wife years ago? Think of all the children you might have had by now if you'd never married your dead warrior."

I knew she was taunting me for throwing up at her how I'd known marriage to one husband, and had been loved well by him alone. But I couldn't respond to her venom if I ever wanted any peace in this place. "Thank you, Jezebel, it is good of God to bless me with a child after my years of barrenness." I put my hand to my womb and smiled. "You know the joy of having a son already. Little Elishua is a fine, sturdy boy, with eyes just like his father's. I pray God will bless me with a son as healthy as yours."

Jezebel stared at me as if to decide if I meant my words. I did, so I knew she'd find no trace of guile on my face.

"Bathsheba, I see you have your lyre in your arms." Abigail said with a warm smile. "Please share with us your gift of music. I'm sure my friends here wouldn't mind singing and dancing with you to help you celebrate."

Her words astonished me, yet I knew she was right to encourage this. How often had I seen music transform a situation for the better. Had this not even happened yesterday with David and me, even when I didn't want it to?

Though only a few of the women expressed their approval of her idea, I quickly slipped my lyre out of its covering, sat down on the thick rug, and began to play and sing. It was the children who began dancing first. I laughed as they pranced, twirled, jumped and leaped around the room. Their joyous giggles filled my heart with delight.

Then, one by one, different of the women began to dance, as others went into their rooms and came out with tambourines and other instruments and joined me. Other women lifted their voices with mine, creating lovely harmonies.

When I glanced over at Abigail, I found her holding Leah while Rebekah danced. She looked up and caught my gaze. Her smile was beatific, with only a hint of smugness. Jezebel scooped up the dancing Elishua and stalked to her room, but only two of the other women followed her.

* * *

After that morning, I felt a definite change in the way many of the women greeted and accepted me. I also discovered how much easier it was for me to adjust to my new life when I didn't feel like I must be constantly on my guard around David's women and their small children. There were more spontaneous times together of singing and dancing, when others would suggest it, or bring out their instruments. But they always asked me to join them.

As I got used to the rhythm of life within the women's quarters, I found unexpected contentment. Each morning after we broke our fast, we would all go together to worship at the tent of meeting. Returning to our quarters, we were usually served a light repast of cheeses and fruits, sweet wine and some juices. The afternoons we napped, and then we'd play games or dance and sing. Some would weave, others embroidered or strung beads, while a few found pleasure grinding grain and making bread. We'd return to worship at the tent in the late afternoon, and in the early evening, we'd be served another meal from the king's table, and soon after we'd go to our individual rooms.

Most evenings, although not every one, one of the wives or concubines would be called by Chilion to join King David. I was interested to note none of the women had more than one night with the king. It made me wonder if in this way, David tried to reduce the tendency of the women toward jealousy and envy of one another.

I was thankful David didn't call me back to him. Although I'd recaptured some of the peace I'd found weeks before, it was still hard to fully forgive David. But I was working with God to do this.

One day David's concubine, Rebekah approached me with Leah asleep in her arms. "Bathsheba, how are you feeling these days? Is your baby sickness still as severe as it was before?"

"No, it isn't, Rebekah," I said, speaking the truth. "Thank you for asking."

She drew me aside with her free hand, still cradling Leah in her arm. "Do not be concerned that our king has not called you back to him," she whispered. "He knows you are not well and will call you back once Abigail reports to him that you've passed your days of nausea. I know, for this happened with me."

I was touched by her concern for me. However, I didn't believe it was Abigail who kept me from him, but David himself. "It's so kind of you to tell me this, as I never knew Abigail reports such things to our king," I said.

"Abigail is like a mother to us all. She has even promised me that when I feel ready to return to the king, she will have Hannah nurse Leah for me so that I can spend the night with him."

"That is very good of her. Would you mind if I held Leah? I admit I've held very few babies, but I promise not to drop her."

Rebekah's laugh was high and joyful. "Oh, Bathsheba, I know you'd never drop her. Here." She handed the babe to me. "You can practice holding my baby before you have your own."

As I held Leah with her head in the crook of my arm, I noted her upturned nose, dark hair and gentle smile. Was I wrong? Would God give me a little girl as tiny and adorable as this one?

"I pray when I'm pregnant again, I might give David a son," Rebekah said. "Although when he asked to see Leah, he seemed quite charmed by her."

"I can understand, for so am I." I wondered why it surprised me that David had asked to see his own daughter. And why I was thankful he had.

* * *

Mama was allowed to visit me every other week, but Abigail became the woman I sought out for wise counsel and acceptance, even as Mama had advised me to do. Somehow, she'd known I'd need to seek out Abigail because she'd been a wife to David for years, which made her wise in understanding David in ways Mama could never be. She also talked more about Rachel during each visit, and I soon recognized how Rachel had become more of a daughter than a servant to her. I thanked God I felt grateful and not envious of this relationship.

It was only Jezebel and two other women who remained aloof and even openly hostile to me. The other wives and concubines became more accepting and friendly with each passing week. Ironically, I also felt this acceptance came because I was never called to David. Whether they believed, as Rebekah did, that this was because of my morning sickness I wasn't sure.

However, an unexpected joy came when I was into my fourth month of pregnancy. David's younger wife, Abijah, began to reach out to me with small acts of kindness. At first, she sat by me in the mornings when we'd break our fast, her son, Ibhar with her. She sympathized with my nausea, and assured me it would soon pass. I didn't tell her it had passed.

She also walked with me to the tent of meeting, and stood with me in the women's court. We both appreciated not only the worship, but the freedom we experienced in our walk to and from the tabernacle.

Abijah's son, Ibhar, was three years old and as fearless as any warrior when he climbed over beds, and ran full-tilt around the courtyard on his chubby little legs. He never cried when he tripped over something and fell. Ibhar had David's unusual copper-colored hair, and the endearing habit of hugging your leg when he wanted you to pick him up. Once I knew Abijah didn't mind, I often did just that.

One afternoon, as I sat with my lyre in my lap after I'd played for her, she asked if she might hold my instrument. When I handed it to Abijah, and showed her the best way to hold it, she gifted me with a huge smile of gratitude that touched me deeply. I watched her tentatively touch the strings, and glow with an inner radiance when the notes vibrated richly through the air. I realized if she had a teacher, she'd probably be a natural to learn how to play.

"Abijah, would you like me to teach you how to play the lyre?" I asked.

Looking up at me, her face shone with a hungry yearning. "Would you really teach me? Am I not too old to learn?"

"No, of course you're not too old, and yes, I'd enjoy teaching you. I even have an instrument you could use. And if you like playing, I'm sure Abigail could arrange for you to have one of your own."

Her eyes lit with hope. "Do you truly believe Abigail could do this for me?"

I smiled at her. "Of course. But first, let's teach you how to play it."

"Perhaps if I learned how to play, David would call me to him more often? It has been a few months since I last was called to him. But then, you shared this gift of music with our king and it's been a month since he called you to him."

"Abijah, do you want to learn to play for yourself or for David?"

"Can I not want to learn this to please our king as well as myself?"

"Yes, of course," I agreed. Suddenly remembering how I'd first wanted to learn to play the lyre to please my father.

* * *

When I entered my fifth month, I couldn't believe how well I felt. Lying half awake on my bed one morning, I was singing softly, my hand resting lightly on the growing mound of my womb. Suddenly, I felt, again, that wondrous inner flutter/tapping which I knew must be my child's way of letting me know he could hear me singing to him.

I wanted to dance out of my room and announce to everyone how I'd felt new life, but knew if I did, it would be to announce to everyone I was farther along than people believed. However, I did tell Abigail later that day when she called me to visit her in her rooms.

After I told her, I was surprised to see her frown instead of smile at the news. "Bathsheba, I must tell you there's an ugly rumor that the sickness you knew at Uriah's death, which Rachel innocently reported to their handmaidens, might not have been from your grief, but from an adulterous pregnancy."

I felt the blood drain out of my face and whoosh from my body, and I swayed on my feet. Abigail quickly grabbed me and helped me sit down on the rug next to her.

"I'd begun to believe God's mercy would cover my shame," I whispered. "Dear Rachel, I'm sure if she said anything about my sickness it was to try and gain their sympathy, not arouse their suspicions."

"Of course it was," Abigail agreed. "And for now, we can only wait and see if these rumors will grow or die. I'd like to keep you closer to me again, but I fear if I appear more protective of you, it would only add fuel to the gossip. Besides, you and Abijah have been together lately much more than you and I have, and I've noticed you've spent time with Rebekah and Leah as well."

"And I've noticed how you've been careful to nourish these friendships by staying away from me."

She gave me a smile full of wisdom. "We both were aware of the jealousy our close relationship stirred up among the other women. And how much more friendly they've been toward you since we seemingly grew apart."

"You're right, for you to suddenly be at my side again might raise their suspicions."

"Yes, I fear it would," Abigail agreed. "I also wanted you to know my handmaiden, Deborah, is the midwife for David's women. She'll check you monthly to be sure all is well."

"Thank you." I was touched by her concern, and thankful the midwife was a woman I could trust.

"And now that we've celebrated our traditional sounding of the trumpets, in a few days we'll travel to the tabernacle in Gibeon. . ."

"Where we'll celebrate our yearly Day of Atonement, when we as a nation and a people confess our sins to God and the high priest enters the Holy of Holies," I added. Thinking of the deaths of Uriah and the other warriors, I began to weep softly. "But has God forgiven me my part in the deaths of Uriah and his comrades? When the priest lays his hand on the scapegoat and sends him away as a sign that our sins have been removed from us, will I finally be free of this burden of unforgiveness that still rises up within me?"

"Ah, little one, you have not wept like this in weeks." She put her arms around me.

"I still grieve the moment it all began in the courtyard," I said. "If David had never seen me, so many would still be alive today."

"Bathsheba, you must let go of this. Please," she begged, "when we fast together through the Day of Atonement, let me pray our loving and forgiving God will remove all thoughts and feelings that so wrongly accuse you, especially of Uriah's and the others' deaths. I would see you experience God's peace, again."

"Oh, that our Lord would answer you, for my prayers seem to go unheeded."

Chapter 35

A few days after the Day of Atonement, Mama came to see me. With wonder, she told me how soon after my pregnancy was announced, Grandfather began visiting her to discuss my health and well-being. I was astounded by her news. She told me how he now treated her well, and even expressed appreciation for her visits to me.

We both thanked God for this miracle clearly initiated by him. I also praised God that no new gossip had surfaced during or after the Day of Atonement.

After Mama had left and we'd returned from our late afternoon worship, Chilion came into the common room to say the Lady Bathsheba would spend the night with the king. I felt happy that no anger or fear surfaced at his announcement, but a sense of – what? Anticipation?

After I ate, I took up my lyre and left the common room to follow the guard to meet David. When I walked in, I saw David sitting by the table, a gold goblet in his hand. Before I prostrated myself at his feet, I caught a glimpse of his ravaged face. I was shocked at his appearance.

"I give you leave to stand, wife," he said, his voice thick and slurred.

I stood and gaped at him in concern. He was staring into

the goblet as he swirled the liquid, which I knew must be wine from the scent that permeated the room. After a few moments, he sighed deeply and looked up at me. His eyes held such pain, I felt an overwhelming compassion for him. I walked over and knelt before him. When he didn't move, I wrapped my arms around his waist, and rested my head in his lap.

"Ah Bathsheba," he whispered as he put his hand on my head, "how is it you can seek to comfort me when I've been the source of all your grief?"

Tears shook loose from my eyes, but words remained trapped in my throat. I knew my only answer was I felt moved by a sympathy even I couldn't explain.

"I dreamed of Uriah the night we celebrated the Day of Atonement." His voice gruff with emotion, he removed his hand from me.

I lifted my head, drawn to seek his face by his astonishing words. Fat, unexpected tears slid down the weathered grooves of his cheeks. He looked over my head, as if he could still see my dead husband. "His black eyes, Bathsheba, held such sadness. They didn't accuse, nor were they filled with anger, but it was as if his eyes held the sorrow of the world within their dark depths. When I tried to run away from him, like the coward I was, my feet couldn't move. They were caught by a snare. I closed my eyes to try and shut out the pain of his gaze. But even with my eyes closed, I felt his grief radiating like the heat of the sun over me."

My head bowed with the weight of his words. Wrenching sobs shook me. With an anguished cry, I slipped away from David, and sat with my arms wrapped around my knees.

"I've been trying to sing what I could remember of your lament for him today, but all that would come were the words I wrote for Jonathan and Saul," he said. "Bathsheba, I called you to me so you might teach me your lament, and we might grieve for Uriah together.

"He was a good friend to me when there weren't many I

could truly call friends," he mused. "And, to all but a few, he seemingly abandoned his honor when he deserted Saul's army to join me and my rebels. When he came to know the one true God, he submitted to being circumcised by Abiathar, and even took on a new name. The name God spoke to me to give him; Uriah, for truly, our God had become his light."

"You were the one to give Uriah his Hebrew name?" I asked, shocked.

"Yes," David murmured.

"And then you condemned him to darkness," I groaned, "robbing him of his light and his life."

With my words, silence settled over me, except for David's heavy breathing. I remained at his feet, too grieved to move. Would he do violence to me for my words?

"Yes," he whispered.

Oh Lord, he just admitted he murdered my husband. I trembled with the force of that one word. Drawing from some source of strength beyond my understanding, I drew myself up. I stood before him and as I looked down on David, it was as if I saw a stranger. The compassion I'd felt so deeply when I'd first seen his pain was transformed into an unquenchable desire to see him suffer even as I had suffered.

I knew I risked my life, and the life of my babe, but the words exploded from me, "I never intended you or anyone else to hear my lamentation for Uriah. If you're finally grieving what you did to your faithful friend, write your own lament."

His head jerked up and he stared at me, his eyes growing wide, as if with sudden recognition.

Without another word, nor a submissive bow, I turned, walked to the door and, without a moment's hesitation, opened it and closed it behind me. I strode past the guard and down the hall to the stairs. I braced myself to hear David's roar for the guard to stop me, or his order to cut me down. It didn't come.

The guard at the door of the women's quarters bowed and opened it for me. I walked into the room, and thanked God the common area was empty. There was no one to observe my quick return from my king. With a sigh of relief, I entered my own rooms and found Naomi embroidering. When she saw me, she jumped up in surprise and dropped the material on the floor.

"Lady?" she asked, her wrinkled face creased with alarm.

"I'm going to bed, and I won't need your help tonight, Naomi, so please finish what you're doing."

"Yes, lady," she said. But her expressive brown eyes spoke her misgivings.

I stepped into my bedchamber and closed the door. Collapsing on the bed, I shook violently. With a silent moan, I pulled the wool covering over me and tried to curl up. But my quaking body wouldn't bend. Flashes of heat mixed with numbing cold, as my mind locked itself back into that place of hopeless grieving for Uriah, even as my heart waited for David's summons. . . to kill me and our child.

The warmth of the soft wool that cocooned me slowly penetrated my body's chill. And, when Naomi didn't run into my room to call me back to David, I stopped shaking. I placed a hand on my womb, and took comfort from the evidence of his growth. How I loved this child. Yet, I'd still risked his and my life with my reckless flight from David.

"I'm sorry, little one," I whispered. "Your father grieves and angers me like no one has ever done in my life, which might be shorter if I don't learn to hold my tongue. Yet, I still live and you with me and, if God wills it, David will spare our lives."

As if in answer to my words, and the pressure of my hand, I felt the babe move within me. This proof of his budding life comforted me, and yet the song I began to sing to him, was the lament for Uriah I refused to sing for his father.

* * *

"Bathsheba, can you hear me?"

Was that Abigail's voice? It sounded so far away, and when I tried to open my eyes, it felt like they'd been sewn shut. My mouth was as dry as the desert, and my body burned with its heat. Had summer not passed already? Why was the sun beating down on me like this?

"Bathsheba, you're sick. You must stop fighting Naomi as she tries to wipe you down with a cool rag," she commanded.

Dear Abigail, is she not always ordering me about? Suddenly, excruciating pain screamed louder than her voice, and I was being drawn into a vortex of darkness. "Uriah, I'm coming."

"Pray, Naomi, pray with me she and the babe will fight this fever and live."

*　　*　　*

I awoke feeling like I'd eaten linen thread and my body had suffered a terrible beating. Had David beaten me? Confusion sifted through my mind at this dreadful thought. With more effort than I'd expected, I slowly opened my eyes. As they focused, I recognized my mother sitting in a chair next to my bed. Was she asleep? Where was I? Didn't I leave my mother's house?

"Anna, she's awake!" Abigail exclaimed.

I moved my head to look where her voice came from and squeezed my eyes shut against the pain.

"Ah, your head still beats with the ache of your fever," Abigail said softly. "But you're alive, little one, when days ago we had little hope you'd live."

I felt Mama's hand upon my brow, and then her lips as she leaned over and kissed me. "The Lord has graciously answered our prayers for your life, praise to his name," she cried.

"I'm so thirsty," I croaked.

Immediately a cup was at my lips and a hand placed behind my neck to help lift my aching head. "Here," Mama said, "but sip it slowly, so you don't choke."

I did as she asked and was relieved by the cool wine that wetted my mouth and soothed my throat. Gently, she put my head down. Even with this small effort, I felt exhaustion sweep over me, and I closed my eyes.

"Yes, you must sleep, Bathsheba," Abigail said, "and regain your strength."

I felt a small smile touch my lips. Mama and Abigail together. How could I not recover when I had my two mothers caring for me and ordering me to get well? Was David pleased I was regaining my strength? Or had he thought God would kill me with a fever so he wouldn't need to?

Chapter 36

Each day, with the help and care of my mother and Naomi, I slowly regained my strength. When Abigail feared for my life on the second day of my illness, she'd asked for and received permission from David for Mama to come to the women's quarters and stay until I died or, if God willed it, recovered. Mama told me Abigail knew if anyone would be able to save my life, it would be her, as she knew how Mama would fight for me against any foe, but especially death.

After a week, Mama felt I was well enough to be allowed out of my bed. She helped me walk, slowly, around my small bedchamber. As we walked, it suddenly struck me I hadn't felt any evidence of my child's continued health.

"Mama," I cried, stopping abruptly, "could I live and my child die with this fever?"

She looked at me as she held my arm. Her eyes darkened with doubt. "Ah, my daughter, I've wondered if you've felt any movement since you've begun your recovery."

"Mama, tell me, could I be well and my child not be?" I demanded again. My heart raced and I slumped down onto my bed.

"Yes, I've known of pregnant women who've recovered from terrible illnesses only to lose their babes soon after. But most of the time, a woman's body works very hard to protect the babe within her."

Dread moved over me with cold fingers that stole my breath, and left me to gasp for air. Mama was immediately at my side. "Breathe, dear one, breathe in, and now let it out." She began breathing with me, as if she'd teach me how to do it.

Once I breathed normally again, she helped me to lie down. As I lay on my back, I closed my eyes and tenderly placed my hands over my womb. Softly, but then with greater volume, I sang David's song that I'd rewritten for my son weeks before. However, new verses of hope flowed out, as my confidence grew that he still lived.

> For it was you, Lord, who took the curse
>   from my dead womb
> And made it blossom with life,
>   like a flower in a garden
> And it is you, Lord,
>   who is forming his inward parts;
> you are knitting him together in my womb.
>   I praise you, for he is being fearfully and wonderfully made.
> Wonderful are your works;
>   that I know very well.
> Lord, awaken my son,
>   who sleeps beneath my heart,
> And call him to your dance of life,
>   with kicks and taps and twirls,
> For I know he hears me sing to him,
>   and delights to hear my voice,
> Even as you, Lord, sing to me,
>   and lift me from despair.

Suddenly, my womb erupted with movement, as if he somersaulted his joy that I sang to him again. I shouted "He's alive!"

Mama's smile radiated her wonder, as her hands pushed mine aside and she firmly kneaded my womb. This time it felt like a small, but strong kick and Mama laughed out loud.

"Ah, daughter, you have a strong son there who clearly loves his mother's singing."

"Yes, but will his father ever want to hear his mother's voice again?"

* * *

Abigail told me the other women had been frightened for their own lives, and the lives of their children when they'd heard of my fever. She explained this was why she wouldn't allow me out of my rooms until two weeks after I'd first been assailed by my illness. She explained that although sickness may be considered a consequence of sin, she'd seen fevers and colds passed from child to mother to handmaiden too often not to believe some sicknesses could be "caught" when you lived close together. For this reason, she'd taken precautions to keep me sequestered in my room.

Because I still wasn't strong enough to walk to the tent of meeting, Abigail encouraged me to wrap up in my hooded robe and go out into the courtyard. It was a rare, sunny day and she believed I could use the exercise and it would be good for me to be out of my room. I took her advice and walked out into the courtyard and sat on the bench. With a sense of deep thankfulness, I lifted up my head to feel the warmth of the sun. "Praise you, Lord, I'm alive and my babe and I didn't die with the fever, nor from David's wrath."

After awhile, I carefully walked around the courtyard, watching the stones so I wouldn't accidentally trip. Was David still as sick as he looked when I'd last seen him? I wondered if he'd written his own lament for his friend and my beloved. Was he sorry I was alive? According to Abigail, he'd sent someone to inquire about my condition each day. This hadn't surprised me, for wouldn't he want to appear the concerned husband of his new and pregnant wife to all his court?

Bathsheba, you're being unfair to him. Would he ever call me back to him so I might find out the answers to these questions? Would I ask him, if he did call me to him? Did I want him to call me to him again? I wasn't sure.

I'd never been so sick before, and I found the experience sobering. As Mama had told Abigail, it wasn't that I'd never had fevers or runny noses as a child, or even as an adult, but by God's mercy, they'd never been life threatening. Mama shared how worried Abigail had been, and how my sickness had brought back all her memories of Kileab's death. She and Mama had prayed at my bedside for hours, and when my fever had broken, Abigail had danced around the room with loud praises to God.

I sat down on the bench in the corner, exhausted by my walk and wrapped my robe more tightly around me. Contentment filled me as I rested, and felt the air stirred by a gentle breeze. I looked up to the refreshing sight of a vivid blue and almost cloudless sky, and the sun making its daily climb up God's invisible ladder. In the distance, I could faintly hear the singing of the priests, as they led our people in worship. I missed my time in worship. How long would it be before I regained the strength to join the women on their daily treks to the tent? The way I felt, I knew it would still be a few more days.

As I thought more about David, it occurred to me that even though I still wasn't at peace with him in my heart, it was as if the fever had burned away the greater part of my renewed anger and bitterness, and even my unforgiveness. Could it be because he'd admitted to me he'd been, "the darkness to Uriah's light?" David hadn't in any way asked my forgiveness, but to admit, even obliquely, he'd killed Uriah. . . it both comforted me and left me wondering how to respond now, weeks after our confrontation.

I closed my eyes, and leaned against the wall. It felt good to absorb the heat of the sun that shone down on me in this small corner of the courtyard. With a smile, I put my hand on my rounded stomach, and felt my babe tap me to tell me he enjoyed being outside, too. I found that I wanted to share this active child with David. Would he ever call me back to him?

* * *

I was so deep into my thoughts, that I hadn't heard the women's return. However, the shrill, arguing voices caught my attention. From my bench, I could see Jezebel and Abijah facing one another, the other women circling them.

"I talked with Michal again after worship," Jezebel said, "and she told me she also believes Bathsheba must have been pregnant when David married her. Even though she's pretty, he'd never have taken a widow to wife if she'd not been carrying his child. And was she not punished by God with a fever and almost died? And do we even know if the child didn't die in her womb? Surely if the child is dead it is because of her sin."

"Jezebel, we all know how much Michal hates David," Abijah cautioned with quiet force. "And how she only comes among us when she wants to stir up strife."

"Well, she was only speaking what we've all suspected," Jezebel defended. "Or, at least those of us who aren't courting Bathsheba's friendship, or getting music lessons," she sneered. "I know why you wanted to learn to play that instrument, so you could play for our king and in this way attract his favor."

"You're only bitter because the king continues to neglect you," Abijah rebuked her.

"Women, stop this," Abigail commanded, as she walked into the room. I'd never heard such a strong note of authority in her voice before.

"You can't mean to defend the adulteress in our midst, even if she's the daughter of your friend," Jezebel mocked, drawing some of the other women's murmurs of agreement, but others shouted Abigail was right, she must stop.

"Jezebel, do you think I won't report all you've accused David and Bathsheba of to our king?" she replied, her sharp gaze focused on the other woman. "David abhors gossip, especially among his women. Why do you think Michal was given her own home and David never touched her again?"

Gasps and mutterings flowed like the sounds of insects in the night.

Slowly turning, Abigail caught the eye of each woman. "Tell me, all of you who want to agree with Jezebel, what man, especially our king, will put up with an angry and bitter woman who spends her time in poisonous gossip against him and his other wives? Does he not have more sweet and adoring wives and concubines to take to his bed than one with the tongue of an asp? And can he not always add more beautiful and agreeable women to his harem if he so chooses? And exile or kill any wife or concubine who dishonors and maligns him?"

Grim silence reigned. I watched her pivot, as she silently challenged them to refute her. "Now, I want each of you to return to your rooms and children, and ponder my words. When David's generous and abundant food is set before us, we'll come together again. Abijah, with all this clamor, I forgot to tell you David has requested that you join him tonight. Speak not of this afternoon's conclave to him, but go and prepare yourself for your night with the king. Hannah will help with Ibhar's care while you're gone."

"Yes, lady," she breathlessly agreed.

"Jezebel, I'll discuss this further with you later." Her voice was full of controlled anger.

I couldn't hear Jezebel's answer, but watched as the women dispersed to their rooms. I bowed my head, closed my eyes, and felt tears drop onto my cheeks.

"Bathsheba," Abigail's voice startled me.

I looked up. She stared down at me before she sat down on the bench. Her arm slipped around my shoulder.

"Oh, little one, you're shaking, we must get you back to bed before you become sick again," she said. "I'm so sorry. I hadn't foreseen this at all, and then I was afraid you might be in the midst of them before I glanced out and saw you on the bench. I made sure every eye was on me and their backs were to you."

"You certainly accomplished that goal," I said, attempting humor. "Truly, Abigail, I don't think I could've moved even if they'd all come storming out with rocks in their hands."

"No, little one, not that," she said. "But now I must take you back to your room to rest. I've already sent a message to David and expect him to send for me shortly."

"But you told Abijah—"

"Don't worry, once I talk with David, I'll convince him to call Abijah to himself to reward her for her defense of you and him, although she'll not be told this is her reward." Her blue eyes twinkled. "But first David and I must talk. I hadn't realized how Jezebel had become almost as bitter and angry as Michal, and the two of them together are dangerous not only to you, my dear, but also to our king." With an agility that defied her years, Abigail stood up and reached a hand to me, helping me to stand beside her. "Come, I'll take you to your room before I see David."

"Do you honestly believe you can stop this gossip so easily by removing Jezebel?" I asked, doubt in my voice.

"Ah Bathsheba, when you remove the head of a poisonous snake, even though its body may move around for a bit, very soon it dies, too." Her eyes gleamed with conviction. "What has become quite clear this day is Jezebel is the snake within these quarters, and she and her poisonous tongue must go. Then I'll wait to make sure another doesn't take her place." Her grin held a touch of danger. "But I think once the women observe the rapid exile of their friend, they'll not want to follow her."

"But won't banishing her for her gossip about David and me only prove to everyone the truth of it?"

"Bathsheba, you've much to learn about court life, and the most important truth is the fact that if the king is displeased with you, you'll soon be exiled or dead."

I stared at her with sudden comprehension. "Yes, of course. How stupid of me not to remember my own experience with this truth."

Abigail grabbed my hand and squeezed it. "I'm so sorry, I didn't think."

"Are you perfect that you can remember everything?" I asked, only half jesting. "Truly, most of your time is spent resolving our problems, giving me and others comfort, and helping us in whatever way you can to make our lives easier," I said. "In many ways, I owe you my life. And what applies to Jezebel, must apply to me, too. You and Mama have been right all along: I must forgive David. For I've decided I truly don't want to end up like Michal or Jezebel. May God have mercy on them and on me."

Chapter 37

Jezebel and Elishua were removed from her rooms and the women's quarters before we went to worship the next morning. I watched from my doorway, as I felt it better not to show myself among David's women at this time. Abigail was in the midst of the servants, to direct them in their tasks to remove all of Jezebel's possessions.

We weren't told where they were going. I'm not sure Jezebel knew herself. There were many tears, but no words of farewell between her and her friends. In fact, she never spoke, which gave me the distinct impression she'd been forbidden to speak. I could only guess what the punishment would be if she had.

In the midst of this sad, but necessary leaving, Abijah walked into the common room. Her face radiated her joy from her night with the king. I also caught her surprise, as well as the look of satisfaction, when she took in the significance of what she saw. Abijah smiled at Jezebel, who looked back on her with venomous hate.

Chilion opened the door but didn't bow, as he normally did to a wife or concubine of David's. He watched her and Elishua as they walked out of our common room. I was puzzled when I realized the servants remained in the room with her baskets.

"Empty the baskets on the rug," Chilion directed the servants.

They gently upended the baskets, and all of Jezebel's possessions of clothing, jewels, cosmetics, and other treasures scattered before the women.

"After you return the baskets to the room that belonged to Jezebel," he said, "leave us."

They quickly did as told, and left. Chilion bowed to Abigail, and followed them out the door. The guard closed it shut.

"Our worthy king and husband, David," Abigail announced, gaining all of our attention, "desires I make his will clear to you. First, if anyone of you gossips against himself and his most worthy wife, Bathsheba, or against any other member of his family, he'll not hesitate to remove you from these quarters and banish you from his presence forever. He will also keep all the gifts he gave you when you became his wife or concubine, even as he's done to Jezebel.

"Second, to reward those of you who remained loyal to him by defending him and Bathsheba against Jezebel's gossip, he's ordered me to allow each of you to choose one of her possessions to keep for yourself. However, because of your strong defense of Bathsheba, you, Abijah, will go first, and you'll choose five treasures for your reward in defending Bathsheba. Whatever is left after all have chosen, will be given to his beloved and most honorable wife, Bathsheba."

I stared at her, trying to absorb the words she'd spoken. Beloved and most honorable wife? Had he truly spoken those words about me to Abigail? Or were they Abigail's words?

Abigail looked around the room at each of the women. "When Jezebel began spewing her lies yesterday, Chilion held the door for me so I might observe you all before I walked into the room. Therefore, I know which of you were agreeing with her, and which of you were standing with Abijah in her defense of Bathsheba. Thus, David ordered the first list of women I name to return to their rooms until it's time to leave for worship. Yes, you'll be fasting until we return to this room after going to the tabernacle," she told them, with a grim smile.

"When I'm done with the first list, I'll begin with the second. These women will have the honor of picking something from among Jezebel's belongings, and will also be served an abundant meal before leaving for worship."

Not wanting to be present as she named all the women who'd gleefully joined Jezebel when she'd assassinated my reputation, I backed into my room and shut the door. I wanted nothing of Jezebel's, but I also knew there was no choice, I must accept whatever was left.

"Lady, let me get you some food," Naomi said, her voice deep with worry.

I felt emotionally exhausted and wanted only to hide from all that was happening. "No."

I slipped down on the floor and smiled, as dark humor gripped me. A tap on the door came and before Naomi could reach it, Abigail sailed into my room and shut the door.

She bowed from her waist and smiled at me. "It's done." Looking at me more closely, she asked, "What has you grinning like a lioness at her prey?"

"It just occurred to me that this is the first time I've ever participated in receiving my own 'spoils of war.' For, dear Abigail, wouldn't you say my receiving part of Jezebel's belongings is very like our men receiving a portion of the victory plunder from our enemies?"

"How astute, Bathsheba," she praised me. "When David told me exactly what I must do, and gave me the words to speak, it never entered my mind how like this is to plundering an enemy." She laughed before she quickly sobered. "You do realize Jezebel was your enemy, and she did mean to destroy you?"

"Yes, Abigail, I saw it plainly yesterday. And although I can't understand why she felt such delight in her poisonous gossip about me, I still feel somewhat sorry for her. Probably because her gossip is true."

"Don't say it! You were a convenient target for her yesterday, but I've heard what she's said about David's other wives and concubines before you. And, you weren't in Hebron to experience the damage of Michal's bitterness and unforgiveness among David's wives there, which she spread for awhile here in the women's quarters of Jerusalem as well."

She stood erect and stared down at me. "It was I who counseled David to give Michal her own home, with servants loyal to him, and to restrict access to his wives and concubines. And so I counseled him to remove Jezebel. Neither David nor I were going to tolerate that woman bringing the same kind of destruction here that Michal had brought before her."

"Abigail, was it you or David who described me as his 'beloved and most honorable wife?'" I asked.

"David, of course," she said, and gave me one of her glorious, dimpled smiles. "Didn't I say you would capture David's heart? Well, it seems you already have."

"But I've never told you what happened at our last meeting," I said.

She put her hand up. "And you won't." She lifted her face and sniffed the air. "Ah, I think we'll now have much more than cheese and wine to break our fast," she crooned. "Come, let's enjoy our victory feast with your fellow victors in this important battle."

I followed her out, but I prayed when my babe arrived early, these women wouldn't turn on me with even more venom than Jezebel.

* * *

After Jezebel left, it was as if a clean, fresh breeze blew threw our living quarters, leaving it smelling like the first scents of spring. Although it wasn't spring, but late fall, and a number of braziers burned in our rooms to keep us warm. It wasn't that all gossip ceased among us, but none of it was contaminated by Jezebel's poison, nor was it aimed at me, for which I was especially grateful.

I was entering into my seventh month when Chilion announced at our evening meal that David had called for me to come to him. Shocked, I looked up and had to smile at the others' astounded expressions, although Abigail couldn't hide her knowing grin.

Within a short time, I again walked the hall which led to David's bedchamber. Since Jezebel had left, it seemed as if God had answered my prayers to root out my own bitterness and unforgiveness. But I knew the true test would be how I'd respond to David when I spent this time with him. I prayed I could be with him and not allow anger or bitterness to upset my commitment to forgive him.

The guard tapped at the door, but we heard no response. Fear tried to grip me, but I refused to allow it. David would call "come," wouldn't he? Surely he'd not decided he didn't want to see me?

The guard tapped again, and opened the door when we both heard a garbled "come."

I entered to find David sitting up on the bed, a blue covering over him, as if he'd just awakened from a nap. His hair was long and disheveled, with added strands of gray streaking it. He blinked his eyes, as if trying to focus. He looked like he'd aged years in the months since I'd last seen him.

I suddenly realized I couldn't prostrate myself before him, as my protruding stomach made that position impossible. I knelt and bowed my head. I heard the rustle of his wool covering and felt his weight hit the floor, and shake the boards as he walked toward me.

He put his hand under my chin and lifted my face. I didn't want to look closely at him, somehow afraid of what I'd see, but I did. Whereas before his face had looked ravaged, now it looked gray and gaunt. His eyes appeared sunken, dull and colorless, and more gray laced his thick beard as well.

"You've grown more beautiful," he rasped. "Abigail told me how you've become radiant with this new life growing within you. I had to see for myself. She was right." He smiled and I saw a quick reflection of his old self. "But Abigail is always right, isn't she?"

I smiled at the truth of it. "Yes, she is."

"Let me help you up." He grabbed my elbow and gently drew me up, then stood and stared at my rounded form. Reaching out, he tenderly put a hand to my belly. "Is he active?"

"Here," I said. Taking David's chapped, broad hand, I pressed it where I could feel my child's movement. "What do you think?"

A smile of wonder moved across his face, lighting up his eyes. They filled with thick tears. "I'm blessed to have been the one to give you this growing child."

I sucked in a breath, both moved and grieved with his words, and the emotions that came with them. Yet, incredibly, I felt no anger. Nor any desire to argue with him. *May God be praised, I'm free of my unforgiveness.*

Removing his hand, David said, "If I ask you to play something other than Uriah's lament, will you play and sing for me, Bathsheba? I've not been able to make music for months now, and it came to me it's your playing and singing I crave, more than anyone else's, including my own."

"Yes, my lord king, I'll play for you. But I forgot my lyre."

"Mine is there on the table, take it."

As I walked over and picked it up, I asked him, "Is there something you'd especially like to hear?"

"Only the lyre and your voice, Bathsheba. Play whatever songs of worship you want. Perhaps with your singing, I might again feel the joy of my Lord's presence."

I wondered at his words, but only said, "Why don't you sit back on the bed, and I'll take this chair and bring it near?"

"Yes." A coughing fit seized him and I set his lyre back on the table while I poured some wine and brought it to him. His hand shook as he sipped the wine. Nodding toward me, he murmured, "Please, play."

As I settled myself into the chair with his lyre, I felt a deep sadness wash over me. I'd wanted David to suffer as I had, and it seemed my prayer had been answered. Yet, I felt no satisfaction or joy in this knowledge. In fact, I felt a strong desire to console him, and I prayed the Lord would allow my singing his songs to do this.

> "Rejoice in the Lord, O you righteous.
> Praise befits the upright.
> Praise the Lord with the lyre;
> make melody to him with the harp of ten strings.
> Sing to him a new song;
> play skillfully on the strings, with loud shouts...."

I played for him for hours. Every time I thought he'd fallen asleep, and I'd put the lyre down, he'd gruffly ask for another song. I stopped a number of times to help him sit up with coughing fits I was sure must kill him. But he'd sip the wine and ask me to play more. So I sang until my voice grew weak, and my body cried out for sleep.

"You're tired, wife, and I've been selfish once again, forcing you to play until you're ready to fall asleep in that chair."

I stared over at him and nodded, but I tempered my agreement with a smile.

He gave me the sweetest smile I'd ever seen on a man. "Thank you for giving me your gift of music this night. You've no idea how it has soothed me." He sat up straighter. "When I was called to play for Saul, I was always exhausted afterwards as well," he said, his voice husky. "Sometimes I'd play until my fingers were wet with blood and my voice was all but gone, and he'd demand I continue." A look of fear crossed his face. "Bathsheba, I've not forced you to play until your fingers are bleeding, have I?"

"No, my king," I reassured him. "I've built up great calluses these last months as I've played often with your women. Besides, I knew you wouldn't want me to play until I hurt."

"Do you really believe that, Bathsheba?" he asked with quiet intensity.

"Yes, David, I know you wouldn't purposefully hurt me," I said. The sudden awareness that I spoke the truth filled me with an inner serenity. "I also want to thank you for how you intervened to protect me against Jezebel and her gossip. My life in the women's quarters has been much improved since she left."

"I'm glad. How soon before your babe is due? I admit I'm not good at keeping track of such things."

"Our son should arrive around the time of the almond blossoms in two months," I told him, amazed I felt a need to stress this child, whom I'd always owned as mine alone, was ours. Yet, it felt right to say this.

"You sound very sure you're carrying our son. Why is that?" he asked curiously.

"I don't know, but ever since I first admitted I was pregnant, I've believed I carried a boy child."

"Well, I must let you go back to your own bed," he said. "Even though I would have you stay with me, I know this cough would only keep you awake, as it has me for more nights and days than I can remember. I want you to be well, Bathsheba, for the child's sake, and my own."

I stared at him from my chair and slowly stood. Feeling stiff, I put the lyre down and stretched. I looked over at him to find his eyes upon me. Yet, I saw no lust in his glance, but a kind of sorrowful yearning.

"Let me have a moment of privacy," I said, "and then I'll join you in your bed and sleep."

He stared at me for a long moment, as if trying to determine my motivation for doing what he'd plainly given me freedom not to do. "I'd like that."

As I took care of my body's needs, I wondered how sick David was. Yet, I felt no fear that whatever sickened him would touch me or our babe.

When I joined him in the bed, he put a soft wool covering over me. Resting on my back, my arms above my head, our son, as he was prone to do, immediately began his nightly dance. I reached out and found David's hand, and placed it on my womb. "Feel him? Every night for over a month, he's been dancing like this. I think he must already be a worshiper of God."

David choked as if on a sob, sat up and began to cough deeply, scaring me. After the fit left him, he got out of the bed and went to the table, where he poured himself some wine and gulped it down. I turned on my side so I could watch him. He sat down in the chair and put his head on his arms that rested on the table. Before long, I heard him loudly snore. I got up, took one of our coverings and slipped it over his shoulders and back. Shaking my head at the irony of him sleeping in a chair while I slept in his bed, I crawled back into bed and was soon asleep.

When I awoke in the morning, David was gone. But next to me on the bed, he'd left a small ivory carving of a lion which looked Egyptian. I knew it was a gift for his son, and I wept with grief for my sick husband.

Chapter 38

David didn't call me to him to sing again. Nor did he summon me at all. In fact, he rarely asked for any of his wives or concubines to join him, except for Abigail. We wondered if he was spending time with his older wives, and although I didn't think this was true, I agreed with the other women this must be so.

However, I'd noticed when Abigail returned from a night with David, although she always wore a smile, her dimples never showed, and her blue eyes were clouded with worry. Had David continued to grow more ill so that his sickness was life-threatening? This thought grieved me, and I repented of my earlier desire for David's death, and prayed for the Lord to intervene in his life and bring him back to health.

As my babe grew within me, and I entered into my ninth month, I saw how the women watched me. I suspected they wondered if Jezebel hadn't been right after all. I knew Abigail worked hard to impede their speculations, but she couldn't spend all her time with the women, and I assumed my protruding belly might look like I was farther along than seven months.

I also imagined the fact that we'd all been shut up by the cold weather in our rooms and common room, except for our twice daily treks to the tabernacle didn't help, either. So I watched and listened as the gossip became more focused on David and his health, Abigail and me.

The gossip made it easier for me to stay in my room. Although I did brave the courtyard if the sun was shining, but only when the other women napped. I still gave Abijah her lessons, and Rebekah still came to visit me with Leah. But the other women avoided me.

Abigail was back in the habit of checking on me each day, and stayed to try and cheer me up. Yet, when I'd ask her how David was, she'd say he was fighting a cough, and would quickly change the subject. Because of this, I knew he wasn't well, and she didn't want me to worry. What I'd come to understand from her, in oblique references, was her concern for me if David died. I knew she believed I'd be open to public censure, and possibly worse, if the truth came out I'd been with David when Uriah was at war. We both knew I couldn't say "no" to the king, but we also knew most people would still blame me, as my ultimate mother, Eve's temptress daughter.

It was a cold, windy day when I felt a deep, inner contraction grip me like a vise around my stomach. A grunt escaped me, and I quickly sat down on the rug in my room. Naomi was immediately kneeling beside me.

"Lady, what are you feeling?" she asked.

I smiled at her. "This contraction was different, Naomi, from the ones I've been feeling lately. It was stronger and deeper, and definitely more painful."

"I must go and get Lady Abigail and Deborah," she said.

"I think perhaps you should," I agreed.

She was out the door before I'd finished speaking and back with Abigail and Deborah long before another contraction came.

"So," Abigail said, entering the room before Deborah and Naomi. "This son of yours has decided it's time to show himself?"

I nodded before asking, "How long does this take?" It suddenly occurred to me I'd never been with a woman delivering her baby, and had no idea what I'd be experiencing, other than painful contractions. I also knew women who'd died in childbirth, yet I felt no fear of this for myself. Why this was, I wasn't sure.

"Deborah can tell you better than I," Abigail said.

"Lady, you'll be having contractions that begin coming closer and stronger together over time. For many women, it can take a day or more to birth a babe, for others, it takes less time. Right now, I'd help you up so you might walk to Lady Abigail's and weave or do something that will hold your attention. If you sit and wait for another contraction to come, you'll find anticipating the pain makes it feel more painful."

I stared at her and, after a moment of thought, smiled. "Deborah, I can tell you're a gifted midwife, for you've already eased my mind. Let's go to our lady's room, and I'll weave until I need to do something that will occupy all of me quite thoroughly; like having a baby."

* * *

Our son chose to make me suffer through all the day and night and into the early morning before he decided he was ready to enter the world. First light had just broken through when I was finally sitting on the birthing stool, after Deborah had massaged and prepared me for the birth, making sure he was positioned just right.

"It's time to push, lady." Deborah's voice was firm, yet soothing. "Hold your breath and push as hard as you can."

The pain came in ever-increasing waves now, and my screams became grunts as the pressure built within me. I closed my eyes and grasped at a breath and held it. I bore down with all my weary strength until I gasped for another breath.

"Good, good, lady, you're getting close, now take more deep breaths and then hold it again."

Abigail wiped the sweat from my brow, as I kept up the excruciating rhythm of holding my breath and pushing, then gasping for breath again.

"Good, lady, I can feel the head. Come now, take another breath and hold it, you're almost there."

I held my breath and bore down until I felt dizzy and was sure I must faint, when suddenly it felt like a log came loose within me and the babe slid out.

"Yes, he's here," Abigail exclaimed, her voice filled with joy and tears.

I looked down and saw Deborah holding up a tiny boy-child, his hair as black as my own, his red face scrunched up in anger. He waved his perfectly formed hands and feet before his affronted cry filled the air. Love gripped me with such strength I was sure I was experiencing another contraction. I'd been given a son. The curse I'd lived with for so many years had been broken and I'd been blessed with a beautiful boy-child.

"Praise our loving and faithful Father," I croaked from dry, cracked lips. "He's perfect."

I saw Abigail take him from Deborah, who knelt before me and massaged my stomach. "I must do this to help you deliver the afterbirth," she explained, as I winced with the pain. "We must be sure to get all of it out of you, or you can become very sick and die."

I closed my eyes and gritted my teeth. She stopped and I glanced up to see Deborah had taken our babe and was wiping him with salt. Feeling another contraction, I squeezed my eyes shut and took small breaths.

As the pain continued, Deborah's voice said, "Here."

I glanced up as she put the swaddled babe on my lap and then helped me put him to my breast.

"His suckling will help your contractions to increase, so you'll deliver the afterbirth sooner," she told me matter-of-factly.

Still sitting on the stool, I was amazed at the strength of his suckling mouth, which I could feel to my curling toes. Deborah was right, within a few minutes of his nursing, my afterbirth had been delivered. But the contractions didn't stop, although they weren't as painful.

"Now, drink this." Abigail held up the cup for me to drink some sweet wine as the baby continued to nurse. The wine tasted sweeter than I'd ever known it to taste, and helped to wet my dry mouth. "I'll go out and tell Chilion to send a servant to give David the news you've given birth to his son, and although he's early, we pray he'll live."

I nodded, somehow knowing her words didn't sound quite right, but I was too exhausted to understand why

"Come, lady, you must rest now," Deborah said, "I'll help you to our lady's bed, as she wishes you to stay with her for a few days."

She put a hand under my arm and helped me up. However, my legs immediately crumpled under me. Instinctively, I held more tightly to the babe in my arms. Naomi quickly took my other arm and between Deborah and Naomi, I was able to make my way to Abigail's bed. There they helped me lie down on the extra cloths. As I slipped into welcome sleep, I reached out to feel my babe next to me. He wasn't there.

* * *

The angry cry of a baby awoke me. I opened my eyes to see Abigail looking down at me with her fully dimpled smile. I felt incredibly well for only having a few hours sleep after such a strenuous birth. I decided it must be a result of my joy.

"I think he has both his father and his mother's voices," she congratulated, "he's sure to be another musician, like my Kileab."

"As you're so often right, I won't argue with you," I said with a grin as I carefully sat up. She handed the babe to me, and I put him to my breast. I grimaced as he latched on with painful vigor.

"David was proud and delighted by the news," Abigail told me. "And sent you back his congratulations and blessings. He was thankful to hear all was well with you both, and plans to visit you soon."

Looking up at her, I caught the shadowed darkness in her

eyes before they cleared as she smiled down upon me. "Because our son was late, he'd only be considered seven weeks early," I said. "I've not been around many newborns, but he's not large, is he? However, I doubt he's as small as I'd think an early babe would be. How far have the rumors flown?"

"Our maidservants, of course, have said nothing," she assured me. "In fact, Deborah lied well, announcing the babe was early, and not very big, and we wouldn't know if he'd live or die for another few days."

I stared at her, as my heart quickened with foreboding. "Couldn't she have said we were sure the Lord would intervene to bless him with health soon?" I cried, disturbing the babe who broke off nursing to cry his distress. I helped reattach him.

"Little one, Abijah asked to see you and the babe. To protect you and him, I told her she must wait, and when others asked, we said the same thing. You must understand, living so close, all the women have been privy to your labor, and heard the child's loud wails," she tried to explain. "If they view the babe now, they'd know for a certainty he's full-term. But Deborah tells me new babes always lose weight their first days of life, so it's best we wait a few days before we dare let anyone but Anna see him."

"And you really believe by saying this we're preventing more rumors about his early birth from flying through the court?" I asked in disbelief.

She sighed deeply. "I know the rumors about your early birth, and the consequent doubts about the time of his conception, will not be stopped by Deborah's lie. But, hopefully, some will pause and question the more deadly gossip that's sure to spread."

"Jezebel's friends are probably saying even now that she was banished for telling the truth and not lies about me and David." Sadness flowed through me. I put my son to my shoulder to burp him as I'd learned to do with Leah.

"Your son burps with the same enthusiasm as his father," Abigail said with a grin.

I put him to my other breast and smiled my joy at her. "Oh,

Abigail, now that I'm holding my son in my arms, the child I prayed for day and night for years, I find myself immune to the gossip. Isn't it amazing how during my whole pregnancy, God was at work not only to knit our son together in my womb, but to lovingly unravel the chains of bitterness, anger and unforgiveness that bound me?

"I'm sorry the sins David tried so hard to cover-up are now being revealed by the early birth of our son. But I can't be sorry for the innocent child who was birthed as a result of those sins." I tenderly brushed the soft tendrils of dark hair from his cheek, before I glanced back at her. "I know you must have experienced this with Kileab, but as soon as Deborah placed him in my arms, love filled me so completely, it was as if I'd never loved before. Truly, it's as if this love has created a shield around me and our son, and no fear of rumors or gossip can penetrate it."

Abigail stared down at me in silence. The suckling noises of my son filled the room, and I watched her smile at the babe with loving wonder. Deep contentment and peace filled me.

"You've truly forgiven David, haven't you." It was a statement, and I heard the awe in her voice.

"Yes, I believe I have," I said, nodding. I drew the babe from my breast to put him on my shoulder and pat his back. "When I saw David two months ago, I was shocked at how sick he was, and knew he was suffering both physically and spiritually. Abigail, you know how I wished and prayed for his suffering, and, at first, I wanted him dead." I stopped as I again remembered the sick and grieving man I'd last seen. "However, when I saw how he was truly suffering, I found no pleasure or satisfaction in it, and began to pray for his healing."

"Which hasn't happened yet, and I'm not sure when or if it will," she murmured.

As I continued to pat his back, I caught a glimpse of the shadow which dimmed her blue eyes. "What else aren't you telling me?"

"When did you get to know me so well?" she demanded with

mock displeasure.

I smiled. "You and Mama are very much alike, which clearly gave me years of practice to know you better. Abigail, please, what else is rumored?"

"No, it's about your mother. She sent me a scroll telling me Ahithophel came by when he'd learned about your early delivery."

I closed my eyes against the dizziness that assailed me.

"Bathsheba, you've grown so pale, what can I do to help?"

"Please, bring me some sweet wine," I said, even as I clutched my son more closely to me. Oh Grandfather, have you put together the myriad strands of my hasty marriage to weave together the whole piece? Do you remember how sick I was even before the news of Uriah's death?

Returning with the goblet, she handed it to me and I sipped it until I felt the blood begin to stir again within me.

"This morning, as soon as the news of your son's birth was announced, he stormed into her home and demanded to know if you were pregnant with David's babe before you wed. If this was why she'd tried to talk Uriah into coming home when he'd come back to Jerusalem."

"What did Mama tell him?"

"She didn't write anymore, but I gave Chilion the other scroll she wrote asking David for his permission to come and see her grandchild, and see you as well."

"What has David answered?" I cried, startling the babe into a wail. My arms trembled as I placed him on my shoulder and gently patted him. Soon he grew limp and I knew he slept. I gently lay him down on the bed next to me, feeling too weak to hold him.

"Bathsheba, I believe she just arrived in my rooms. Shall I go and get her?" She looked down upon the child. "As the babe sleeps, let Naomi care for him while we talk."

I could only nod. Abigail carefully picked him up and handed him to Naomi, who stood near. I knew Mama would hold him a moment before she came to me. She must be anxious to meet the child she'd once cursed, but then blessed because I'd begged her to be thankful for his unexpected but precious life. Would she now curse him again because of Grandfather?

Chapter 39

Mama rushed into the room, sat on the bed and gently hugged me. "My dear Bathsheba, you're now a blessed mother of a son," she declared with pride.

"Oh Mama, I'm so glad you're happy for me, even after having to face Grandfather and his anger again." I hugged her tightly. "I feared he might put all the pieces together."

She pressed a kiss to my forehead before she pulled away from me and stood up. "Daughter, I've told you many times, I've lived with his rejection since we first met, except for the last few months. That he's angry again isn't a hardship for me, although I'm concerned for you," she said with a tender smile. "What's most important now is you're well and have a beautiful son who looks much like you did as a babe."

"Mama, thank you, but you must tell me about your talk with Grandfather."

"Yes," Abigail agreed, walking into the room. "I want to hear, too."

"It was as I wrote you, he came to me this morning, breathing curses against David and telling me he remembered your unusual sadness, which became a lingering illness," she said, her voice low and intense. "Then, he recalled how David called Uriah to Jerusalem to report on the war, and his apparent displeasure when Uriah refused to go home. Next he noted how I'd gone against all I knew as the wife of a warrior to come to the palace to beg Uriah to come to you. Suddenly it all made sense to him." She looked at me, her dark eyes bright with tears. "He knows now how Joab must have been ordered by David to put Uriah close to the gate to assure his death."

"I feared when I delivered our babe early, it would be Grandfather who'd have the wisdom to put it all together," I said. "Yet, I knew I wasn't to tell him."

"I know, dear one. I tried to tell him he was wrong," Mama said with quiet dignity. "For I feared what he might do. . . ."

"What will Grandfather do?" I asked, anxious for all of us, but especially him. I'd seen David banish Jezebel, and have Uriah killed. I knew he could have Grandfather killed as well, if my irate relative didn't show the wisdom he was known for at court. Surely, he'd keep his tongue and say nothing which might be construed as treason?

Mama shrugged. "I tried to reason with him, making him see the danger not only to himself, but to all of us if he chose to confront David. He promised me he wouldn't challenge our king, but bide his time. What 'biding his time' means, I don't know. But, I think he finally saw the wisdom of my appeals for him to accept the way God broke your curse, and gave you a child. His great-grandson is the son of the king of Israel. And he's heard from David's own lips how he honors you. I also told him that you've forgiven David, as have I, and it would be wise for him to do so, too."

She slumped down into the chair by my bed. "However, we both know your grandfather, and how his nature has always been to hold grudges. So, God alone knows what he might eventually do to wreak his own kind of revenge, and how it might affect our lives when he does."

"I can't worry about that right now," I replied, my exhaustion pulling at me.

"Dear one, you're weary from your labor. Forgive me for

adding to your fatigue." She suddenly smiled with renewed joy. "I'll go and hold my grandson while you rest. God has given us the joy of new life this day, and however he came to us, we must celebrate his birth."

She kissed me again, and I carefully settled myself so I might sleep. But as much as I didn't want to think about Grandfather, I was haunted by his wrathful face.

* * *

When I awoke from my nap, Mama was standing by my bed holding my son with an exquisite smile of pleasure on her face.

"I hadn't realized how much these old arms longed to hold my grandchild until I held him," she said. "I've been told by other women how being a grandmother was one of the sweetest joys of life, and now I know they're right. However, although grandmothers can do many things for their grandchildren, we can't nurse them." Waiting while I sat up, she carefully handed him to me. "I don't think I've ever seen you so content, dear one."

I looked up and smiled at her. "That's because I have never been so content before, Mama," I agreed. "I know I'm the innocent victim of David's transgressions. Yet, others are holding me as responsible as he for his actions, and some hate me for them. But I can only love and rejoice in this child, even though his birth revealed the probable cause of Uriah's death, and David's rushed marriage to his widow."

"Abigail told me David hasn't been well for months," she said, "and she believes it's been his guilt that has made him ill."

"I remember you telling me there would be a time David would avoid me because I'd remind him of his sin. You were right."

Sadness filled her eyes. "Some things you'd rather not be right about."

"Will you stay here with us? I'm sure others in the neighborhood must have confronted you with their suspicions as well."

"Yes, they have. Even though the king announced the baby was premature, there have been others who don't believe him," Mama said. "Ah, daughter, Lilith was the hardest one to face, for her grief over Barak has been devastating. Yet, incredibly, she didn't blame you, but our king. She said she knew how much you loved Uriah, for hadn't she seen you two together for years? Thus, she reasoned, if you became pregnant with David's child, it would only be because he'd called you to him. And what can a woman do, married or not, faced by a king's command?"

Tears slid from my eyes, and I caught them with a finger before they splashed upon my suckling child. "Ah, Mama, I'm humbled by her faith in me, and her perception of the truth."

"Of course, Mara—"

"Please, I know how she must be proclaiming my complicity with the king to all."

"So, I'm in the midst of a war, with some defending you and others condemning you. Abigail has invited Rachel and me to stay in your rooms while you remain in hers, and visit you during the day. I've decided this is a wise plan and I'll do it. I'd rather not have to face your grandfather's wrath again."

* * *

It was very late at night when I woke up to our son crying next to me on the bed. Gently, I lifted him. Feeling how wet he was, I was just moving to get out of bed when Naomi was there to take him.

"Here, lady, let me change his cloths and bring him back to you."

"Thank you, Naomi."

As she took care of the babe, I painfully took care of my own needs. As I slipped back into the bed, I thought about Mama's visit. Grandfather had cursed David and our child, but he'd also sworn he wouldn't risk the lives of us all by confronting David. For this grace I was thankful.

Naomi brought a wailing babe to me, but I noticed immediately it wasn't the strong, lusty cry he'd had during the day and early evening. When she put him in my arms, I felt the unusual heat of him and fear gripped me with fierce tenacity.

"Naomi, did he seem warm to you?"

"Yes, lady, do you want me to wake up Deborah? She's asleep in the next room."

"Yes. And please call Abigail, too," I said.

"My lady, the king called Lady Abigail to him only moments ago. She's not here."

"Go and awaken Deborah," I ordered her.

She bowed and left me. I put my babe to my breast, but he didn't latch on and suckle with the vigor he'd shown earlier. As I stroked his forehead and hair while he nursed, the heat of his forehead heightened my fear.

Too worried over my son to think about why David would call Abigail to him so late into the night, I watched as our son nursed, then pulled his head back to cry, and then latched on again. My heart broke as I watched him, for I knew he must be in pain.

"Lady Bathsheba, Naomi says the babe is fevered," Deborah said, kneeling next to the bed.

I looked at Deborah, and could see her eyes held deep concern. "Yes, and he's not nursing like he did earlier today."

Reaching out, she put two fingers to my son's forehead. "Yes, he's feverish."

"What do we do?" I cried.

"For one so young, as for those who are older, we try to cool them, and pray he eats and sleeps and the Lord God delivers him to health, even as he did for you."

"He acts as if it hurts to swallow," I whispered. "He keeps pulling away, then latching on for a moment, and then pulling away again."

Deborah watched him before she closed her eyes and bowed her head. I stared at her bowed head, and dread squeezed my heart with tight bands of iron. My babe's pitiful wail brought my attention back to him. Where was the strong voice he'd been born with? How could it disappear so quickly? He wasn't even a full day old! I must sing to him. That'll soothe him, and help him rid himself of this fever. Even in the womb he enjoyed my songs.

> "Hear a just cause, O Lord; attend to my cry;
>   give ear to my prayer from lips free of deceit.
> From you let my vindication come;
>   let your eyes see the right.
> If you try my heart, if you visit me by night,
>   if you test me, you will find no wickedness in me;
> my mouth does not transgress.
>   As for what others do, by the word of your lips
> I have avoided the ways of the violent.
>   My steps have held fast to your paths;
> my feet have not slipped.
>   I call upon you, for you will answer me, O God;
> incline your ear to me, hear my words.
>   Wondrously show your steadfast love,
> O savior of those who seek refuge
>   from their adversaries at your right hand...."

"He's asleep, lady," Deborah whispered beside me. "Would you like me to put him—"

"No, I want to hold him."

"He'd remain cooler if you put him down," she said quietly.

Unreasoning anger filled me. I wanted to scream at her, but stopped myself, for it would wake my child. "I will hold him," I snapped.

She bowed, touching her head to the floor. Suddenly I was aware of the power I had to demand her life if she displeased me. The thought staggered me as I recognized her alarm in that one act of obeisance. Hadn't I done the same thing with David? *Lord, I don't want this dear woman to fear me.*

"Rest, Deborah. I'll call if I need you."

"As you wish, lady."

I watched her struggle to stand, straighten her small body, and slowly walk away before I stared down at our son. Fervently, I prayed for our son's healing.

* * *

By morning, my son's fever hadn't abated, and my panic grew. I held him as he slept, sang to him, nursed him and changed him. I didn't want anyone to touch him but me, not my mother, not Abigail, nor Deborah. I was jealous of any hands upon him but mine. If he were to die. . . no, I couldn't allow my mind to think it. I just wanted to enjoy every minute of my child's precious new life.

I dozed on the bed with him, my arms propped up by pillows, when I caught the subtle scent of Abigail's unique flower perfume. I slowly opened my eyes. Surely that haggard looking woman was not my. . . "Abigail?" I whispered.

She stumbled across the floor, slid down and knelt next to the bed. Her head rested near my lap, and she silently wept, gulping air like it was water to a thirsty man. She'd been with David. Called to him in the darkest hours of the night. Why was she so distressed?

"Has David died?" I cried in disbelief.

She shook her head, as the tears continued to flow down her face like liquid grief. With obvious effort, she pulled herself up and wiped her eyes with one of the cloths I had near for the babe. She saw the chair, pulled it next to the bed, and sat down. "Bathsheba, God's prophet, Nathan, came to David yesterday afternoon. He told him a story about a rich man with many flocks of sheep and a poor man with only one precious ewe lamb. A lamb that he loved so much, he treated it like one of his own daughters."

I stared at her, trying to understand why a prophet of God would tell David such a story. "Yes? Was there more?"

She nodded. "Nathan told David that when a traveler came to the rich man, he didn't want to prepare one of his own sheep to feed the visitor, so he took the poor man's lamb, slaughtered it, and fed it to his guest." Her voice trembled so strongly she stopped.

"Abigail?" I whispered.

She forced herself to breath slowly. "Hearing the story, David became irate and told Nathan the man deserved to die, for doing such an odious thing and showing no pity, but as the law didn't prescribe death, the rich man must therefore pay the lawful price, and restore the lamb fourfold to the poor man."

As I sat listening and held my babe, I shivered with an inner recognition. Yet, I knew I hadn't heard this story before.

"Bathsheba, when David pronounced his judgment on the rich man, Nathan looked him straight in the eye and proclaimed to him, 'You are the man!'"

I jerked up, startling my poor babe, who began to cry weakly. With a trembling hand, I gave him my breast, and gently stroked his fevered brow as he suckled. "Yes," I whispered, "he is that rich man, isn't he? Did you know, Abigail, Uriah used to call me his 'lamb?' God knew that, didn't he? Which is why Nathan used the image of a ewe lamb." I moaned softly. "And yet, it was Uriah who was slaughtered."

"Yes, little one, and after Nathan told David all the ways God blessed him through the years, giving him his kingdom, and more, he clearly exposed the full extent of David's sin of despising the Lord and His word by killing Uriah with the sword of the Ammonites and taking you to wife," she gulped down a sob. "Nathan then pronounced God's judgment on David, telling him that the sword would never leave his family, and what he did in secret, would be done to him by someone in his own house, who'd take his wives in plain view of his people."

Gently, I wiped the drop of milk from the corner of my babe's open mouth and covered my breast. He'd fallen asleep again as the fever raged in his tiny body. I looked across at Abigail, who was staring at me, as if waiting for my response.

"The Lord has vindicated me, and yet, I feel no joy, no relief, truly, I feel nothing."

"Bathsheba, with this declaration, David humbly confessed his sin against his God, and Nathan proclaimed the Lord forgave him, and he'd not die for his sins. But the Lord pronounced one more judgment against David, a judgment he is pleading with God to relent from with fasting and prayer." Abigail jumped out of the chair, and again knelt by me. "Dear one, the Lord proclaimed that because of how David's sin gave cause for God's enemies to utterly scorn him, David's child will die."

"Nooooo—" I wailed.

With my son held tightly in my arms, I scrambled off the bed and ran toward the door. I had to protect his innocent life. He was not only David's child, but mine! Where could I go? "Take me to Carmel," I shouted. "I'll live with him far away from David's court. Within months we'll be forgotten. It will be as if we never lived," I sobbed. "Surely that will be enough to appease our God."

Abigail stood up and slowly walked toward me, her arms outstretched. My babe's weak, mewling cry rent my heart. "Our God is a God of mercy, not vengeance," I cried out. "Oh God, you can't take my child! Please God, no! If you must take someone, take *me*! Not my babe, not my son. . . Abigail, help me!"

I sank to my knees, wanting only to die. "Let my son live, Lord, he's innocent of everything. Take me. Please, take me." I clutched my son's hot, fevered body to my breast.

Abigail's arms came from behind me and surrounded my waist. "Dear one, you're bleeding, let me take the babe."

"Yes, let me bleed to death," I agreed, pulling away from her. "Don't, Lord, don't let my son dry up with fever like a green shoot in the desert. Let him live!

"Abigail, I know his name!" I cried, seeing it blaze across my mind. "He's my Ben-Oni! My 'son of labor and sorrow.' Like Jacob, David can rename him Benjamin, the 'son of his right hand.'" I dragged myself upright and held my son up to God in my hands. "Let me die, Lord, like Jacob's Rachel died, and as you let her son live, let my son live as well!" Hysterical laughter poured out of me until I choked on it.

"Jonathan was of the tribe of Benjamin," I sang, "it's said David loved him better than anyone. David will honor Jonathan's memory, yes, he'll call him Benjamin. I'll call him Ben-Oni until I die." My arms grew weak, I lowered him to my breast. Black spots flew into my vision. I swayed.

Abigail screamed, "Deborah, help me catch them!"

Chapter 40

Was that David's voice singing? No, it couldn't be. Where was I? How long had I been sleeping? I opened my eyes. They blurred and slowly focused on the man sitting beside my bed. He was holding my son and singing to him. It was David. He looked terrible, even worse than when I'd last seen him. His beard and hair were in wild disarray and full of ashes... I gasped, suddenly remembering. I struggled to sit up, but dizziness felled me. I sank back against a pillow, groaning.

"Give me my son," I demanded. I wanted to snatch him out of David's deadly embrace, but didn't have the strength.

"He's my beloved son, with beautiful black hair like his mother," he praised.

"He's dying for your sins," I snarled. "You should be the one to die, not him." I lifted my trembling arms and reached for my babe.

"Bathsheba, please forgive me," he implored.

He slowly stood and gently placed Ben-Oni in my arms, I clasped him to my chest. His hot, sweating body felt boneless in my arms.

"Besides our God, I've sinned most against you," David said.

I'd waited so long to hear those words, and never thought

I'd hear them. I had even told myself I'd forgiven him without them. I knew now I hadn't. "Your sinful arrogance and lust took my honor, and your fear killed my husband. And now, the only true gift I believed you'd given me, the life of my son, is forfeit to God to save your own. The child I never expected to carry and birth, the son I love with every fiber of my being."

I looked down at Ben-Oni. Even as he slept, I saw how the fever was slowly leeching his fragile life from me. "Abigail told me you've been fasting and praying for the life of. . . our son, Ben-Oni," I murmured, breaking the laden silence.

"She's also the one who told me I must come and claim my son and try and comfort you," he admitted. "I wanted to come to you, Bathsheba, when you first had the babe, but I was so weighed down with guilt."

His confession astonished me "And is it gone now, my king?" I asked scornfully.

"Bathsheba, I don't know why God has chosen to take the child and not me," he said, falling to his knees by the bed. "Truly, for what I did to Uriah and to you, I deserve to die. Not just because God and his law demand it, but because as king, I'd demand it of my own subject." He stopped, took a deep breath, and slowly released it. Hesitantly, he reached out and put a calloused finger to the heat-flushed cheek of our son and lightly stroked him.

"For months now, I've lived with the burden of my sins." He gazed at me, his eyes full of sorrow. "When I asked you to come and sing for me, I hoped your presence and gift of music might somehow lift the heaviness of God's convicting hand from me."

His finger left our son to catch a tear silently falling down my cheek. He brought it to his lips and kissed it. "Your generosity of spirit toward me was like an arrow to my hardened heart, and when you placed my hand on your belly so I might feel our 'dancing son' whom you proclaimed would be another worshiper of our God. . . ." Choking up, he stopped.

I watched in silence as he worked to find his voice again,

tears streaking his pale, grief-ravaged face. "Please, beloved, believe me when I tell you I'd gladly give my life for the life of our son, and I've pleaded with our Lord to do this. He's the innocent one."

"Yes," I whispered, "he is."

"But as I live, I haven't given up hope that our loving God might relent and grant us our child's life, too." His voice rang with a note of hope I didn't have. He leaned down and kissed Ben-Oni on his forehead. "You're our beloved Ben-Oni," he declared with quiet force.

He moved his head and softly kissed my lips. "You're my honored and beloved wife." He stood up and bowed to me. "I'll leave you now to return to my prayers and fasting. Send word through Abigail if there's any change."

I watched him walk slowly toward the door, noting his torn garment, and the dirt that clung to him. Our babe began to cry in my arms, as if bewailing his father's departure. I kissed him and put him to my breast, praying he'd nurse vigorously again, but having no hope he would. He didn't.

I looked up to see David standing in front of the closed door, his bent body shaking. . . with silent weeping? Did I really tell him I wanted him dead and our son alive? Yes. With a clarity that staggered me, the Lord showed me how my unwillingness to forgive David was that closed door. If I was ever to heal and love again, I needed to forgive David – and speak the words. What was holding me back? Could David have been more repentant? No.

"David, husband," I rasped.

He turned slowly, like an old man expecting a death blow. I cried out at the stark anguish etched in every rugged line of his grief-stricken face, and the hopeless bent to his shoulders.

"I told myself I forgave you months ago, for your sins against me and Uriah, but I didn't," I confessed. "For every time we came together, I'd take offense by something you said or did, and I'd embrace my right to my anger and unforgiveness."

I looked down and gently stroked Ben-Oni's cheek. "Then I saw you sick and in agony when you called me to sing for you, and I remembered how I'd prayed you'd suffer the way I had. Yet, when I saw how you suffered, I grieved, and asked our Lord to heal you."

"I felt those prayers in your music, and the way you chose to lie with me that night."

I glanced up to see the light of hope brighten his eyes. "I'm glad. But I must admit when Abigail told me of Nathan's judgment against our innocent babe, like a rain of arrows to my heart, all the old anger and bitterness struck." I tried to catch a breath, but caught a hiccupping sob instead.

David rushed to me, and knelt by the bed. "Beloved, please, don't cry."

"Husband, I forgive you," I cried. Ben-Oni immediately joined me. "I forgive you."

Trembling, David hugged us both, with arms suddenly strong and comforting. "May the Lord God bless you, my wife, and our son."

"And you, my husband." I kissed his gaunt, wet cheek. The latched door of my heart swung open, admitting forgiveness, but also a soul-deep grief.

* * *

On the seventh day, my precious son's life burned out. I sat on the bed, my eyes closed as I held him, quietly singing. When I realized his tiny, shriveled body was cooling in my arms, my eyes snapped open. It wasn't renewed life that cooled his fevered form, but death. Our son was dead.

My anguished wail caused Mama and Abigail to jump out of their chairs and move to my side. Their eyes filled with tears when they saw me clutching my lifeless child to my breast.

"It is finished," Abigail whispered. "I'll send word to David that our God did not relent." She turned and shuffled toward the door.

"Oh, my poor, sweet daughter," Mama lamented. She sat on

the bed, wrapped her arms around both of us, and her grievous cry mixed with my agonized keening.

*   *   *

Although all of David's women knew of the "premature" birth of our son, and his death days afterwards, only Abijah and Rebekah showed any sympathy toward me. Abijah brought me the bread of mourning to our rooms, and Rebekah the cup of consolation. For their gifts of mercy, Abigail showed them Ben-Oni's tiny, wrapped body. I didn't care if they believed the rumors or not, I only cared they'd valued our friendship enough to share in my grief. I blessed them for it.

The day after Ben-Oni's death, all the court, including David's other wives and concubines, participated in the funeral procession. I found no comfort, for I knew that all but two of them were there at the command of the king. Not out of any real sense of grief or desire to mourn with us. And although most joined in our cries of grief, it was only my own anguished voice I heard.

As we walked, I saw my grandfather was among the men who followed David ahead of us. He strolled beside Absalom, whose face appeared quietly pleased with whatever Grandfather was saying to him. Obviously they weren't talking about my loss. Did Grandfather have no grief over his great-grandson's death? No desire to grieve with his granddaughter? Apparently not.

Our son would be buried uncircumcised and unnamed on the day when, if he'd lived, he would have been circumcised and named. Others might believe, because of this, he wasn't a true Israelite, but I knew the truth. He belonged fully to God now, and his name was Ben-Oni. Hadn't I carried him for nine months beneath my heart? Experiencing the wonder of God weaving him within me, and dancing to my singing? Didn't I hold him for seven days, nursing him at my breasts? God gave him life, as surely as he took it. Blessed be the name of the Lord.

Because I was still ritually unclean, I didn't follow the

others to David's family tomb, but stood at a distance, watching. Abiathar took our death-wrapped child and walked him into the family's tomb. I stood and watched David. He was dressed now in his kingly attire and not the rent clothing he'd worn for the seven days of our child's life. He had changed. The death of our son had transformed him. He was no longer the arrogant king-husband I'd experienced so often in the last months. Instead, he appeared to be tangibly cloaked in regal humility.

As tears filled my eyes, I wondered if this could be our son's gift to him. . . to return to David the mantle of humility and grace I knew he'd worn years before. For I not only recalled the stories of him I'd heard from Abigail, Uriah and my parents; but I remembered that man, too.

Abiathar walked out of the tomb empty-handed, and my arms ached with the loss of my son's precious weight. With renewed grief, I cried out my loss. My mother and some of the other women began to weep with me. I heard my husband's loud groans as they rose antiphonally to our cries.

David's slow gait led us away from the tomb and back to the palace. Leaving the rest of the mourners in the palace courtyard, he continued to walk before me until we reached the door to the women's quarters. There he stopped, kissed my forehead and left. Mama and Abigail appeared pleased by his unusual consideration. I was too grief-stricken to feel anything.

Chilion opened the door to us and bowed as we entered. I didn't note the entrance of the other women, but went directly to my own rooms. I couldn't return to Abigail's, they held all the painful memories of my son I could not bear right now.

* * *

Two weeks after Ben-Oni's death, Mama and Rachel had left to return home. I was so deep into my grief, I really didn't miss them.

"You should keep those for your next child," Abigail said, walking into my bedchamber.

I was sorting through some of the baby things I'd used with

Ben-Oni. I looked up at her and shook my head. "No."

"You never told either your mother or me about your time with David," she reminded me. She sat on a pillow on the floor and faced me. "Do you want to talk about it?"

"You're the one who called David to me, so I was sure he must have shared with you what happened between us," I replied. I was surprised, yet grateful David had kept those intimate and cherished moments to himself.

"I sent for him because he'd yet to claim his son or praise you for the birth of him, like every new father must do. I only reminded him of his duty."

"Even knowing all Nathan prophesied to him from the Lord, you encouraged him to come?" I asked, suddenly remembering that terrible detail.

"Especially after hearing Nathan's prophecies," she said. "Bathsheba, David sinned grievously against our God, Uriah, you and his people. The Lord chose to save his life, although God alone knows how the sword will come against his family, and how deep the grief will be when it comes. Your son is dead. My son died of a fever, as well. Although I was given eighteen years with him, I still grieve his death. And why I was never given more children, I don't know." She gave me a wistful smile. "But I've learned to trust God with my questions. And I know you, who have become the daughter of my heart, will have more sons."

I laughed. I couldn't help it. She spoke with such absurd confidence. And once I began to laugh, I couldn't stop, until my laughter became weeping, and Abigail was holding me tightly against her.

"Why didn't David's long days of prayer and fasting change God's heart?"

With a gentle push, I was out of her arms and she was staring intently into my tearful eyes. "Little one, I've been praying," she said, as if it was not something she often did. "And although I don't claim to speak for God as Nathan does, one of the truths that came to me is the fact Ben-Oni was your first-born son. Yet, because he was conceived outside of your marriage to David, he was illegitimate. Bathsheba, he could never have ascended to David's throne."

I couldn't stop a bark of laughter. "Abigail, you know better than I how Amnon stands even now as David's heir. And there are more sons who are alive and very well who would inherit if Amnon died," I reasoned. "Truly, it's hardly likely a son of mine would inherit David's throne." I paced the room, unsettled by her words.

"Have you forgiven David for Ben-Oni's death?"

I stopped in front of her and gave her a bittersweet smile. "Oh Abigail, the Lord showed me if I could forgive David for his rape of me and murder of Uriah, how could I not also forgive him for the death of our son?

"I also witnessed how he fasted and prayed for the life of Ben-Oni," I said. "And I saw David hold and bless our son, and even sing over him, the son whose premature birth revealed his sins to all. Yet, I swear to you, he loved our son, perhaps not as much as I, who carried him so close to my heart for all those months, but he called him his 'beloved son.' And I know David truly would have given his life for him, even as I would have, if God had allowed us our substitutions. But the Lord did not."

"So, you have truly forgiven David from your heart?"

"Yes, I've forgiven him with all my heart, and David knows this."

"Have you thought if God had taken one of you, God couldn't raise up more sons from the two of you?"

"No, dear Abigail," I said with a sad smile, "it's you who reminds me of this."

"Bathsheba, I had a dream the other night I must share with you. Again, I don't claim to have dreams or words from God like the Prophet Nathan, or our ancestor, Joseph," she said, as if she had to make sure I understood she was making no claims as a prophet. "But when I have such vivid dreams and remember them, I believe they're important.

"In my dream you're in a fairly large courtyard playing with a small boy, perhaps of two years. He's a strong, sturdy child, with brown hair mixed with the burnished copper of David's. The two of you are stacking stones when David strides into the courtyard carrying a thick stick. David gives the stick to the child, who playfully swings it around. Laughing, David lifts the boy with his stick, and puts him on his shoulders. Reaching out to you, David grasps your hand with his, and with the child on his shoulders, the three of you leave the courtyard. You walked toward a large building in the distance, which I somehow knew to be a house of worship, although I've never seen its like before."

I was trembling when she finished, although I couldn't explain why, other than the fact her words seemed to resonate with truth within me. "What do you think it means?"

She shrugged her shoulders and gave me a mysterious smile. "As I said, I'm not a dreamer like Joseph, but I believe the thick stick may symbolize a scepter, and David putting him atop his shoulders, well it could mean he'll rule after him."

"And the large building which you knew to be for worship?"

"I don't think you knew this, but years ago, after David's palace was completed here in Jerusalem, he wanted to build a house for the name of his God. However, through Nathan, the Lord told David how he was going to build David's hereditary house and bless him, but also encouraged him with the promise a house for his God would be constructed, but it would be accomplished by David's son, and not David."

I stared at her as my whole body shook.

"Truthfully, little one, when I first heard the amazing gift of worship God gave you, and saw how well it complimented David's own gifts at your wedding banquet... well, I've wondered if the two of you wouldn't produce the child who'd honor our God in this way. Would it not be remarkably like our God of redemption to bless David and you with a son, who not only inherited your gifts of music, but your hearts for God, and used him to build our Lord's house of worship?"

With a cry, I wrapped my arms around Abigail and hugged her with all my strength. In sudden insight, I pulled back so I could see her face. "Was this once a dream you had for Kileab, dearest Abigail? To see him be the son of David who'd build God's house for him?"

She nodded and began to weep loudly. Soon, we were both weeping.

Chapter 41

Of David's women, all but Abijah and Rebekah shunned me. I grieved this, but also understood it, as Abigail told me not only did they blame me for Jezebel's banishment, but also for the fact David no longer called Jezebel's friends to him.

I sat in the chair in my room and tried to play something other than a lament on my lyre. Abigail opened my door and strode into the room before Naomi could greet her.

"I've talked with David," she announced. "We both agreed you can't thrive here amidst all these bitter women. So, as it would be easier for David to move one woman than all, he's bought you a house and you'll move into it tomorrow."

I stared at her with open-mouthed wonder. "I'm moving. . . tomorrow?"

"Yes, so you need to begin supervising Naomi in your packing, and you should probably begin right now."

As what she said slowly penetrated my grieving mind, a smile of deep joy moved across my face. Jumping up from the chair, I hugged her. "Thank you, I hadn't even considered this. I didn't know it was possible! Oh, you're amazing."

"Yes, I know," she said with one of her obnoxious grins. "But you do realize I'll miss you terribly, and you me?"

"Yes." Her grin disappeared and she enfolded me in a breath-robbing hug.

*   *   *

My new home was an easy walk up the road from the palace and to the west of it. It was larger than the one I'd shared with Uriah, with a good sized courtyard blessed with a large palm tree, as well as a pomegranate tree and flowering bushes. After living in my two small rooms, and even Abigail's four larger rooms in the women's quarters, it felt blessedly spacious.

Because I was still in the midst of completing my thirty-three days of ritual purification after Ben-Oni's birth, I wasn't able to join the women at the tent of meeting each day. It grieved me I couldn't attend worship, for I knew my sorrow would be eased by being able to be there. However, the second day in my new home I discovered that because of our proximity to the tent of meeting, if I climbed the ladder to our roof, I could sit and hear the music as it was carried on a blessed breeze, directly to me. For this grace, I thanked my God.

*   *   *

Spring was perfuming the air with the glorious fragrance of blossoming life, when I completed the days of my purification with the required sacrifices at the tabernacle in Gibeon. Within a day of completing this ritual, I received a messenger from my kingly husband telling me to expect his visit the next morning after worship.

Anticipation of David's arrival seemed to make my hands awkward, as I tried to dress and prepare. Naomi smiled at me with gentle understanding as she helped me with my hair and cosmetics.

"You look beautiful, my lady." Naomi smiled her approval.

I smoothed down the new tunic I wore. It was blue, with embroidery at the neck and sleeves that both Naomi and I had worked on this last week. "I feel like a new bride."

She looked intently into my eyes, which she'd never done before. "You are a new bride, my lady."

The truth of her words brought a sense of such overwhelming

peace; I took a breath, as if to inhale the sweetness more deeply. Yes, this was the beginning of the marriage I could now welcome and accept, and even find pleasure in. For David had become a man I could honor, respect and love in a way I could not before. Truly, God was merciful in his redeeming power.

A short tap sounded, and before Naomi could reach the courtyard door, the guard opened it and David walked in. He looked very fine in his blue tunic and short robe, and he had his lyre tucked under his arm.

Naomi quickly bowed and scuttled away, leaving us staring at each other. We both smiled at the same time, before I remembered myself and bowed deeply.

"Rise, beloved," he said, sounding anxious. "I've something I want to share with you. Shall we go to your bedchamber?"

"As you wish, my lord," I said, bowing my head and waiting for him to go before me. When he didn't, I looked up to see him signal me to walk before him, so I did. As I turned, I caught his sudden grin, which both shocked and captivated me.

Walking into the room behind me, he directed, "Sit in this chair close to me and let me sing to you. The Lord has graciously restored my gift of music, as well as my health," he told me with joy coloring every word. "I believe this song will speak to your heart, as I wrote it in praise of our God, but also for you."

He sat down in the chair across from my own. With a nod, he took up his lyre and began to play.

"Have mercy on me, O God,
    according to your steadfast love;
according to your abundant mercy
    blot out my transgressions.
Wash me thoroughly from my iniquity
    and cleanse me from my sin.
For I know my transgressions
    and my sin is always before me
Against you, you only have I sinned

and done what is evil in your sight,
    so that you are justified in your sentence
and blameless when you pass judgment. . .
    Purge me with hyssop, and I shall be clean;
wash me and I shall be whiter than snow.
    Let me hear joy and gladness;
let the bones that you have crushed rejoice . . .
    Create in me a pure heart, O God,
and put a new and right spirit within me.
    Do not cast me from your presence,
and do not take your Holy Spirit from me.
    Restore to me the joy of your salvation
and sustain in me a willing spirit.
    Then will I teach transgressors your ways,
and sinners will return to you.
    Deliver me from bloodshed, O God,
O God of my salvation,
    and my tongue will sing aloud of your deliverance. . .
The sacrifice acceptable to God is a broken spirit;
    a broken and contrite heart, O God, you will not despise. . . ."

As the last note hung in the air, I looked at him, tears welling in my eyes. "Abigail and I both saw how you were wasting away," I said. "Abigail was even afraid for your life." I stared at him, noting how healthy he looked, his face ruddy again and no longer pale, his hazel eyes clear and alert. "It's as if you've regained the years taken from you when you were sick all those months, and even after Ben-Oni. . ." I stopped and swallowed "After he died."

"It's as I sang," he explained. "I grieved what I'd done to you, and how I betrayed my good and faithful friend, Uriah, but I refused to admit my sin to myself or my God. The King of Israel could do anything he wanted, take anyone he desired, betray and kill if it was necessary, was he not a great king?" David bowed his head and took a ragged breath. "This king was too proud to admit he'd sinned, and could sin so grievously against his God, his friends and his people." He looked at me, pain filling his eyes.

"Somehow I lost the shepherd boy who knew his job was always to protect his sheep from being killed by wild animals or stolen by thieves. And he didn't recognize himself when he became a wild animal and a thief."

"So, in his mercy, God sent Nathan to help you remember who you are, and repent of who you'd become."

"But not before you, beloved, lost your honor, your husband and your cherished child." He leaned across the space between us and took my hands in his own. "How do I restore to you what I so sinfully took?"

"David, only our God can restore and redeem what was lost to me and to us," I said. "And I rejoice that he has already begun to do this in both our lives."

David lifted my hand and kissed it. "I've prayed our God would show his forgiveness of me by allowing me to comfort you and give you more sons. Beloved, I know how your heart aches with the loss of our babe."

"And I've prayed this same prayer, my husband," I said, discovering a smile among my tears. "Although I wouldn't mind having a daughter, too."

Again, we looked at each other and smiled. I'm not sure if he rose first or I did, but as soon as we both stood, we were in each other's arms. And, incredibly, in his embrace, I felt safe and cherished.

Chapter 42

David left me after two weeks of joyful celebration. When he left, I felt a deep inner assurance he'd given me the blessed seed of a new life. By the end of the third week after he'd returned to the palace, I knew without doubt I was with child.

However, this time I could delight in the news and in giving it to David, personally, and see his joy matched my own as I called him back to me to tell him. After Naomi served us a celebratory meal, we came together with a deep gratitude to God. And in my heart, I believed I carried a son who'd be blessed by God with health and long life.

When Abigail heard our news a few days later, she sent word she'd visit me to give her congratulations as well, with permission from the king, of course. And as Naomi had been sent to tell Mama, I knew she might very well be at my door with Abigail, if not sooner.

In the early afternoon of the following day, Naomi was at our gate to greet Abigail. She strolled into the courtyard and stopped. With a look of awe on her face, she moved in a slow circle.

"Bathsheba," she said, wonder ringing in her voice. "This is the courtyard in my dream. It's here where I saw you playing with your son, and David coming in to put him on his shoulders."

I gazed at her and marveled at her prophetic words. Was I

even now carrying David's heir to his throne? I danced, my arms held high in worship. Abigail danced with me before I fell into her arms and we laughed with all the joy of God's promise.

"As always, your words, my dearest friend, give me great hope and make my heart sing with joy."

"It's a wonder, isn't it, how God works to redeem our deepest sorrows? I've grieved Kileab's death these past years, never dreaming the Lord would bless me with a daughter who was even more gifted in music than my son, and who would bring me new life and great delight."

I hugged her close before I released her and stepped back. "Having you here again, reminds me of how very much I've missed you," I said.

"I've missed you, too," she admitted, kissing my cheeks. "It's not the same without you in our women's quarters. Even in your grief, you were a blessing to me. And Abijah asked if you might return to see her sometime? She and Ibhar miss you, too."

"That is sweet of her, but I don't believe I'll be returning soon to the women's quarters."

"No, I didn't think so." Abigail gave me a wistful smile. "So, how are you feeling?"

I put my hand to my womb and smiled with delight. "I can tell already this pregnancy is different. It's not as if I don't expect to have all the symptoms once again, but I know my grief at Uriah's death intensified and increased them. So, I'm trusting they won't be as pronounced as they were before."

"And you've come to truly love our kingly husband."

I smiled. "Yes, I have."

"I do enjoy being right," she said, with only a touch of pride dripping from her voice. "Didn't I tell you you'd come to love and appreciate David and he you?"

"Indeed, you did," I agreed, bowing to her in acknowledgment of her great wisdom.

She stood and reached a hand to me. "I must go now, and prepare for our Passover. I asked David if we might travel together to stand in the women's court at the tent of meeting in Gibeon during the celebration, and he agreed."

"Thank you. That will make the celebration all the more memorable."

She kissed me. "Be well, little one." Leaning forward, she whispered in my ear, "I look forward to awaiting David's new heir with you, although for now, this is our secret with God."

* * *

The Lord blessed my pregnancy, for although I was often nauseous, I rarely was sick, and even this didn't linger beyond my third month. I felt this was another way God was demonstrating his goodness and mercy in my life.

David delighted me by coming to be with me at least one day each week, and when I was feeling better, and entered my fourth month, he came more, and stayed longer. He also called me to the Palace to join him in special banquets, which pleased me, as well. But when we were alone, we spent much of our time singing and playing our lyres, for one of our greatest joys was to worship together. And the babe would often respond to our singing with kicks and bumps that delighted us both.

Abigail would come to check on me at least once a month, and more often as my pregnancy advanced. It was to her I expressed my fears and doubts about whether I truly would have a healthy son. It wasn't that I didn't have faith, but after losing Ben-Oni, fear still assailed me with tenacious doubts. She always listened to me in great sympathy, understanding my fears, and would hold me. But then she'd assure me that the Lord was growing a strong, healthy son within me, who'd one day grow up to be the king of Israel.

Restoring my faith in God's promise, she'd hand me Kileab's lyre and tell me to play and sing her one of the new songs God had given me. And I would.

* * *

When I was into my ninth month, it was decided Abigail would move into our second bedchamber, and Deborah would join Naomi so they both could be near when I went into labor. As neither Abigail nor I liked to be idle, we wove and embroidered together, as well as spent hours talking about David and his history, the court and the continuing war. But as the weather became colder, and I grew bigger, we often sat in front of a brazier talking. When it wasn't raining, I bundled up to walk around the courtyard, while Abigail stayed close to the warmth of the brazier.

Mama frequently visited as well, and as the days drew near to the time I should deliver, it was Abigail who approached David to get his blessing for Mama to move in with us, too. At the invitation, Mama quickly agreed, and arranged for her male servant, Lilith's son, Abner, to watch the house, and Rachel to stay with Sarai. She brought a basket of her things and moved into Abigail's room. Thus it was when David came to see how I was doing a few days later, he discovered my mother with us, as well.

It warmed and touched my heart when his response to her presence was one of laughter and an affectionate greeting. In fact, soon Mama, David and Abigail were all sharing an anecdote from their lives in Ziklag, with each of them adding separate and delightful details to their story. Listening to them, I was thankful for the legacy of their lives together, which carried over and extended into the blessing God had given us by integrally weaving my life to David's. As I listened, I rubbed the strong, tiny foot within me until it moved away from my rib. This little one seemed to be more of a kicker than a dancer, and my sore ribs testified to his strength.

* * *

The sun rose with glittering light on the day our son was born, and I welcomed it after we'd had two days of cold rain. I was walking in the courtyard, to take advantage of the sunshine, when I felt a sharp pain and a rush of wetness between my legs. Mama, who'd taken to following me everywhere, immediately noticed the puddle that formed at my feet.

"Well, daughter, it seems this child has decided to arrive today, and with your waters breaking so quickly, he'll most likely come faster than his brother did."

"Bathsheba's in labor," Abigail crooned. She walked out of the weaving room, which was also the room where our maidservants slept. "Deborah, we need you."

I doubled over with another contraction. Deborah put her hand lightly to my back. "Your mother's right, lady, when the waters break so soon, the babe usually comes quickly, but if he doesn't, well, we'll trust the Lord means for you not to labor so long for this child."

"I'll send Naomi with a message to David, so he can be praying for you, dear one," Abigail said. She knew I'd be comforted knowing this.

"Thank you."

Although I didn't labor as long for our second son, it was more intense, the contractions beginning long and hard almost from the beginning. By late afternoon Deborah sat me down on the birthing stool, and I commenced again the rhythm of my delivery.

Within minutes and not hours, our son was pushed into Deborah's waiting arms. With an expression of great satisfaction, she held his beautiful, healthy body up for us all to see, and grinned when he loudly expressed his displeasure at coming into this cold, inhospitable world with a loud cry of offense.

"I believe he's bigger than his brother," Mama praised.

"Look at that brown hair, and can you see the copper highlights?" Abigail exclaimed. She looked over at me and smiled her delight.

Mama took the babe from Deborah after she'd cleaned him, and put salt and oil on him before swaddling him.

Abigail received him from Mama and quietly proclaimed, "He's the child I saw, little one, I know it. Although the copper highlights are barely visible now, in two years, I know they'll shine in the sun like I saw them in my dream."

With a soft smile of joy, and eyes full of happy tears, she handed him to me. I took him, kissed his red face and wept as I gently placed him at my breast. Feeling him grab hold and suckle, I ignored the pain and silently thanked God for his amazing goodness in giving David and me a strong, healthy son. I also remembered our beloved Ben-Oni, and thanked God for him as well.

* * *

David didn't wait for the next morning to meet his new son, but arrived the same evening he was born.

I was dozing, our son in my arms, when he strode into our bedchamber. Smelling his distinct perfume, I opened my eyes and smiled at him with all the love in my full heart.

He bowed to me. "Thank you for our son, beloved. May I hold him?"

"Of course," I said, joy dancing through me. I carefully handed him to David, who had knelt beside the bed, to make it easier for me to give him our son.

I watched David as he gazed at our babe, his eyes full of pride and wonder. Soon his son opened his eyes and looked back at his father with first unfocused, then focused eyes. David put a finger against his tiny hand, and he immediately grabbed it tightly. Joy filled his voice, "This son of mine has a strong grip, and he looks like me, doesn't he?"

I smiled at his loving boast. "Yes, he does."

"And as we agreed, we'll call him 'Solomon.' For truly he represents how our God brought his 'peace and wholeness' into our lives after so much pain and bitterness."

"Yes, husband, he is our 'Solomon,'" I agreed. There was something in David's eyes that drew me to ask. "What else did you want to tell me?"

"My love, after news of his birth was proclaimed, Nathan came to me again."

My stomach cramped and I closed my eyes against the pain. David's hand immediately cupped my cheek. I opened my eyes to see the love and assurance that filled his own.

"Bathsheba, do not grieve, for Nathan came to tell us how much our God loves our son as well, and how he's named him 'Jedidiah' which means 'beloved of the Lord.'"

"Blessed are you, O Most High," I lifted my arms and proclaimed with wonder. "Who names our son his beloved."

Mama and Abigail appeared at the door. "We heard you praising God," Abigail said, her face alight with curiosity.

"The Lord has given us his name for our son today; 'Jedidiah, beloved of the Lord,'" I marveled, as exquisite peace bubbled up like a well-spring within, overflowing into delighted laughter.

David's deep laughter joined mine. He held our son up in his open hands, as if an offering unto the Lord. "We do praise you, my Rock and my Redeemer, for our blessed son."

Mama and Abigail walked into the room and stood at the foot of the bed, watching David with Solomon.

"Our God has blessed you both by giving you a son and naming him Jedidiah, even as you have named him Solomon,'" Abigail proclaimed. "And may the Lord bless his beloved's reign with peace throughout all of Israel."

David drew Solomon to his heart, sat down on the bed, and slipped his other arm around me. We were both awestruck by her prophesy.

"My heart overflows with gratitude for the gift God has given us," I said. And as I thought of my journey to forgiveness and how the Lord had given me his love and peace for my bitterness and pain, a song of David's resonated within me. I raised my voice and sang:

> "Sing praises to the Lord, O you faithful ones,
>   and give thanks to his holy name.
> For his anger is but for a moment;
>   his favor is for a lifetime;
> Weeping may linger for a night,
>   but joy comes with the morning...."

PSALMS USED IN THE MANUSCRIPT – NRSV

Miriam's Song – Exodus 15
"Song of the Bow" David's Lament for Saul and Jonathan
– 1 Samuel 1:19-27
Psalm 5:11-12
Psalm 13:1-2
Psalm 13:3-6
Psalm 17: 1-7
Psalm 23:1-4
Psalm 28:1-2
Psalm 30:4-5
Psalm 31:9-10
Psalm 33:1-3
Psalm 34:17-20, 22
Psalm 35:4.10
Psalm 36:7-9
Psalm 39:1b
Psalm 42:1-2, 3-5
Psalm 43:1
Psalm 51:1-4, 7-8, 10-14, 17
Psalm 57:1-3
Psalm 63:1-3
Psalm 139:13-14
Psalm 139:23-24

Study questions by Theme

Barrenness:

1. Bathsheba (and her culture) interpreted her barrenness as a curse from God. If you have experienced barrenness or infertility, what made you feel cursed by God?

2. How can you identify with Bathsheba's struggle to discover the root cause/sin that would cause her barrenness?

3. Given the fact that Bathsheba was impregnated by David, the infertility seems to have been with Uriah – how does that change the issue?

4. In Old Testament times, barrenness was seen as a judgment against the woman – do you believe this is still the case in the New Covenant under Jesus? Why or why not

5. What allowed you to identify with Bathsheba's bittersweet acceptance of her pregnancy?

6. Can you understand Bathsheba's mother's desire to protect her daughter by ending the pregnancy before it became known? Why did her suggestion shock you?

7. What might you have done in Bathsheba's circumstances?

Rape/physical abuse:

1. Could Bathsheba have resisted the King more effectively? How?

2. Do you see the King's actions as rape? If so, how? If not, why not?

3. The church has often vilified Bathsheba over the years as the

seductress – What's your view?

4. Why has the church believed Bathsheba was complicit in her own "seduction?" Is it because we can't imagine how David, as "a man after God's own heart" could have raped her?

5. In 2 Samuel 12, Nathan comes to David to pronounce his judgment – who do you think the poor man was in Nathan's story? The ewe lamb? The rich man?

6. If you, the reader, have ever been abused or raped, have you believed the lie that it was your fault? Why is that a lie?

7. Do you believe that you have to stay with your abuser, especially if you're married to him? Do you think God could hate abuse even more than he hates divorce?

8. Bathsheba lived in a time and place different from our own culture, yet similar to many other cultures today. As women, do we support the abused among us? If so, how? If not, why not?

** A resource for you if you are experiencing abuse is: Peace and Safety in the Christian Home – PASCH; http://www.peaceandsafety.com/home

Betrayal:

1. If there is not a strong trust relationship already in place, there can be no betrayal. In what ways did David betray Bathsheba? In what ways did he betray Uriah?

2. In sending for Uriah, and then sending him home to his wife, what is David trying to do?

3. If David had wanted to claim Bathsheba's child as his own,

would he not have just ordered Uriah's death and not called him back to Jerusalem? How would the story have been altered if David had done this?

4. What do you think made David believe he could get away with the whole scheme?

5. Do you think he ever considered that God would judge his actions?

6. How do you identify with Bathsheba's desire to end her own life? Was Bathsheba's fear for her life legitimate? Was Bathsheba's fear for the well being and safety of her family legitimate, especially after Uriah was killed?

7. How were David's actions a betrayal of his God-anointed kingship?

Forgiveness:

1. Were Abigail and Anna unfair in their persistence that Bathsheba must forgive? How?

2. How does Bathsheba resolve her anger towards God?

3. How does that enable her to both forgive herself, and begin the journey to forgive David?

4. What was the role that Abigail played? How important was that?

5. Unforgiveness can be like a cancer or a poison to the soul. Would you have taken the same stance as Anna and Abigail?

6. How can you identify with Bathsheba's emotional and spiritual journey to forgiveness?

7. What do you think Bathsheba's life would have been like if she hadn't forgiven David?

8. Do you believe that Bathsheba could have borne another child with David if she had not forgiven him?

9. Are there issues of unforgiveness in your life that you need to acknowledge and address? What are the steps you need to take to do this?

10. Bathsheba's journey to forgiveness was full of obstacles – what obstacles are in your path?

11. Do you believe it is necessary for the person to ask for your forgiveness before you grant it? If so, why? If not, why not?

12. How can forgiveness be proactive, that is, is it possible to live a lifestyle of active forgiveness?

Hearing God's voice:

1. Who in the story spoke for God into Bathsheba's life experience?

2. Whose voice did you identify with?

3. Think about the ways she listened – whose voice had the most impact?

4. What did Bathsheba have to overcome internally in order to hear the voices?

5. Did she recognize God's presence in the voices?

6. Has God ever spoken into your life through others? Was it difficult to hear those words spoken?

7. The Psalms (David's songs and others) also spoke to Bathsheba. How has God used his Word to speak into your life?

8. Music played a big role in Bathsheba's journey – has music had an impact on your journey? If so, how?

9. God also spoke to Bathsheba through a small stone. Has God ever used nature to speak into your life? If so, how?

Loss of a child:

1. Was Bathsheba's response to the news of her child's impending death believable?

2. Do you think her heart softened to David when she found out he was fasting and praying for their son's life? Is it all right to be angry with God in circumstances like these?

3. How did you feel when God did not relent and save the child?

4. Why do you think God spared David's life and took their son's life?

5. How did Bathsheba resolve her anger and find hope again after the death of her child?

6. In what way is God's grace and power at work in the lives of David and Bathsheba and their next child, Solomon?

7. How did you feel when you read that God's name for Solomon was Jedidiah "Beloved of God?"

8. If you have lost a child, do you believe that it was God's judgment on you? Why or why not?

9. Jesus established a New Covenant and fulfilled the Law, and in so doing, took God's judgment upon himself. Do you believe that? Do you believe it is possible that there is "no condemnation for all who are in Christ Jesus?" Do you believe that you are free from "the law of sin and death?" (Rom. 8) What steps do you need to take to realize such freedom?

About The Author

Lorita Boyle loves research. As a history major, English minor, she dreamed of doing research for a writer, and then became that writer! She's a California native transplanted to Madison, Wisconsin in mid-life. She's been married thirty-nine years, and has three married children and two grandchildren. You can visit her website at: www.loritaboyle.com

Publishing That Works For You

Do you need a speaker?

Do you want Lorita Boyle to speak to your group or event? Then contact Larry Davis at: **(623) 337-8710** or email: **ldavis@intermediapr.com** or use the contact form at: **www.intermediapr.com**.

Whether you want to purchase bulk copies of *Bathsheba's Lament* or buy another book for a friend, get it now at: **www.imprbooks.com**.

If you have a book that you would like to publish, contact Terry Whalin, Publisher, at Intermedia Publishing Group, (623) 337-8710 or email: twhalin@intermediapub.com or use the contact form at: www.intermediapub.com.